A Smaller History of Greece

William Smith

Contents

- CHAPTER I. GEOGRAPHY OF GREECE. 7
- CHAPTER II. ORIGIN OF THE GREEKS AND THE HEROIC AGE. 10
- CHAPTER III. GENERAL SURVEY OF THE GREEK PEOPLE-
  -NATIONAL INSTITUTIONS. 17
- CHAPTER IV. EARLY HISTORY OF PELOPONNESUS AND SPARTA,
  DOWN TO THE END OF THE MESSENIAN WARS, B.C. 668. 21
- CHAPTER V. THE EARLY HISTORY OF ATHENS, DOWN TO
  THE ESTABLISHMENT OF DEMOCRACY BY CLISTHENES, B.C. 510. 31
- CHAPTER VI. THE GREEK COLONIES. 44
- CHAPTER VII. THE PERSIAN WARS.--FROM THE IONIC REVOLT TO
  THE BATTLE OF MARATHON, B.C. 500-490. 48
- CHAPTER VIII. THE PERSIAN WARS.--THE BATTLES OF THERMOPYLAE,
  SALAMIS, AND PLATAEA, B.C. 480-479. 59
- CHAPTER IX. FROM THE END OF THE PERSIAN WARS TO THE BEGINNING
  OF THE PELOPONNESIAN WAR, B.C. 479-431. 72
- CHAPTER X. ATHENS IN THE TIME OF PERICLES. 87
- CHAPTER XI. THE PELOPONNESIAN WAR.--FIRST PERIOD, FROM THE
  COMMENCEMENT OF THE WAR TO THE PEACE OF NICIAS, B.C. 431-421. 95
- CHAPTER XII. THE PELOPONNESIAN WAR. SECOND PERIOD, FROM
  THE PEACE OF NICIAS TO THE DEFEAT OF THE ATHENIANS
  IN SICILY, B.C. 421-413. 107
- CHAPTER XIII. THE PELOPONNESIAN WAR.--THIRD PERIOD, FROM
  THE SICILIAN EXPEDITION TO THE END OF THE WAR, B.C. 413-404. 119
- CHAPTER XIV THE THIRTY TYRANTS, AND THE DEATH OF SOCRATES,
  B.C. 404-399. 131
- CHAPTER XV. THE EXPEDITION OF THE GREEKS UNDER CYRUS, AND
  RETREAT OF THE TEN THOUSAND, B.C. 401-400. 138
- CHAPTER XVI. THE SUPREMACY OF SPARTA, B.C. 404-371. 145
- CHAPTER XVII. THE SUPREMACY OF THEBES, B.C. 371-361. 160
- CHAPTER XVIII. HISTORY OF THE SICILIAN GREEKS FROM THE DESTRUCTION
  OF THE ATHENIAN ARMAMENT TO THE DEATH OF TIMOLEON. 166
- CHAPTER XIX. PHILIP OF MACEDON, B.C. 359-336. 170
- CHAPTER XX. ALEXANDER THE GREAT, B.C. 336-323. 179
- CHAPTER XXI. FROM THE DEATH OF ALEXANDER THE GREAT TO
  THE CONQUEST OF GREECE BY THE ROMANS, B.C. 323-146. 199
- CHAPTER XXII. SKETCH OF THE HISTORY OF GREEK LITERATURE FROM
  THE EARLIEST TIMES TO THE REIGN OF ALEXANDER THE GREAT. 219

A SMALLER HISTORY OF GREECE

BY

William Smith

CHAPTER I.
GEOGRAPHY OF GREECE.

Greece is the southern portion of a great peninsula of Europe, washed on three sides by the Mediterranean Sea. It is bounded on the north by the Cambunian mountains, which separate it from Macedonia. It extends from the fortieth degree of latitude to the thirty-sixth, its greatest length being not more than 250 English miles, and its greatest breadth only 180. Its surface is considerably less than that of Portugal. This small area was divided among a number of independent states, many of them containing a territory of only a few square miles, and none of them larger than an English county. But the heroism and genius of the Greeks have given an interest to the insignificant spot of earth bearing their name, which the vastest empires have never equalled.

The name of Greece was not used by the inhabitants of the country. They called their land HELLAS, and themselves HELLENES. At first the word HELLAS signified only a small district in Thessaly, from which the Hellenes gradually spread over the whole country. The names of GREECE and GREEKS come to us from the Romans, who gave the name of GRAECIA to the country and of GRAECI to the inhabitants.

The two northerly provinces of Greece are THESSALY and EPIRUS, separated from each other by Mount Pindus. Thessaly is a fertile plain enclosed by lofty mountains, and drained by the river Peneus, which finds its way into the sea through the celebrated Vale of Tempe. Epirus is covered by rugged ranges of mountains running from north to south, through which the Achelous the largest river of Greece, flows towards the Corinthian gulf.

In entering central Greece from Thessaly the road runs along the coast through the narrow pass of Thermopylae, between the sea and a lofty range of mountains.

The district along the coast was inhabited by the EASTERN LOCRIANS, while to their west were DORIS and PHOCIS, the greater part of the latter being occupied by Mount Parnassus, the abode of the Muses, upon the slopes of which lay the town of Delphi with its celebrated oracle of Apollo. South of Phocis is Boeotia, which is a large hollow basin, enclosed on every side by mountains, which prevent the waters from flowing into the sea. Hence the atmosphere was damp and thick, to which circumstance the witty Athenians attributed the dullness of the inhabitants. Thebes was the chief city of Boeotia. South of Boeotia lies ATTICA, which is in the form of a triangle, having two of its sides washed by the sea and its base united to the land. Its soil is light and dry and is better adapted for the growth of fruit than of corn. It was particularly celebrated for its olives, which were regarded as the gift of Athena (Minerva), and were always under the care of that goddess. Athens was on the western coast, between four and five miles from its port, Piraeus. West of Attica, towards the isthmus, is the small district of MEGARIS.

The western half of central Greece consists of WESTERN LOCRIS, AETOLIA and ACARNANIA. These districts were less civilised than the other countries of Greece, and were the haunts of rude robber tribes even as late as the Peloponnesian war.

Central Greece is connected with the southern peninsula by a narrow isthmus, on which stood the city of Corinth. So narrow is this isthmus that the ancients regarded the peninsula as an island, and gave to it the name of PELOPONNESUS, or the island of Pelops, from the mythical hero of this name. Its modern name, the MOREA, was bestowed upon it from its resemblance to the leaf of the mulberry.

The mountains of Peloponnesus have their roots in the centre of the country, from which they branch out towards the sea. This central region, called ARCADIA, is the Switzerland of the peninsula. It is surrounded by a ring of mountains, forming a kind of natural wall, which separates it from the remaining Peloponnesian states. The other chief divisions of Peloponnesus were Achaia, Argolis, Laconia, Messenia, and Elis. ACHAIA is a narrow slip of country lying between the northern barrier of Arcadia and the Corinthian gulf. ARGOLIS, on the east, contained several independent states, of which the most important was Argos. LACONIA and MESSENIA occupied the whole of the south of the peninsula from sea to sea: these two countries were separated by the lofty range of Taygetus, running from north to south, and terminating in the promontory of Taenarum (now Cape Matapan), the southernmost point of Greece and Europe. Sparta, the chief town of Laconia, stood in the valley of the Eurotas, which opens out into a plain of considerable extent towards the Laconian gulf. Messenia, in like manner, was drained by the Pamisus, whose plain is still more extensive and fertile than that of the Eurotas. ELIS, on the west of Arcadia, contains the memorable plain of Olympia, through which the Alpheus flows, and in which the city of Pisa stood.

Of the numerous islands which line the Grecian shores, the most important was Euboea, stretching along the coasts of Boeotia and Attica. South of Euboea was the group of islands called the CYCLADES, lying around Delos as a centre; and east of these were the SPORADES, near the Asiatic coast. South of these groups are the large islands of CRETE and RHODES.

The physical features of the country exercised an important influence upon the political destinies of the people. Greece is one of the most mountainous countries of Europe. Its surface is occupied by a number of small plains, either entirely surrounded by limestone mountains or open only to the sea. Each of the principal Grecian cities was founded in one of these small plains; and, as the mountains which separated it from its neighbours were lofty and rugged, each city grew up in solitary independence. But at the same time it had ready and easy access to the sea, and Arcadia was almost the only political division that did not possess some territory upon the coast. Thus shut out from their neighbours by mountains, the Greeks were naturally attracted to the sea, and became a maritime people. Hence they possessed the love of freedom and the spirit of adventure, which have always characterised, more or less the inhabitants of maritime districts.

CHAPTER II.
ORIGIN OF THE GREEKS AND THE HEROIC AGE.

No nation possesses a history till events are recorded in written documents; and it was not till the epoch known by the name of the First Olympiad, corresponding to the year 776 B.C., that the Greeks began to employ writing as a means for perpetuating the memory of any historical facts. Before that period everything is vague and uncertain; and the exploits of the heroes related by the poets must not be regarded as historical facts.

The PELASGIANS are universally represented as the most ancient inhabitants of Greece. They were spread over the Italian as well as the Grecian peninsula; and the Pelasgic language thus formed the basis of the Latin as well as of the Greek. They were divided into several tribes, of which the Hellenes were probably one: at any rate, this people, who originally dwelt in the south of Thessaly, gradually spread over the rest of Greece. The Pelasgians disappeared before them, or were incorporated with them, and their dialect became the language of Greece. The Hellenes considered themselves the descendants of one common ancestor, Hellen, the son of Deucalion and Pyrrha. To Hellen were ascribed three sons, Dorus, Xuthus, and AEolus. Of these Dorus and AEolus gave their names to the DORIANS and AEOLIANS; and Xuthus; through his two sons Ion and Achaeus, became the forefather of the IONIANS and ACHAEANS. Thus the Greeks accounted for the origin of the four great divisions of their race. The descent of the Hellenes from a common ancestor, Hellen, was a fundamental article in the popular faith. It was a general practice in antiquity to invent fictitious persons for the purpose of explaining names of which the origin was buried in obscurity. It was in this way that Hellen and his sons came into being; but though they never had any real existence, the tales about them may be regarded as the traditional history of the races to whom they gave their names.

The civilization of the Greeks and the development of their language bear all the marks of home growth, and probably were little affected by foreign influence. The traditions, however, of the Greeks would point to a contrary conclusion. It was a general belief among them that the Pelasgians were reclaimed from barbarism by Oriental strangers, who settled in the country and introduced among the rude inhabitants the first elements of civilization. Attica is said to have been indebted for the arts of civilized life to Cecrops, a native of Sais in Egypt. To him is ascribed the foundation of the city of Athens, the institution of marriage, and the introduction of religious rites and ceremonies. Argos, in like manner, is said to have been founded by the Egyptian Danaus, who fled to Greece with his fifty daughters, to escape from the persecution of their suitors, the fifty sons of his brother AEgyptus. The Egyptian stranger was elected king by the natives, and from him the tribe of the Danai derived their name, which Homer frequently uses as a general appellation for the Greeks. Another colony was the one led from Asia by Pelops, from whom the southern peninsula of Greece derived its name of Peloponnesus. Pelops is represented as a Phrygian, and the son of the wealthy king Tantalus. He became king of Mycenae, and the founder of a powerful dynasty, one of the most renowned in the Heroic age of Greece. From him was descended Agamemnon, who led the Grecian host against Troy.

The tale of the Phoenician colony, conducted by Cadmus, and which founded Thebes in Boeotia, rests upon a different basis. Whether there was such a person as the Phoenician Cadmus, and whether he built the town called Cadmea, which afterwards became the citadel of Thebes, as the ancient legends relate, cannot be determined; but it is certain that the Greeks were indebted to the Phoenicians for the art of writing; for both the names and the forms of the letters in the Greek alphabet are evidently derived from the Phoenician. With this exception the Oriental strangers left no permanent traces of their settlements in Greece; and the population of the country continued to be essentially Grecian, uncontaminated by any foreign elements.

The age of the heroes, from the first appearance of the Hellenes in Thessaly to the return of the Greeks from Troy, was supposed to be a period of about two hundred years. These heroes were believed to be a noble race of beings, possessing a superhuman though not a divine nature, and superior to ordinary men in strength of body and greatness of soul.

Among the heroes three stand conspicuously forth: Hercules, the national hero of Greece; Theseus, the hero of Attica; and Minos, king of Crete, the principal founder of Grecian law and civilization.

Hercules was the son of Zeus (Jupiter) and Alcmena; but the jealous anger of Hera (Juno) raised up against him an opponent and a master in the person of Eurystheus at whose bidding the greatest of all heroes was to achieve those wonderful labours which filled the whole world with his fame. In these are realized, on a magnificent scale, the two great objects of ancient heroism, the destruction of physical and moral evil, and the acquisition of wealth and power. Such, for instance, are the labours in which he destroys the terrible Nemean lion and Lernean hydra, carries off the girdle of Ares from Hippolyte, queen of the Amazons, and seizes the golden apples of the Hesperides, guarded by a hundred-headed dragon.

Theseus was a son of AEgeus, king of Athens, and of AEthra, daughter of Pittheus, king of Troezen. Among his many memorable achievements the most famous was his deliverance of Athens from the frightful tribute imposed upon it by Minos for the murder of his son. This consisted of seven youths and seven maidens whom the Athenians were compelled to send every nine years to Crete, there to be devoured by the Minotaur, a monster with a human body and a bull's head, which Minos kept concealed in an inextricable labyrinth. The third ship was already on the point of sailing with its cargo of innocent victims, when Theseus offered to go with them, hoping to put an end for ever to the horrible tribute. Ariadne, the daughter of Minos, became enamoured of the hero, and having supplied him with a clue to trace the windings of the labyrinth, Theseus succeeded in killing the monster, and in tracking his way out of the mazy lair. Theseus, on his return, became king of Attica, and proceeded to lay the foundations of the future greatness of the country. He united into one political body the twelve independent states into which Cecrops had divided Attica, and made Athens the capital of the new kingdom. He then divided the citizens into three classes, namely, EUPATRIDAE, or nobles; GEOMORI, or husbandmen; and DEMIURGI, or artisans.

Minos, king of Crete, whose history is connected with that of Theseus, appears, like him, the representative of an historical and civil state of life. Minos is said to have received the laws of Crete immediately from Zeus; and traditions uniformly present him as king of the sea. Possessing a numerous fleet, he reduced the surrounding islands, especially the Cyclades, under his dominion, and cleared the sea of pirates.

The voyage of the Argonauts and the Trojan war were the most memorable enterprises undertaken by collective bodies of heroes.

The Argonauts derived their name from the Argo, a ship built For the adventurers by Jason, under the superintendence of Athena (Minerva). They embarked in the harbour of Iolcus in Thessaly for the purpose of obtaining the golden fleece which was preserved in AEa in Colchis, on the eastern shores of the Black Sea, under the guardianship of a sleepless dragon. The most renowned heroes of the age took part in the expedition. Among them were Hercules and Theseus, as well as the principal leaders in the Trojan war; but Jason is the central figure and the real hero of the enterprise. Upon arriving at AEa, after many adventures, king AEtes promised to deliver to Jason the golden fleece, provided he yoked two fire-breathing oxen with brazen feet, and performed other wonderful deeds. Here, also, as in the legend of Theseus, love played a prominent part. Medea, the daughter of AEtcs, who was skilled in magic and supernatural arts, furnished Jason with the means of accomplishing the labours imposed upon him; and as her father still delayed to surrender the fleece, she cast the dragon asleep during the night, seized the fleece, and sailed away in the Argo with her beloved Jason.

The Trojan war was the greatest of all the heroic achievements. It formed the subject of innumerable epic poems, and has been immortalised by the genius of Homer. Paris, son of Priam, king of Troy, abused the hospitality of Menelaus, king of Sparta, by carrying off his wife Helen, the most beautiful woman of the age. All the Grecian princes looked upon the outrage as one committed against themselves. Responding to the call of Menelaus, they assembled in arms, elected his brother Agamemnon, king of Mycenae, leader of the expedition, and sailed across the AEgean in nearly 1200 ships to recover the faithless fair one. Several of the confederate heroes excelled Agamemnon in fame. Among them Achilles, chief of the Thessalian Myrmidons, stood pre-eminent in strength, beauty, and valour; whilst Ulysses, king of Ithaca; surpassed all the rest in the mental qualities of counsel and eloquence. Among the Trojans, Hector, one of the sons of Priam, was most distinguished for heroic qualities and formed a striking contrast to his handsome but effeminate brother Paris. Next to Hector in valour stood AEneas, son of Anchises and Aphrodite (Venus). Even the gods took part in the contest, encouraging their favourite heroes, and sometimes fighting by their side or in their stead.

It was not till the tenth year of the war that Troy yielded to the inevitable decree of fate; and it is this year which forms the subject of the Iliad. Achilles, offended by Agamemnon, abstains from the war; and in his absence the Greeks are no match for Hector. The Trojans drive them back into their camp, and are already setting fire to their ships, when Achilles gives his armour to his friend Patroclus, and allows him to charge at the head of the Myrmidons. Patroclus repulses the Trojans from the ships, but the god Apollo is against him, and he falls under the spear of Hector. Desire to avenge the death of his friend proves more powerful in the breast of Achilles than anger against Agamemnon. He appears again in the field in new and gorgeous armour, forged for him by the god Hephrastus (Vulcan) at the prayer of Thetis. The Trojans fly before him, and, although Achilles is aware that his own death must speedily follow that of the Trojan hero, he slays Hector in single combat.

The Iliad closes with the burial of Hector. The death of Achilles and the capture of Troy were related in later poems. The hero of so many achievements perishes by an arrow shot by the unwarlike Paris, but directed by the hand of Apollo. The noblest combatants had now fallen on either side, and force of arms had proved unable to accomplish what stratagem at length effects. It is Ulysses who now steps into the foreground and becomes the real conqueror of Troy. By his advice a wooden horse is built, in whose inside he and other heroes conceal themselves. The infatuated Trojans admit the horse within their walls. In the dead of night the Greeks rush out and open the gates to their comrades. Troy is delivered over to the sword, and its glory sinks in ashes. The fall of Troy is placed in the year 1184 B.C.

The return of the Grecian leaders from Troy forms another series of poetical legends. Several meet with tragical ends. Agamemnon is murdered on his arrival at Mycenae, by his wife Clytaemnestra and her paramour AEgisthus. But of these wanderings the most celebrated and interesting are those of Ulysses, which form the subject of the Odyssey. After twenty years' absence he arrives at length in Ithaca, where he slays the numerous suitors who devoured his substance and contended for the hand of his wife Penelope.

The Homeric poems must not be regarded as a record of historical persons and events, but, at the same time, they present a valuable picture of the institutions and manners of the earliest known state of Grecian society.

In the Heroic age Greece was already divided into a number of independent states, each governed by its own king. The authority of the king was not limited by any laws; his power resembled that of the patriarchs in the Old Testament; and for the exercise of it he was responsible only to Zeus, and not to his people. But though the king was not restrained in the exercise of his power by any positive laws, his authority was practically limited by the BOULE; or council of chiefs, and the Agora, or general assembly of freemen. These two bodies, of little account in the Heroic age, became in the Republican age the sole depositories of political power.

The Greeks in the Heroic age were divided into the three classes of nobles, common freemen, and slaves. The nobles were raised far above the rest of the community in honour, power, and wealth. They were distinguished by their war-like prowess, their large estates, and their numerous slaves. The condition of the general mass of freemen is rarely mentioned. They possessed portions of land as their own property, which they cultivated themselves; but there was another class of poor freemen, called Thetes, who had no land of their own, and who worked for hire on the estates of others. Slavery was not so prevalent in the Heroic age as at a later time, and appears in a less odious aspect. The nobles alone possessed slaves, and they treated them with a degree of kindness which frequently secured for the masters their affectionate attachment.

Society was marked by simplicity of manners. The kings and nobles did not consider it derogatory to their dignity to acquire skill in the manual arts. Ulysses is represented as building his own bed-chamber and constructing his own raft, and he boasts of being an excellent mower and ploughman. Like Esau, who made savoury meat for his father Isaac, the Heroic chiefs prepared their own meals and prided themselves on their skill in cookery. Kings and private persons partook of the same food, which was of the simplest kind. Beef, mutton, and goat's flesh were the ordinary meats, and cheese, flour, and sometimes fruits, also formed part of the banquet; wine was drunk diluted with water, and the entertainments were never disgraced by intemperance, like those of our northern ancestors. The enjoyment of the banquet was heightened by the song and the dance, and the chiefs took more delight in the lays of the minstrel than in the exciting influence of the wine.

The wives and daughters of the chiefs, in like manner, did not deem it beneath them to discharge various duties which were afterwards regarded as menial. Not only do we find them constantly employed in weaving, spinning and embroidery, but like the daughters of the patriarchs they fetch water from the well and assist their slaves in washing garments in the river.

Even at this early age the Greeks had made considerable advances in civilization. They were collected in fortified towns, which were surrounded by walls and adorned with palaces and temples. The massive ruins of Mycenae and the sculptured lions on the gate of this city belong to the Heroic age, and still excite the wonder of the beholder. Commerce, however, was little cultivated, and was not much esteemed. It was deemed more honourable for a man to enrich himself by robbery and piracy than by the arts of peace. Coined money is not mentioned in the poems of Homer. Whether the Greeks were acquainted at this early period with the art of writing is a question which has given rise to much dispute, and must remain undetermined; but poetry was cultivated with success, though yet confined to epic strains, or the narration of the exploits and adventures of the Heroic chiefs. The bard sung his own song, and was always received with welcome and honour in the palaces of the nobles.

In the battle, as depicted by Homer, the chiefs are the only important combatants, while the people are an almost useless mass, frequently put to rout by the prowess of a single hero. The chief is mounted in a war chariot, and stands by the side of his charioteer, who is frequently a friend.

CHAPTER III.
GENERAL SURVEY OF THE GREEK PEOPLE--NATIONAL INSTITUTIONS.

The Greeks, as we have already seen, were divided into many independent communities, but several causes bound them together as one people. Of these the most important were community of blood and language--community of religious rites and festivals--and community of manners and character.

All the Greeks were descended from the same ancestor and spoke the same language. They all described men and cities which were not Grecian by the term BARBARIAN. This word has passed into our own language, but with a very different idea; for the Greeks applied it indiscriminately to every foreigner, to the civilized inhabitants of Egypt and Persia, as well as to the rude tribes of Scythia and Gaul.

The second bond of union was a community of religious rites and festivals. From the earliest times the Greeks appear to have worshipped the same gods; but originally there were no religious meetings common to the whole nation. Such meetings were of gradual growth, being formed by a number of neighbouring towns, which entered into an association for the periodical celebration of certain religious rites. Of these the most celebrated was the AMPHICTYONIC COUNCIL. It acquired its superiority over other similar associations by the wealth and grandeur of the Delphian temple, of which it was the appointed guardian. It held two meetings every year, one in the spring at the temple of Apollo at Delphi, and the other in the autumn at the temple of Demeter (Ceres) at Thermopylae. Its members, who were called the Amphictyons, consisted of sacred deputies sent from twelve tribes, each of which contained several independent cities or states. But the Council was never considered as a national congress, whose duty it was to protect and defend the common interests of Greece; and it was only when the rights of the Delphian god had been violated that it invoked the aid of the various members of the league.

The Olympic Games were of greater efficacy than the amphictyonic council in promoting a spirit of union among the various branches of the Greek race, and in keeping alive a feeling of their common origin. They were open to all persons who could prove their Hellenic blood, and were frequented by spectators from all parts of the Grecian world. They were celebrated at Olympia, on the banks of the Alpheus, in the territory of Elis. The origin of the festival is lost in obscurity; but it is said to have been revived by Iphitus, king of Elis, and Lycurgus the Spartan legislator, in the year 776 B.C.; and, accordingly, when the Greeks at a later time began to use the Olympic contest as a chronological era, this year was regarded as the first Olympiad. It was celebrated at the end of every four years, and the interval which elapsed between each celebration was called an Olympiad. The whole festival was under the management of the Eleans, who appointed some of their own number to preside as judges, under the name of the Hellanodicae. During the month in which it was celebrated all hostilities were suspended throughout Greece. At first the festival was confined to a single day, and consisted of nothing more than a match of runners in the stadium; but in course of time so many other contests were introduced, that the games occupied five days. They comprised various trials of strength and skill, such as wrestling boxing, the Pancratium (boxing and wrestling combined), and the complicated Pentathlum (including jumping, running, the quoit, the javelin, and wrestling), but no combats with any kind of weapons. There were also horse-races and chariot-races; and the chariot-race, with four full-grown horses, became one of the most popular and celebrated of all the matches.

The only prize given to the conqueror was a garland of wild olive; but this was valued as one of the dearest distinctions in life. To have his name proclaimed as victor before assembled Hellas was an object of ambition with the noblest and the wealthiest of the Greeks. Such a person was considered to have conferred everlasting glory upon his family and his country, and was rewarded by his fellow-citizens with distinguished honours.

During the sixth century before the Christian era three other national festivals--the Pythian, Nemean, and Isthmian games--which were at first only local became open to the whole nation. The Pythian games were celebrated in every third Olympic year, on the Cirrhaean plain in Phocis, under the superintendence of the Amphictyons. The games consisted not only of matches in gymnastics and of horse and chariot races, but also of contests in music and poetry. They soon acquired celebrity, and became second only to the great Olympic festival. The Nemean and Isthmian games occurred more frequently than the Olympic and Pythian. They were celebrated once in two years--the Nemean in the valley of Nemea between Phlius and Cleonae--and the Isthmian by the Corinthians, on their isthmus, in honour of Poseidon (Neptune). As in the Pythian festival, contests in music and in poetry, as well as gymnastics and chariot-races, formed part of these games. Although the four great festivals of which we have been speaking had no influence in promoting the political union of Greece, they nevertheless were of great importance in making the various sections of the race feel that they were all members of one family, and in cementing them together by common sympathies and the enjoyment of common pleasures. The frequent occurrence of these festivals, for one was celebrated every gear, tended to the same result.

The Greeks were thus annually reminded of their common origin, and of the great distinction which existed between them and barbarians. Nor must we forget the incidental advantages which attended them. The concourse of so large a number of persons from every part of the Grecian world afforded to the merchant opportunities for traffic, and to the artist and the literary man the best means of making their works known. During the time of the games a busy commerce was carried on; and in a spacious hall appropriated for the purpose, the poets, philosophers, and historians were accustomed to read their most recent works.

The habit of consulting the same oracles in order to ascertain the will of the gods was another bond of union. It was the universal practice of the Greeks to undertake no matter of importance without first asking the advice of the gods; and there were many sacred spots in which the gods were always ready to give an answer to pious worshippers. The oracle of Apollo at Delphi surpassed all the rest in importance, and was regarded with veneration in every part of the Grecian world. In the centre of the temple of Delphi there was a small opening in the ground, from which it was said that a certain gas or vapour ascended. Whenever the oracle was to be consulted, a virgin priestess called PYTHIA took her seat upon a tripod which was placed over the chasm. The ascending vapour affected her brain, and the words which she uttered in this excited condition were believed to be the answer of Apollo to his worshippers. They were always in hexameter verse, and were reverently taken down by the attendant priests. Most of the answers were equivocal or obscure; but the credit of the oracle continued unimpaired long after the downfall of Grecian independence.

A further element of union among the Greeks was the similarity of manners and character. It is true the difference in this respect between the polished inhabitants of Athens and the rude mountaineers of Acarnania was marked and striking; but if we compare the two with foreign contemporaries, the contrast between them and the latter is still more striking. Absolute despotism human sacrifices, polygamy, deliberate mutilation of the person as a punishment, and selling of children into slavery, existed in some part or other of the barbarian world, but are not found in any city of Greece in the historical times.

The elements of union of which we have been speaking only bound the Greeks together in common feelings and sentiments: they never produced any political union. The independent sovereignty of each city was a fundamental notion in the Greek mind. This strongly rooted feeling deserves particular notice. Careless readers of history are tempted to suppose that the territory of Greece was divided among comparatively small number of independent states, such as Attica, Arcadia, Boeotia, Phocis, Locris, and the like; but this is a most serious mistake, and leads to a total misapprehension of Greek history. Every separate city was usually an independent state, and consequently each of the territories described under the general names of Arcadia, Boeotia, Phocis, and Locris, contained numerous political communities independent of one another. Attica, it is true, formed a single state, and its different towns recognised Athens as their capital and the source of supreme power; but this is an exception to the general rule.

CHAPTER IV.
EARLY HISTORY OF PELOPONNESUS AND SPARTA, DOWN TO THE END OF THE MESSENIAN WARS, B.C. 668.

In the heroic age Peloponnesus was occupied by tribes of Dorian conquerors. They had no share in the glories of the Heroic age; their name does not occur in the Iliad, and they are only once mentioned in the Odyssey; but they were destined to form in historical times one of the most important elements of the Greek nation. Issuing from their mountain district between Thessaly, Locris and Phocis, they overran the greater part of Peloponnesus, destroyed the ancient Achaean monarchies and expelled or reduced to subjection the original inhabitants of the land, of which they became the undisputed masters. This brief statement contains all that we know for certain respecting this celebrated event, which the ancient writers placed eighty years after the Trojan war (B.C. 1104). The legendary account of the conquest of Peloponnesus ran as follows:--The Dorians were led by the Heraclidae, or descendants of the mighty hero Hercules. Hence this migration is called the Return of the Heraclidae. The children of Hercules had long been fugitives upon the face of the earth. They had made many attempts to regain possession of the dominions in the Peloponnesus, of which their great sire had been deprived by Eurystheus, but hitherto without success. In their last attempt Hyllus, the son of Hercules, had perished in single combat with Echemus of Tegea; and the Heraclidae had become bound by a solemn compact to renounce their enterprise for a hundred years. This period had now expired; and the great-grandsons of Hyllus--Temenus, Cresphontes, and Aristodemus--resolved to make a fresh attempt to recover their birthright. They were assisted in the enterprise by the Dorians. This people espoused their cause in consequence of the aid which Hercules himself had rendered to the Dorian king, AEgimius, when the latter was hard pressed in a contest with the Lapithae. The invaders were warned by an oracle not to enter Peloponnesus by the Isthmus of Corinth, but across the mouth of the Corinthian gulf. The inhabitants of the northern coast of the gulf were favourable to their enterprise. Oxylus, king of the AEtolians, became their guide; and from Naupactus they crossed over to Peloponnesus. A single battle decided the contest. Tisamenus, the son of Orestes, was defeated and retired with a portion of his Achaean subjects to the northern coast of Peloponnesus, then occupied by the Ionians. He expelled the Ionians, and took possession of the country, which continued henceforth to be inhabited by the Achaeans, and to be called after them. The Ionians withdrew to Attica, and the greater part of them afterwards emigrated to Asia Minor.

The Heraclidae and the Dorians now divided between them the dominions of Tisamenus and of the other Achaean princes. The kingdom of Elis was given to Oxylus as a recompense for his services as their guide; and it was agreed that Temenus, Cresphontes, and Eurysthenes and Procles, the infant sons of Aristodemus (who had died at Naupactus), should draw lots for Argos, Sparta, and Messenia. Argos fell to Temenus, Sparta to Eurysthenes and Procles, and Messenia to Cresphontes.

Such are the main features of the legend of the Return of the Heraclidae. In order to make the story more striking and impressive, it compresses into a single epoch events which probably occupied several generations. It is in itself improbable that the brave Achaeans quietly submitted to the Dorian invaders after a momentary struggle. We have, moreover, many indications that such was not the fact, and that it was only gradually and after a long protracted contest that the Dorians became undisputed masters of the greater part of Peloponnesus.

Argos was originally the chief Dorian state in Peloponnesus, but at the time of the first Olympiad its power had been supplanted by that of Sparta. The progress of Sparta from the second to the first place among the states in the peninsula was mainly owing to the military discipline and rigorous training of its citizens. The singular constitution of Sparta was unanimously ascribed by the ancients to the legislator Lycurgus, but there were different stories respecting his date, birth, travels, legislation, and death. His most probable date however is B.C. 776, in which year he is said to have assisted Iphitus in restoring the Olympic games. He was the son of

Eunomus, one of the two kings who reigned together in Sparta. On the death of his father, his elder brother, Polydectes, succeeded to the crown, but died soon afterwards, leaving his queen with child. The ambitious woman offered to destroy the child, if Lycurgus would share the throne with her. Lycurgus pretended to consent; but as soon as she had given birth to a son, he presented him in the market-place as the future king of Sparta. The young king's mother took revenge upon Lycurgus by accusing him of entertaining designs against his nephew's life. Hereupon he resolved to withdraw from his native country and to visit foreign lands. He was absent many years, and is said to have employed his time in studying the institutions of other nations, in order to devise a system of laws and regulations which might deliver Sparta from the evils under which it had long been suffering. During his absence the young king had grown up, and assumed the reins of government; but the disorders of the state had meantime become worse than ever, and all parties longed for a termination to their present sufferings. Accordingly the return of Lycurgus was hailed with delight, and he found the people both ready and willing to submit to an entire change in their government and institutions. He now set himself to work to carry his long projected reforms into effect; but before he commenced his arduous task he consulted the Delphian oracle, from which he received strong assurances of divine support. Thus encouraged by the god, he suddenly presented himself in the market-place, surrounded by thirty of the most distinguished Spartans in arms. His reforms were not carried into effect without violent opposition, and in one of the tumults which they excited, his eye is said to have been struck out by a passionate youth. But he finally triumphed over all obstacles, and succeeded in obtaining the submission of all classes in the community to his new constitution. His last act was to sacrifice himself for the welfare of his country. Having obtained from the people a solemn oath to make no alterations in his laws before his return, he quitted Sparta for ever. He set out on a journey to Delphi, where he obtained an oracle from the god, approving of all he had done, and promising prosperity to the Spartans as long as they preserved his laws. Whither he went afterwards, and how and where he died, nobody could tell. He vanished from earth like a god, leaving no traces behind him but his spirit: and his grateful countrymen honoured him with a temple, and worshipped him with annual sacrifices down to the latest times.

The population of Laconia was divided into the three classes of Spartans, Perioeci and Helots.

I. The SPARTANS were the descendants of the leading Dorian conquerors. They formed the sovereign power of the state, and they alone were eligible to honours and public offices. They lived in Sparta itself and were all subject to the discipline of Lycurgus. They were divided into three tribes,--the HYLLEIS, the PAMPHILI, and the DYMANES,--which were not, however, peculiar to Sparta, but existed in all the Dorian states.

II. The PERIOECI were personally free, but politically subject to the Spartans. [This word signifies literally DWELLERS AROUND THE CITY, and was generally used to indicate the inhabitants in the country districts, who possessed inferior political privileges to the citizens who lived in the city.] They possessed no share in the government, and were bound to obey the commands of the Spartan magistrates. They appear to have been the descendants of the old Achaean population of the country, and they were distributed into a hundred townships, which were spread through the whole of Laconia.

III. The HELOTS were serfs bound to the soil, which they tilled for the benefit of the Spartan proprietors. Their condition was very different from that of the ordinary slaves in antiquity, and more similar to the villanage of the middle ages. They lived in the rural villages, as the Perioeci did in the towns, cultivating the lands and paying over the rent to their masters in Sparta, but enjoying their homes, wives, and families, apart from their master's personal superintendence. They appear to have been never sold, and they accompanied the Spartans to the field as light armed troops. But while their condition was in these respects superior to that of the ordinary slaves in other parts of Greece, it was embittered by the fact that they were not strangers like the latter, but were of the same race and spoke the same language as their masters, being probably the descendants of the old inhabitants, who had offered the most obstinate resistance to the Dorians, and had therefore been reduced to slavery. As their numbers increased, they became objects of suspicion to their masters, and were subjected to the most wanton and oppressive cruelty.

The functions of the Spartan government were distributed among two kings, a senate of thirty members, a popular assembly, and an executive directory of five men called the Ephors.

At the head of the state were the two hereditary kings. The existence of a pair of kings was peculiar to Sparta, and is said to have arisen from the accidental circumstance of Aristodemus having left twin sons, Eurysthenes and Procles. This division of the royal power naturally tended to weaken its influence and to produce jealousies and dissensions between the two kings. The royal power was on the decline during the whole historical period, and the authority of the kings was gradually usurped by the Ephors, who at length obtained the entire control of the government, and reduced the kings to a state of humiliation and dependence.

The Senate, called GERUSIA, or the COUNCIL OF ELDERS, consisted of thirty members, among whom the two kings were included. They were obliged to be upwards of sixty years of age, and they held their office for life. They possessed considerable power and were the only real check upon the authority of the Ephors. They discussed and prepared all measures which were to be brought before the popular assembly, and they had some share in the general administration of the state. But the most important of their functions was, that they were judges in all criminal cases affecting the life of a Spartan citizen.

The Popular Assembly was of little importance, and appears to have been usually summoned only as a matter of form for the election of certain magistrates, for passing laws, and for determining upon peace and war. It would appear that open discussion was not allowed and that the assembly rarely came to a division.

The Ephors were of later origin, and did not exist in the original constitution of Lycurgus. They may be regarded as the representatives of the popular assembly. They were elected annually from the general body of Spartan citizens, and seem to have been originally appointed to protect the interests and liberties of the people against the encroachments of the kings and the senate. They correspond in many respects to the tribunes of the people at Rome. Their functions were at first limited and of small importance; but in the end the whole political power became centred in their hands.

The Spartan government was in reality a close oligarchy, in which the kings and the senate, as well as the people, were alike subject to the irresponsible authority of the five Ephors.

The most important part of the legislation of Lycurgus did not relate to the political constitution of Sparta, but to the discipline and education of the citizens. It was these which gave Sparta her peculiar character, and distinguished her in so striking a manner from all the other states of Greece. The position of the Spartans, surrounded by numerous enemies, whom they held in subjection by the sword alone, compelled them to be a nation of soldiers. Lycurgus determined that they should be nothing else; and the great object of his whole system was to cultivate a martial spirit, and to give them a training which would make them invincible in battle. To accomplish this the education of a Spartan was placed under the control of the state from his earliest boyhood. Every child after birth was exhibited to public view, and, if deemed deformed and weakly, was exposed to perish on Mount Taygetus. At the age of seven he was taken from his mother's care, and handed over to the public classes. He was not only taught gymnastic games and military exercises but he was also subjected to severe bodily discipline, and was compelled to submit to hardships and suffering without repining or complaint. One of the tests to which he was subjected was a cruel scourging at the altar of Artemis (Diana), until his blood gushed forth and covered the altar of the goddess. It was inflicted publicly before the eyes of his parents and in the presence of the whole city; and many Spartan youths were known to have died under the lash without uttering a complaining murmur. No means were neglected to prepare them for the hardships and stratagems of war. They were obliged to wear the same garment winter and summer, and to endure hunger and thirst, heat and cold. They were purposely allowed an insufficient quantity of food, but were permitted to make up the deficiency by hunting in the woods and mountains of Laconia. They were even encouraged to steal whatever they could; but if they were caught in the fact, they were severely punished for their want of dexterity. Plutarch tells us of a boy, who, having stolen a fox, and hid it under his garment, chose rather to let it tear out his very bowels than be detected in the theft.

The literary education of a Spartan youth was of a most restricted kind. He was taught to despise literature as unworthy of a warrior, while the study of eloquence and philosophy, which were cultivated at Athens with such extraordinary success, was regarded at Sparta with contempt. Long speeches were a Spartan's abhorrence, and he was trained to express himself with sententious brevity.

A Spartan was not considered to have reached the full age of manhood till he had completed his thirtieth year. He was then allowed to marry, to take part in the public assembly, and was eligible to the offices of the state. But he still continued under the public discipline, and was not permitted even to reside and take his meals with his wife. It was not till he had reached his sixtieth year that he was released from the public discipline and from military service.

The public mess--called SYSSITIA--is said to have been instituted by Lycurgus to prevent all indulgence of the appetite. Public tables were provided, at which every male citizen was obliged to take his meals. Each table accommodated fifteen persons, who formed a separate mess, into which no new member was admitted, except by the unanimous consent of the whole company. Each sent monthly to the common stock a specified quantity of barley-meal, wine, cheese, and figs and a little money to buy flesh and fish. No distinction of any kind was allowed at these frugal meals. Meat was only eaten occasionally; and one of the principal dishes was black broth. Of what it consisted we do not know. The tyrant Dionysius found it very unpalatable; but, as the cook told him, the broth was nothing without the seasoning of fatigue and hunger.

The Spartan women in their earlier years were subjected to a course of training almost as rigorous as that of the men, and contended with each other in running, wrestling and boxing. At the age of twenty a Spartan woman usually married, and she was no longer subjected to the public discipline. Although she enjoyed little of her husband's society, she was treated by him with deep respect, and was allowed a greater degree of liberty than was tolerated in other Grecian states. Hence she took a lively interest in the welfare and glory of her native land, and was animated by an earnest and lofty spirit of patriotism. The Spartan mother had reason to be proud of herself and of her children. When a woman of another country said to Gorgo, the wife of Leonidas, "The Spartan women alone rule the men," she replied, "The Spartan women alone bring forth men." Their husbands and their sons were fired by their sympathy to deeds of heroism. "Return either with your shield, or upon it," was their exhortation to their sons when going to battle.

Lycurgus is said to have divided the land belonging to the Spartans into 9000 equal lots and the remainder of Laconia into 30,000 equal lots, and to have assigned to each Spartan citizen one of the former of these lots, and to each Perioecus one of the latter.

Neither gold nor silver money was allowed in Sparta, and nothing but bars of iron passed in exchange for every commodity. As the Spartans were not permitted to engage in commerce, and all luxury and display in dress, furniture, and food was forbidden, they had very little occasion for a circulating medium, and iron money was found sufficient for their few wants. But this prohibition of the precious metals only made the Spartans more anxious to obtain them; and even in the times of their greatest glory the Spartans were the most venal of the Greeks, and could rarely resist the temptation of a bribe.

The legislation of Lycurgus was followed by important results. It made the Spartans a body of professional soldiers, all trained and well disciplined, at a time when military training and discipline were little known, and almost unpractised in the other states of Greece. The consequence was the rapid growth of the political power of Sparta, and the subjugation of the neighbouring states. At the time of Lycurgus the Spartans held only a small portion of Laconia: they were merely a garrison in the heart of an enemy's country. Their first object was to make themselves masters of Laconia, in which they finally succeeded after a severe struggle. They next turned their arms against the Messenians, Arcadians, and Argives. Of these wars the two waged against Messenia were the most celebrated and the most important. They were both long protracted and obstinately contested. They both ended in the victory of Sparta, and in the subjugation of Messenia. These facts are beyond dispute; but of the details we have no trustworthy narrative.

The FIRST MESSENIAN WAR lasted from B.C. 743 to 724. During the first four years the Lacedaemonians made little progress; but in the fifth a great battle was fought, and although its result was indecisive, the Messenians did not venture to risk another engagement, and retired to the strongly fortified mountain of Ithome. In their distress they sent to consult the oracle at Delphi, and received the appalling answer that the salvation of Messenia required the sacrifice of a virgin of the royal house to the gods of the lower world. Aristodemus, who is the Messenian hero of the first war, slew his own daughter, which so disheartened the Spartans, that they abstained from attacking the Messenians for some years. In the thirteenth year of the war the Spartan king marched against Ithome, and a second great battle was fought, but the result was again indecisive. The Messenian king fell in the action; and Aristodemus, who was chosen king in his place, prosecuted the war with vigour. In the fifth year of his reign a third great battle was fought. This time the Messenians gained a decisive victory, and the Lacedaemonians were driven back into their own territory. They now sent to ask advice of the Delphian oracle, and were promised success upon using stratagem. They therefore had recourse to fraud: and at the same time various prodigies dismayed the bold spirit of Aristodemus. His daughter too appeared to him in a dream, showed him her wounds, and beckoned him away. Seeing that his country was doomed to destruction, Aristodemus slew himself on his daughter's tomb. Shortly afterwards, in the twentieth year of the war, the Messenians abandoned Ithome, which the Lacedaemonians razed to the ground, and the whole country became subject to Sparta. Many of the inhabitants fled into other countries; but those who remained were reduced to the condition of Helots, and were compelled to pay to their masters half of the produce of their lands.

For thirty-nine years the Messenians endured this degrading yoke. At the end of this time they took up arms against their oppressors. The SECOND MESSENIAN WAR lasted from B.C. 685 to 668. Its hero is Aristomenes, whose wonderful exploits form the great subject of this war. It would appear that most of the states in Peloponnesus took part in the struggle. The first battle was fought before the arrival of the allies on either side, and, though it was indecisive, the valour of Aristomenes struck fear into the hearts of the Spartans. To frighten the enemy still more, the hero crossed the frontier, entered Sparta by night, and affixed a shield to the temple of Athena (Minerva), with the inscription, "Dedicated by Aristomenes to the goddess from the Spartan spoils." The Spartans in alarm sent to Delphi for advice. The god bade them apply to Athens for a leader. Fearing to disobey the oracle, but with the view of rendering no real assistance, the Athenians sent Tyrtaeus, a lame man and a schoolmaster. The Spartans received their new leader with due honour; and he was not long in justifying the credit of the oracle. His martial songs roused their fainting courage; and so efficacious were his poems that to them is mainly ascribed the final success of the Spartan arms.

Encouraged by the strains of Tyrtaeus, the Spartans again marched against the Messenians. But they were not at first successful. A great battle was fought at the Boar's Grave in the plain of Stenyclerus, in which they were defeated with great loss. In the third year of the war another great battle was fought, in which the Messenians suffered a signal defeat. So greet was their loss, that Aristomenes no longer ventured to meet the Spartans in the open field. Following the example of the Messenian leaders in the former war, he retired to the mountain fortress of Ira. The Spartans encamped at the foot of the mountain; but Aristomenes frequently sallied from the fortress, and ravaged the lands of Laconia with fire and sword. It is unnecessary to relate all the wonderful exploits of this hero in his various incursions. Thrice was he taken prisoner; on two occasions he burst his bonds, but on the third he was carried to Sparta, and thrown with his fifty companions into a deep pit, called Ceadas. His comrades were all killed by the fall; but Aristomenes reached the bottom unhurt. He saw, however, no means of escape, and had resigned himself to death; but on the third day perceiving a fox creeping among the bodies, he grasped its tail, and, following the animal as it struggled to escape, discovered an opening in the rock, and on the next day was at Ira to the surprise alike of friends and foes. But his single prowess was not sufficient to avert the ruin of his country. One night the Spartans surprised Ira, while Aristomenes was disabled by a wound; but he collected the bravest of his followers, and forced his way through the enemy. Many of the Messenians went to Rhegium, in Italy, under the sons of Aristomenes, but the hero himself finished his days in Rhodes.

The second Messenian war was terminated by the complete subjugation of the Messenians, who again became the serfs of their conquerors. In this condition they remained till the restoration of their independence by Epaminondas in the year 369 B.C. During the whole of the intervening period the Messenians disappear from history. The country called Messenia in the map became a portion of Laconia, which thus extended across the south of Pelponnesus from the eastern to the western sea.

CHAPTER V.
THE EARLY HISTORY OF ATHENS, DOWN TO THE ESTABLISHMENT OF DEMOCRACY BY CLISTHENES, B.C. 510.

Sparta was the only state in Greece which continued to retain the kingly form of government during the brilliant period of Grecian history. In all other parts of Greece royalty had been abolished at as early age, and various forms of republican government established in its stead. The abolition of royalty was first followed by an Oligarchy or the government of the Few. Democracy, or the government of the Many, was of later growth. It was not from the people that the oligarchies received their first and greatest blow. They were generally overthrown by the usurpers, to whom the Greeks gave the name of TYRANTS. [The Greek word Tyrant does not correspond in meaning to the same word in the English language. It signifies simply an irresponsible ruler, and may, therefore, be more correctly rendered by the term Despot.]

The rise of the Tyrants seems to have taken place about the same time in a large number of the Greek cities. In most cases they belonged to the nobles, and they generally became masters of the state by espousing the cause of the commonalty, and using the strength of the people to put down the oligarchy by force. At first they were popular with the general body of the citizens, who were glad to see the humiliation of their former masters. But discontent soon began to arise; the tyrant had recourse to violence to quell disaffection; and the government became in reality a tyranny in the modern sense of the word.

Many of the tyrants in Greece were put down by the Lacedaemonians. The Spartan government was essentially an oligarchy, and the Spartans were always ready to lend their powerful aid in favour of the government of the Few. Hence they took an active part in the overthrow of the despots, with the intention of establishing the ancient oligarchy in their place. But this rarely happened; and they found it impossible in most cases to reinstate the former body of nobles in their ancient privileges. The latter, it is true, attempted to regain them and were supported in their attempts by Sparta. Hence arose a new struggle. The first contest after the abolition of royalty was between oligarchy and the despot, the next was between oligarchy and democracy.

The history of Athens affords the most striking illustration of the different revolutions of which we have been speaking.

Little is known of Athens before the age of Solon. Its legendary tales are few, its historical facts still fewer. Cecrops, the first ruler of Attica, is said to have divided the country into twelve districts, which are represented as independent communities, each governed by a separate king. They were afterwards united into a single state, having Athens as its capital and the seat of government. At what time this important union was effected cannot be determined; but it is ascribed to Theseus, as the national hero of the Athenian people.

A few generations after Theseus, the Dorians are said to have invaded Attica. An oracle declared that they would be victorious if they spared the life of the Athenian King; whereupon Codrus, who then reigned at Athens, resolved to sacrifice himself for the welfare of his country. Accordingly he went into the invaders' camp in disguise, provoked a quarrel with one of the Dorian soldiers and was killed by the latter. Upon learning the death of the Athenian king, the Dorians retired from Attica without striking a blow: and the Athenians, from respect to the memory of Codrus, abolished the title of king, and substituted for it that of Archon or Ruler. The office, however, was held for life, and was confined to the family of Codrus. His son Medon was the first archon, and he was followed in the dignity by eleven members of the family in succession. But soon after the accession Alcmaeon, the thirteenth in descent from Medon, another change was introduced, and the duration of the archonship was limited to ten years (B.C. 752). The dignity was still confined to the descendants of Medon; but in the time of Hippomenes (B.C. 714) this restriction was removed, and the office was thrown open to all the nobles in the state. In B.C. 683 a still more important change took place. The archonship was now made annual, and its duties were distributed among nine persons, all of whom bore the title. The last of the decennial archons was Eryxias, the first of the nine annual archons Creon.

Such is the legendary account of the change of government at Athens, from royalty to an oligarchy. It appears to have taken place peaceably and gradually, as in most other Greek states. The whole political power was vested in the nobles; from them the nine annual archons were taken, and to them alone these magistrates were responsible. The people, or general body of freemen, had no share in the government.

The Athenian nobles were called EUPATRIDAE, the two other classes in the state being the GEOMORI or husbandmen, and DEMIURGI or artisans. This arrangement is ascribed to Theseus; but there was another division of the people of still greater antiquity. As the Dorians were divided into three tribes, so the Ionians were usually distributed into four tribes. The latter division also existed among the Athenians, who were Ionians, and it continued in full vigour down to the great revolution of Clisthenes (B.C. 509). These tribes were distinguished by the names of GELEONTES (or TELEONTES) "cultivators," HOPLETES "warriors," AEGICORES "goat-herds," and ARGADES "artisans." Each tribe contained three Phratriae, each Phratry thirty Gentes, and each Gens thirty heads of families.

The first date in Athenian history on which certain reliance can be placed is the institution of annual archons, in the year 683 B.C. The duties of the government were distributed among the nine archons in the following manner. The first was called THE ARCHON by way of pre-eminence, and sometimes the Archon Eponymus, because the year was distinguished by his name. The second archon was called THE BASILEUS or THE KING, because he represented the king in his capacity as high-priest of the nation. The third archon bore the title of THE POLEMARCH, or Commander-in-chief and was, down to the time of Clisthenes, the commander of the troops. The remaining six had the common title of THESMOTHETAE, or Legislators. Their duties seem to have been almost exclusively judicial.

The government of the Eupatrids was oppressive; and the discontent of the people at length became so serious, that Draco was appointed in 624 B.C. to draw up a written code of laws. They were marked by extreme severity. He affixed the penalty of death to all crimes alike; to petty thefts, for instance, as well as to sacrilege and murder. Hence they were said to have been written not in ink but in blood; and we are told that he justified this extreme harshness by saying that small offences deserved death, and that he knew no severer punishment for great ones.

The legislation of Draco failed to calm the prevailing discontent. The people gained nothing by the written code, except a more perfect knowledge of its severity; and civil dissensions prevailed as extensively as before. The general dissatisfaction with the government was favourable to revolutionary projects; and accordingly, twelve years after Draco's legislation (B.C. 612), Cylon, one of the nobles, conceived the design of depriving his brother Eupatrids of their power, and making himself tyrant of Athens. Having collected a considerable force, he seized the Acropolis; but he did not meet with support from the great mass of the people, and he soon found himself closely blockaded by the forces of the Eupatrids. Cylon and his brother made their escape, but the remainder of his associates, hard pressed by hunger, abandoned the defence of the walls, and took refuge at the altar of Athena (Minerva). They were induced by the archon Megacles, one of the illustrious family of the Alcmaeonidae, to quit the altar on the promise that their lives should be spared; but directly they had left the temple they were put to death, and some of them were murdered even at the altar of the Eumenides or Furies.

The conspiracy thus failed; but its suppression was attended with a long train of melancholy consequences. The whole family of the Alcmaeonidae was believed to have become tainted by the daring act of sacrilege committed by Megacles; and the friends and partisans of the murdered conspirators were not slow in demanding vengeance upon the accursed race. Thus a new element of discord was introduced into the state, In the midst of these dissensions there was one man who enjoyed a distinguished reputation at Athens, and to whom his fellow citizens looked up as the only person in the state who could deliver them from their political and social dissensions, and secure them from such misfortunes for the future. This man was Solon, the son of Execestides, and a descendant of Codrus. He had travelled through many parts of Greece and Asia, and had formed acquaintance with many of the most eminent men of his time. On his return to his native country he distinguished himself by recovering the island of Salamis, which had revolted to Megara (B.C. 600). Three years afterwards he persuaded the Alcmaeonidae to submit their case to the judgment of three hundred Eupatridae, by whom they were adjudged guilty of sacrilege, and were expelled from Attica. The banishment of the guilty race did not, however, deliver the Athenians from their religious fears. A pestilential disease with which they were visited was regarded as an unerring sign of the divine wrath. Upon the advice of the Delphic oracle, they invited the celebrated Cretan prophet and sage, Epimenides, to visit Athens, and purify their city from pollution and sacrilege. By performing certain sacrifices and expiatory acts, Epimenides succeeded in staying the plague.

The civil dissensions however still continued. The population of Attica was now divided into three hostile factions, consisting of the PEDIEIS or wealthy Eupatrid inhabitants of the plains; of the DIACRII, or poor inhabitants of the hilly districts in the north and east of Attica; and of the PARALI, or mercantile inhabitants of the coasts, who held an intermediate position between the other two. Their disputes were aggravated by the miserable condition of the poorer population. The latter were in a state of abject poverty, They had borrowed money from the wealthy at exorbitant rates of interest upon the security of their property and their persons. If the principal and interest of the debt were not paid, the creditor had the power of seizing the person as well as the land of his debtor, and of using him as a slave. Many had thus been torn from their homes and sold to barbarian masters, while others were cultivating as slaves the lands of their wealthy creditors in Attica. Matters had at length reached a crisis; the existing laws could no longer be enforced; and the poor were ready to rise in open insurrection against the rich.

In these alarming circumstances the ruling oligarchy were obliged to have recourse to Solon; and they therefore chose him Archon in B.C. 594, investing him under that title with unlimited powers to effect any changes he might consider beneficial to the state. His appointment was hailed with satisfaction by the poor; and all parties were willing to accept his mediation and reforms.

Solon commenced his undertaking by relieving the poorer class of debtors from their existing distress. He cancelled all contracts by which the land or person of a debtor had been given as security; and he forbad for the future all loans in which the person of the debtor was pledged. He next proceeded to draw up a new constitution and a new code of laws. As a preliminary step he repealed all the laws of Draco, except those relating to murder. He then made a new classification of the citizens, distributing them into four classes according to the amount of their property, thus making wealth and not birth the title to the honours and offices of the state. The first class consisted of those whose annual income was equal to 500 medimni of corn and upwards, and were called PENTACOSIOMEDIMNI. [The medimnus was one bushel and a half.] The second class consisted of those whose incomes ranged between 300 and 500 medimni and were called KNIGHTS, from their being able to furnish a war-horse. The third class consisted of those who received between 200 and 300 medimni, and were called ZEUGITAE from their being able to keep a yoke of oxen for the plough. The fourth class, called THETES, included all whose property fell short of 200 medimni. The first class were alone eligible to the archonship and the higher offices of the state. The second and third classes filled inferior posts, and were liable to military service, the former as horsemen, and the latter as heavy-armed soldiers on foot. The fourth class were excluded from all public offices, and served in the army only as light-armed troops. Solon, however, allowed them to veto in the public assembly, where they must have constituted by far the largest number. He gave the assembly the right of electing the archons and the other officers of the state; and he also made the archons accountable to the assembly at the expiration of their year of office.

This extension of the duties of the public assembly led to the institution of a new body. Solon created the Senate, or Council of Four Hundred with the special object of preparing all matters for the discussion of the public assembly, of presiding at its meetings, and of carrying its resolutions into effect. No subject could be introduced before the people, except by a previous resolution of the Senate. The members of the Senate were elected by the public assembly, one hundred from each of the four ancient tribes, which were left untouched by Solon. They held their office for a year, and were accountable at its expiration to the public assembly for the manner in which they had discharged their duties.

The Senate of the Areopagus [It received its name from its place of meeting, which was a rocky eminence opposite the Acropolis, called the hill of Ares (Mars Hill)], is said by some writers to have been instituted by Solon; but it existed long before his time, and may be regarded as the representative of the Council of Chiefs in the Heroic age. Solon enlarged its powers, and intrusted it with the general supervision of the institutions and laws of the state, and imposed upon it the duty of inspecting the lives and occupations of the citizens. All archons became members of it at the expiration of their year of office.

Solon laid only the foundation of the Athenian democracy by giving the poorer classes a vote in the popular assembly, and by enlarging the power of the latter; but he left the government exclusively in the hands of the wealthy. For many years after his time the government continued to be an oligarchy, but was exercised with more moderation and justice than formerly.

Solon enacted numerous laws, containing regulations on almost all subjects connected with the public and private life of the citizens. He encouraged trade and manufactures, and invited foreigners to settle in Athens by the promise of protection and by valuable privileges. To discourage idleness a son was not obliged to support his father in old age, if the latter had neglected to teach him some trade or occupation.

Solon punished theft by compelling the guilty party to restore double the value of the property stolen. He forbade speaking evil either of the dead or of the living.

Solon is said to have been aware that he had left many imperfections in his laws. He described them not as the best laws which he could devise, but as the best which the Athenians could receive. Having bound the government and people of Athens by a solemn oath to observe his institutions for at least ten years, he left Athens and travelled in foreign lands. During his absence the old dissensions between the Plain, the Shore, and the Mountain broke out afresh with more violence than ever. The first was headed by Lycurgus, the second by Megacles, an Alcmaeonid, and the third by Pisistratus, the cousin of Solon. Of these leaders, Pisistratus was the ablest and the most dangerous. He had espoused the cause of the poorest of the three classes, in order to gain popularity, and to make himself master of Athens. Solon on his return to Athens detected the ambitious designs of his kinsman, and attempted to disuade him from them. Finding his remonstrances fruitless, he next denounced his projects in verses addressed to the people. Few, however, gave any heed to his warnings: and Pisistratus, at length finding his schemes ripe for action, had recourse to a memorable strategem to secure his object. One day he appeared in the market-place in a chariot, his mules and his own person bleeding with wounds inflicted with his own hands. These he exhibited to the people, telling them that he had been nearly murdered in consequence of defending their rights. The popular indignation was excited; and a guard of fifty clubmen was granted him for his future security. He gradually increased the number of his guard and soon found himself strong enough to throw off the mask and seize the Acropolis (B.C. 560). Megacles and the Alcmaeonidae left the city. Solon alone had the courage to oppose the usurpation, and upbraided the people with their cowardice and their treachery. "You might," said he, "with ease have crushed the tyrant in the bud; but nothing now remains but to pluck him up by the roots." But no one responded to his appeal. He refused to fly; and when his friends asked him on what he relied for protection, "On my old age," was his reply. It is creditable to Pisistratus that he left his aged relative unmolested, and even asked his advice in the administration of the government. Solon did not long survive the overthrow of the constitution. He died a year or two afterwards at the advanced age of eighty. His ashes are said to have been scattered by his own direction round the island of Salamis, which he had won for the Athenian people.

Pisistratus however did not retain his power long. The leaders of the factions of the Shore and the Plain combined and drove the usurper into exile. But the Shore and the Plain having quarrelled, Pisistratus was recalled and again became master of Athens. Another revolution shortly afterwards drove him into exile a second time, and he remained abroad ten years. At length, with the assistance of mercenaries from other Grecian states and with the aid of his partisans in Athens, he became master of Athens for the third time, and henceforth continued in possession of the supreme power till the day of his death. As soon as he was firmly established in the government, his administration was marked by mildness and equity. He maintained the institutions of Solon, taking care, however, that the highest offices should always be held by some members of his own family. He not only enforced strict obedience to the laws, but himself set the example of submitting to them. Being accused of murder, he disdained to take advantage of his authority, and went in person to plead his cause before the Areopagus, where his accuser did not venture to appear. He courted popularity by largesses to the citizens and by throwing open his gardens to the poor. He adorned Athens with many public buildings. He commenced on a stupendous scale a temple to the Olympian Zeus, which remained unfinished for centuries, and was at length completed by the emperor Hadrian. He was a patron of literature, as well as of the arts. He is said to have been the first person in Greece who collected a library, which he threw open to the public; and to him posterity is indebted for the collection of the Homeric poems. On the whole it cannot be denied that he made a wise and noble use of his power.

Pisistratus died at an advanced age in 527 B.C., thirty-three years after his first usurpation. He transmitted the sovereign power to his sons, Hippias and Hipparchus, who conducted the government on the same principles as their father. Hipparchus inherited his father's literary tastes. He invited several distinguished poets, such as Anacreon and Simonides, to his court. The people appear to have been contented with their rule; and it was only an accidental circumstance which led to their overthrow and to a change in the government.

Their fall was occasioned by the conspiracy of Harmodius and Aristogiton, who were attached to each other by a most intimate friendship. Harmodius having given offence to Hippias, the despot revenged himself by putting a public affront upon his sister. This indignity excited the resentment of the two friends, and they now resolved to slay the despots at the festival of the Great Panathenaea, when all the citizens were required to attend in arms. Having communicated their design to a few associates, the conspirators appeared armed at the appointed time like the rest of the citizens, but carrying concealed daggers besides. Harmodius and Aristogiton had planned to kill Hippias first as he was arranging the order of the procession outside the city, but, upon approaching the spot where he was standing, they were thunderstruck at beholding one of the conspirators in close conversation with the despot. Believing that they were betrayed, they rushed back into the city with their daggers hid in the myrtle boughs which they were to have carried in the procession, and killed Hipparchus. Harmodius was immediately cut down by the guards. Aristogiton died under the tortures to which he was subjected in order to compel him to disclose his accomplices.

Hipparchus was assassinated in B.C. 514, the fourteenth year after the death of Pisistratus. From this time the character of the government became entirely changed. His brother's murder converted Hippias into a cruel and suspicious tyrant. He put to death numbers of the citizens, and raised large sums of money by extraordinary taxes.

The Alcmaeonidae, who had lived in exile ever since the third and final restoration of Pisistratus to Athens, now began to form schemes to expel the tyrant. Clisthenes, the son of Megacles, who was the head of the family, secured the Delphian oracle by pecuniary presents to the Pythia, or priestess, henceforth, whenever the Spartans came to consult the oracle, the answer of the priestess was always the same, "Athens must be liberated." This order was so often repeated, that the Spartans at last resolved to obey. Cleomenes, king of Sparta, defeated the Thessalian allies of Hippias; and the tyrant, unable to meet his enemies in the field, took refuge in the Acropolis. Here he might have maintained himself in safety, had not his children been made prisoners as they were being secretly carried out of the country. To procure their restoration, he consented to quit Attics in the space of five days. He sailed to Asia, and took up his residence at Sigeum in the Troad, which his father had wrested from the Mytilenaeans in war.

Hippias was expelled in B.C. 510, four years after the assassination of Hipparchus. These four years had been a time of suffering and oppression for the Athenians, and had effaced from their minds all recollection of the former mild rule of Pisistratus and his sons. Hence the expulsion of the family was hailed with delight. The memory of Harmodius and Aristogiton was cherished with the fondest reverence; and the Athenians of a later age, overlooking the four years which had elapsed from their death to the overthrow of the despotism, represented them as the liberators of their country and the first martyrs for its liberty. Their statues were erected in the market-place soon after the expulsion of Hippias; their descendants enjoyed immunity from all taxes and public burdens; and their deed of vengeance formed the favourite subject of drinking songs.

The Lacedaemonians quitted Athens soon after Hippias had sailed away, leaving the Athenians to settle their own affairs. Clisthenes, to whom Athens was mainly indebted for its liberation from the despotism, aspired to be the political leader of the state but he was opposed by Isagoras, the leader of the party of the nobles. By the Solonian constitution, the whole political power was vested in the hands of the nobles; and Clisthenes soon found that it was hopeless to contend against his rival under the existing order of things. For this reason he resolved to introduce an important change in the constitution, and to give to the people an equal share in the government.

The reforms of Clisthenes gave birth to the Athenian democracy, which can hardly be said to have existed before this time. His first and most important measure was a redistribution of the whole population of Attica into ten new tribes. He abolished the four ancient Ionic tribes, and enrolled in the ten new tribes all the free inhabitants of Attica, including both resident aliens and even emancipated slaves. He divided the tribes into a certain number of cantons or townships, called DEMI, which at a later time were 174 in number. Every Athenian citizen was obliged to be enrolled in a demus, each of which, like a parish in England, administered its own affairs. It had its public meetings it levied rates, and was under the superintendence of an officer called DEMARCHUS.

The establishment of the ten new tribes led to a change in the number of the Senate. It had previously consisted of 400 members, but it was now enlarged to 500, fifty being selected from each of the ten new tribes. The Ecclesia, or formal assembly of the citizens, was now summoned at certain fixed periods; and Clisthenes transferred the government of the state, which had hitherto been in the hands of the archons, to the senate and the ecclesia. He also increased the judicial as well as the political power of the people; and enacted that all public crimes should be tried by the whole body of citizens above thirty years of age, specially convoked and sworn for the purpose. The assembly thus convened was called HELIAEA and its members HELIASTS. Clisthenes also introduced the OSTRACISM, by which an Athenian citizen might be banished without special accusation, trial, or defence for ten years, which term was subsequently reduced to five. It must be recollected that the force which a Greek government had at its disposal was very small; and that it was comparatively easy for an ambitious citizen, supported by a numerous body of partisans, to overthrow the constitution and make himself despot. The Ostracism was the means devised by Clisthenes for removing quietly from the state a powerful party leader before he could carry into execution any violent schemes for the subversion of the government. Every precaution was taken to guard this institution from abuse. The senate and the ecclesia had first to determine by a special vote whether the safety of the state required such a step to be taken. If they decided in the affirmative, a day was fixed for the voting, and each citizen wrote upon a tile or oyster-shell [OSTRACON, whence the name OSTRACISM] the name of the person whom he wished to banish. The votes were then collected, And if it was found that 6000 had been recorded against any one person, he was obliged to withdraw from the city within ten days: if the number of votes did not amount to 6000, nothing was done.

The aristocratical party, enraged at these reforms called in the assistance of Cleomenes, king of the Lacedaemonians. Athens was menaced by foreign enemies and distracted by party struggles. Clisthenes was at first compelled to retire from Athens; but the people rose in arms against Cleomenes, expelled the Lacedaemonians, who had taken possession of the city, and recalled Clisthenes. Thereupon Cleomenes collected a Peloponnesian army in order to establish Isagoras as a tyrant over the Athenians, and at the same time he concerted measures with the Thebans and the Chalcidians of Euboea for a simultaneous attack upon Attica. The Peloponnesian army, commanded by the two kings, Cleomenes and Demaratus, entered Attica, and advanced as far as Eleusis; but when the allies became aware of the object for which they had been summoned, they refused to march farther, and strongly protested against the attempt to establish a tyranny at Athens. Their remonstrances being seconded by Demaratus, Cleomenes found it necessary to abandon the expedition and return home. At a later period (B.C. 491) Cleomenes took revenge upon Demaratus by persuading the Spartans to depose him upon the ground of illegitimacy. The exiled king took refuge at the Persian court.

The unexpected retreat of the Peloponnesian army delivered the Athenians from their most formidable enemy, and they lost no time in turning their arms against their other foes. Marching into Boeotia, they defeated the Thebans and then crossed over into Euboea, where they gained a decisive victory over the Chalcidians. In order to secure their dominion in Euboea, and at the same time to provide for their poorer citizens, the Athenians distributed the estates of the wealthy Chalcidian landowners among 4000 of their citizens, who settled in the country under the name of CLERUCI.

The successes of Athens excited the jealousy of the Spartans, and they now resolved to make a third attempt to overthrow the Athenian democracy. They had meantime discovered the deception which had been practised upon them by the Delphic oracle; And they invited Hippias to come from Sigeum to Sparta, in order to restore him to Athens. The experience of the last campaign had taught them that they could not calculate upon the co-operation of their allies without first obtaining their approval of the project; and they therefore summoned deputies from all their allies to meet at Sparta, in order to determine respecting the restoration of Hippias. But the proposal was received with universal repugnance; and the Spartans found it necessary to abandon their project. Hippias returned to Sigeum, and afterwards proceeded to the court of Darius.

Athens had now entered upon her glorious career. The institutions of Clisthenes had given her citizens a personal interest in the welfare and the grandeur of their country. A spirit of the warmest patriotism rapidly sprang up among them; and the history of the Persian wars, which followed almost immediately, exhibits a striking proof of the heroic sacrifices which they were prepared to make for the liberty and independence of their state.

CHAPTER VI.
THE GREEK COLONIES.

The vast number of the Greek colonies, their wide-spread diffusion over all parts of the Mediterranean, which thus became a kind of Grecian lake, and their rapid growth in wealth, power, and intelligence, afford the most striking proofs of the greatness of this wonderful people. Civil dissensions and a redundant population were the chief causes of the origin of most of the Greek colonies. They were usually undertaken with the approbation of the cities from which they issued, and under the management of leaders appointed by them. But a Greek colony was always considered politically independent of the mother-city and emancipated from its control. The only connexion between them was one of filial affection and of common religious ties. Almost every colonial Greek city was built upon the sea-coast, and the site usually selected contained a hill sufficiently lofty to form an acropolis.

The Grecian colonies may be arranged in four groups: 1. Those founded in Asia Minor and the adjoining islands; 2. Those in the western parts of the Mediterranean, in Italy, Sicily, Gaul, and Spain; 3. Those in Africa; 4. Those in Epirus, Macedonia, and Thrace.

1. The earliest Greek colonies were those founded on the western shores of Asia Minor. They were divided into three great masses, each bearing the name of that section of the Greek race with which they claimed affinity. The AEolic cities covered the northern part of this coast, together with the islands of Lesbos and Tenedos; the Ionians occupied the centre, with the islands of Chios and Samos; and the Dorians the southern portion, with the islands of Rhodes and Cos. Most of these colonies were founded in consequence of the changes in the population of Greece which attended the conquest of Peloponnesus by the Dorians. The Ionic cities were

early distinguished by a spirit of commercial enterprise, and soon rose superior in wealth and in power to their AEolian and Dorian neighbours. Among the Ionic cities themselves Miletus and Ephesus were the most flourishing, Grecian literature took its rise in the AEolic and Ionic cities of Asia Minor. Homer was probably a native of Smyrna. Lyric poetry flourished in the island of Lesbos, where Sappho and Alcaeus were born. The Ionic cities were also the seats of the earliest schools of Grecian philosophy. Thales, who founded the Ionic school of philosophy, was a native of Miletus. Halicarnassus was one of the most important of the Doric cities, of which Herodotus was a native, though he wrote in the Ionic dialect.

2. The earliest Grecian settlement in Italy was Cumae in Campania, situated near Cape Misenum, on the Tyrrhenian sea. It is said to have been a joint colony from the AEolic Cyme in Asia and from Chalcis in Euboea, and to have been founded, according to the common chronology, in B.C. 1050. Cumae was for a long time the most flourishing city in Campania; and it was not till its decline in the fifth century before the Christian era that Capua rose into importance.

The earliest Grecian settlement in Sicily was founded in B.C. 735. The extraordinary fertility of the land soon attracted numerous colonists from various parts of Greece, and there arose on the coasts of Sicily a succession of flourishing cities. Of these, Syracuse and Agrigentum, both Dorian colonies, became the most powerful. The former was founded by the Corinthians in B.C. 734, and at the time of its greatest prosperity contained a population of 500,000 souls, and was surrounded by walls twenty-two miles in circuit. Its greatness, however, belongs to a later period of Grecian history.

The Grecian colonies in southern Italy began to be planted at nearly the same time as in Sicily. They eventually lined the whole southern coast, as far as Cumae on the one sea and Tarentum on the other. They even surpassed those in Sicily in number and importance; and so numerous and flourishing did they become, that the south of Italy received the name of Magna Graecia. Of these, two of the earliest and most prosperous were Sybaris and Croton, both situated upon the gulf of Tarentum, and both of Achaean origin. Sybaris was planted in B.C. 720 and Croton in B.C. 710. For two centuries they seem to have lived in harmony, and we know scarcely anything of their history till their fatal contest in B.C. 510, which ended in the ruin of Sybaris. During the whole of this period they were two of the most flourishing cities in all Hellas. Sybaris in particular attained to an extraordinary degree of wealth, and its inhabitants were so notorious for their luxury, effeminacy, and debauchery, that their name has become proverbial for a voluptuary in ancient and modern times. Croton was the chief seat of the Pythagorean philosophy. Pythagroras was a native of Samos, but emigrated to Croton, where he met with the most wonderful success in the propagation of his views. He established a kind of religious brotherhood, closely united by a sacred vow. They believed in the transmigration of souls, and their whole training was designed to make them temperate and self-denying. The doctrines of Pythagoras spread through many of the other cities of Magna Graecia.

Of the numerous other Greek settlements in the south of Italy, those of Locri, Rhegium, and Tarentum were the meet important. Locri was founded by the Locrians from the mother-country in B.C. 683. The laws of this city were drawn up by one of its citizens, named Zaleucus, and so averse were the Locrians to any change in them, that whoever proposed a new law had to appear in the public assembly with a rope round his neck, which was immediately tightened if he failed to convince his fellow-citizens of the necessity of the alteration. Rhegium, situated on the straits of Messina, opposite Sicily, was colonised by the Chalcidians, but received a large body of Messenians, who settled here at the close of the Messenian war. Anaxilas, tyrant of Rhegium about B.C. 500, was of Messenian descent. He seized the Sicilian Zancle on the opposite coast, and changed its name into Messana, which it still bears. Tarentum was a colony from Sparta and was founded about B.C. 708. After the destruction of Sybaris it was the most powerful and flourishing city in Magna Graecia, and continued to enjoy great prosperity till its subjugation by the Romans. Although of Spartan origin, it did not maintain Spartan habits, and its citizens were noted at a later time for their love of luxury and pleasure.

The Grecian settlements in the distant countries of Gaul and Spain were not numerous. The most celebrated was Massalia, the modern Marseilles, founded by the Ionic Phocaeans in B.C. 600.

3. The northern coast of Africa, between the territories of Carthage and Egypt, was also occupied by Greek colonists. The city of Cyrene was founded about B.C. 630. It was a colony from the island of Thera in the AEgean, which was itself a colony from Sparta. The situation of Cyrene was well chosen. It stood on the edge

of a range of hills, at the distance of ten miles from the Mediterranean, of which it commanded a fine view. These hills descended by a succession of terraces to the port of the town, called Apollonia. The climate was most salubrious, and the soil was distinguished by extraordinary fertility. With these advantages Cyrene rapidly grew in wealth and power; and its greatness is attested by the immense remains which still mark its desolate site. Cyrene planted several colonies in the adjoining district, of which Barca, founded about B.C. 560, was the most important.

4. There were several Grecian colonies situated on the eastern side of the Ionian sea, in Epirus and its immediate neighbourhood. Of these the island of Corcyra, now called Corfu, was the most wealthy and powerful. It was founded by the Corinthians about B.C. 700, and in consequence of its commercial activity it soon became a formidable rival to the mother-city. Hence a war broke out between these two states at an early period; and the most ancient naval battle on record was the one fought between their fleets in B.C. 664. The dissensions between the mother-city and her colony are frequently mentioned in Grecian history, and were one of the immediate causes of the Peloponnesian war. Notwithstanding their quarrels they joined in planting four Grecian colonies upon the same line of coast--Leucas, Anactorium, Apollonia, and Epidamnus.

The colonies in Macedonia and Thrace were very numerous, and extended all along the coast of the AEgean, of the Hellespont, of the Propontis, and of the Euxine, from the borders of Thessaly to the mouth of the Danube. Of these we can only glance at the most important. The colonies on the coast of Macedonia were chiefly founded by Chalcis and Eretria in Euboea; and the peninsula of Chalcidice, with its three projecting headlands, was covered with their settlements, and derived its name from the former city. The Corinthians likewise planted a few colonies on this coast, of which Potidaea, on the narrow isthmus of Pallene, most deserves mention.

Of the colonies in Thrace, the most flourishing were Selymbria and Byzantium, both founded by the Megarians, who appear as an enterprising maritime people at an early period.

CHAPTER VII.
THE PERSIAN WARS.--FROM THE IONIC REVOLT TO THE BATTLE OF MARATHON, B.C. 500-490.

The Grecian cities on the coast of Asia Minor were the neighbours of an Asiatic power which finally reduced them to subjection. This was the kingdom of Lydia, of which Sardis was the capital. Croesus, the last and most powerful of the Lydian kings, who ascended the throne B.C. 560, conquered in succession all the Grecian cities on the coast. His rule, however, was not oppressive, and he permitted the cities to regulate their own affairs. He spoke the Greek language, welcomed Greek guests, and reverenced the Greek oracles, which he enriched with the most munificent offerings. He extended his dominions in Asia Minor as far as the river Halys, and he formed a close alliance with Astyages, king of the Medes, who were then the ruling race in Asia. Everything seemed to betoken uninterrupted prosperity, when a people hitherto almost unknown suddenly became masters of the whole of western Asia.

The Persians were of the same race as the Medes and spoke a dialect of the same language. They inhabited the mountainous region south of Media, which slopes gradually down to the low grounds on the coast of the Persian gulf. While the Medes became enervated by the corrupting influences to which they were exposed, the Persians preserved in their native mountains their simple and warlike habits. They were a brave and hardy nation, clothed in skins, drinking only water, and ignorant of the commonest luxuries of life. Cyrus led these fierce warriors from their mountain fastnesses, defeated the Medes in battle, took Astyages prisoner, and deprived him of his throne. The other nations included in the Median empire submitted to the conqueror, and the sovereignty of Upper Asia thus passed from the

Medes to the Persians. The accession of Cyrus to the empire is placed in B.C. 559. A few years afterwards Cyrus turned his arms against the Lydians, took Sardis, and deprived Croesus of his throne (B.C. 546). The fall of Croesus was followed by the subjection of the Greek cities in Asia to the Persian yoke. They offered a brave but ineffectual resistance, and were taken one after the other by Harpagus the Persian general. Even the islands of Lesbos and Chios sent in their submission to Harpagus, although the Persians then possessed no fleet to force them to obedience. Samos, on the other hand, maintained its independence, and appears soon afterwards one of the most powerful of the Grecian states.

During the reign of Cambyses (B.C. 529-521), the son and successor of Cyrus, the Greek cities of Asia remained obedient to their Persian governors. It was during this reign that Polycrates, tyrant of Samos, became the master of the Grecian seas. The ambition and good fortune of this enterprising tyrant were alike remarkable. He possessed a hundred ships of war, with which he conquered several of the islands; and he aspired to nothing less than the dominion of Ionia, as well as of the islands in the AEgean. The Lacedaemonians, who had invaded the island at the invitation of the Samian exiles, for the purpose of overthrowing his government, were obliged to retire, after besieging his city in vain for forty days. Everything which he undertook seemed to prosper; but his uninterrupted good fortune at length excited the alarm of his ally Amasis, the king of Egypt. According to the tale related by Herodotus, the Egyptian king, convinced that such amazing good fortune would sooner or later incur the envy of the gods, wrote to Polycrates, advising him to throw away one of his most valuable possessions and thus inflict some injury upon himself. Thinking the advice to be good, Polycrates threw into the sea a favourite ring of matchless price and beauty; but unfortunately it was found a few days afterwards in the belly of a fine fish which a fisherman had sent him as a present. Amasis now foresaw that the ruin of Polycrates was inevitable, and sent a herald to Samos to renounce his alliance. The gloomy anticipations of the Egyptian monarch proved well founded. In the midst of all his prosperity Polycrates fell by a most ignominious fate. Oroetes, the satrap of Sardis, had for some unknown cause conceived a deadly hatred against the Samian despot. By a cunning stratagem the satrap allured him to the mainland, where he was immediately arrested and hanged upon a cross (B.C. 522).

The reign of Darius, the third king of Persia. (B.C. 521-485), is memorable in Grecian history. In his invasion of Scythia, his fleet, which was furnished by the Asiatic Greeks, was ordered to sail up the Danube and throw a bridge of boats across the river. The King himself, with his land forces, marched through Thrace; and, crossing the bridge, placed it under the care of the Greeks, telling them that, if he did not return within sixty days, they might break it down, and sail home. He then left them, and penetrated into the Scythian territory. The sixty days had already passed away, and there was yet no sign of the Persian army; but shortly afterwards the Greeks were astonished by the appearance of a body of Scythians, who informed them that Darius was in full retreat, pursued by the whole Scythian nation, and that his only hope of safety depended upon that bridge. They urged the Greeks to seize this opportunity of destroying the Persian army, and of recovering their own liberty, by breaking down the bridge. Their exhortations were warmly seconded by the Athenian Miltiades, the tyrant of the Thracian Chersonesus, and the future conqueror of Marathon. The other rulers of the Ionian cities were at first disposed to follow his suggestion; but as soon as Histiaeus of Miletus reminded them that their sovereignty depended upon the support of the Persian king, and that his ruin would involve their own, they changed their minds and resolved to await the Persians. After enduring great privations and sufferings Darius and his army at length reached the Danube and crossed the bridge in safety. Thus the selfishness of these Grecian despots threw away the most favourable opportunity that ever presented itself of delivering their native cities from the Persian yoke. To reward the services of Histiaeus, Darius gave him the town of Myrainus, near the Strymon. Darius, on his return to Asia, left Megabazus in Europe with an army of 80,000 men to complete the subjugation of Thrace and of the Greek cities upon the Hellespont. Megabazus not only subdued the Thracians, but crossed the Strymon, conquered the Paeonians, and penetrated as far as the frontiers of Macedonia. He then sent heralds into the latter country to demand earth and water, the customary symbols of submission. These were immediately granted by Amyntas, the reigning monarch (B.C. 510); and thus the Persian dominions were extended to the borders of Thessaly. Megabazus, on his return to Sardis, where Darius awaited him, informed the Persian monarch that Histiaeus was collecting the elements of a power which might hereafter prove formidable to the Persian sovereignty, since Myrcinus commanded the navigation of the Strymon, and consequently the commerce with the interior of Thrace. Darius, perceiving that the apprehensions of his general were not without foundation, summoned Histiaeus to his presence, and, under the pretext that he could not bear to be deprived of the company of his friend, carried him with the rest of the court to Susa. This apparently trivial circumstance was attended with important consequences to the Persian empire and to the whole Grecian race.

For the next few years everything remained quiet in the Greek cities of Asia; but about B.C. 502 a revolution in Naxos, one of the islands in the AEgean Sea, first disturbed the general repose, and occasioned the war between Greece and Asia. The aristocratical exiles, who had been driven out of Naxos by a rising of the people, applied for aid to Aristagoras, the tyrant of Miletus and the son-in-law of Histiaeus. Aristagoras readily promised his assistance, knowing that, if they were restored by his means, he should become master of the island. He obtained the co-operation of Artaphernes, the satrap of western Asia by holding out to him the prospect of annexing not only Naxos, but all the islands of the AEgean sea, to the Persian empire. He offered at the same time to defray the expense of the armament. Artaphernes placed at his disposal a fleet of 200 ships under the command of Megabates, a Persian of high rank; but Aristagoras having affronted the Persian admiral, the latter revenged himself by privately informing the Naxians of the object of the expedition, which had hitherto been kept a secret. When the Persian fleet reached Naxos they experienced a vigorous resistance; and at the end of four months they were compelled to abandon the enterprise and return to Miletus. Aristagoras was now threatened with utter ruin. Having deceived Artaphernes, and incurred the enmity of Megabates, he could expect no favour from the Persian government, and might be called upon at any moment to defray the expenses of the armament. In these difficulties he began to think of exciting a revolt of his countrymen; and while revolving the project he received a message from his father-in-law, Histiaeus, urging him to this very step. Afraid of trusting any one with so dangerous a message, Histiaeus had shaved the head of a trusty slave, branded upon it the necessary words, and as soon as the hair had grown again sent him off to Miletus. His only motive for urging the Ionians to revolt was the desire of escaping from captivity at Susa, thinking that Darius would set him at liberty in order to put down an insurrection of his countrymen. The message from Histiaeus fixed the wavering resolution of

Aristagoras. He forthwith called together the leading citizens of Miletus, laid before them the project of revolt, and asked them for advice. They all approved of the scheme, with the exception of Hecataeus, one of the earliest Greek historians. Aristagoras laid down the supreme power in Miletus, and nominally resigned to the people the management of their own affairs. A democratical form of government was established in the other Greek cities of Asia, which thereupon openly revolted from Persia (B.C. 500).

Aristagoras now resolved to cross over to Greece, in order to solicit assistance. The Spartans, to whom he first applied, refused to take any part in the war; but at Athens he met with a very different reception. The Athenians sympathised with the Ionians as their kinsmen and colonists, and were incensed against the satrap Artaphernes, who had recently commanded them to recall Hippias. Accordingly they voted to send a squadron of twenty ships to the assistance of the Ionians; and in the following year (B.C. 499) this fleet, accompanied by five ships from Eretria in Euboea, crossed the AEgean. The troops landed at Ephesus, and, being reinforced by a strong body, of Ionians, marched upon Sardis. Artaphernes was taken unprepared; and not having sufficient troops to man the walls, he retired into the citadel, leaving the town a prey to the invaders. Accordingly they entered it unopposed; and while engaged in pillage, one of the soldiers set fire to a house. As most of the houses were built of wickerwork and thatched with straw, the flames rapidly spread, and in a short time the whole city was in flames. The Greeks, on their return to the coast, were overtaken by a large Persian force and defeated with great slaughter. The Athenians hastened on board their ships and sailed home.

When Darius heard of the burning of Sardis, he burst into a paroxysm of rage. It was against the obscure strangers who had dared to burn one of his capitals that his wrath was chiefly directed. "The Athenians!" he exclaimed, "who are they?" Upon being informed he took his bow, shot an arrow high into the air, saying, "Grant me, Jove, to take vengeance upon the Athenians!" And he charged one of his attendants to remind him thrice every day at dinner "Sire, remember the Athenians." Meantime the insurrection spread to the Greek cities in Cyprus, as well as to those on the Hellespont and the Propontis, and seemed to promise permanent independence to the Asiatic Greeks; but they were no match for the whole power of the Persian empire, which was soon brought against them. Cyprus was subdued, and siege laid to the cities upon the coast of Asia. Aristagoras now began to despair, and basely deserted his countrymen, whom he had led into peril. Collecting a large body of Milesians, he set sail for the Thracian coast, where he was slain under the walls of a town to which he had laid siege. Soon after his departure, his father-in-law, Histiaeus came down to the coast. The artful Greek not only succeeded in removing the suspicions which Darius first entertained respecting him, but he persuaded the king to send him into Ionia, in order to assist the Persian generals in suppressing the rebellion. Artaphernes, however, was not so easily deceived as his master, and plainly accused Histiaeus of treachery when the latter arrived at Sardis. "I will tell you how the facts stand" said Artaphernes to Histiaeus; "it was you who made the shoe, and Aristagoras has put it on." Finding himself unsafe at Sardis, he escaped to the island of Chios; but he was regarded with suspicion by all parties. At length he obtained eight galleys from Lesbos, with which he sailed towards Byzantium, and carried on piracies as well against the Grecian as the barbarian vessels. This unprincipled adventurer met with a traitor's death. Having landed on the coast of Mysia, he was surprised by a Persian force and made prisoner. Being carried to Sardis, Artaphernes at once caused him to be crucified, and sent his head to Darius, who ordered it to be honourably buried, condemning the ignominious execution of the man who had once saved the life of the Great King.

In the sixth year of the revolt (B.C. 495), when several Grecian cities had already been taken by the Persians, Artaphernes laid siege to Miletus by sea and by land. A naval engagement took place at Lade a small island off Miletus, which decided the fate of the war. The Samians deserted at the commencement of the battle, and the Ionian fleet was completely defeated. Miletus was soon afterwards taken, and was treated with signal severity. Most of the males were slain; and the few who escaped the sword were carried with the women and children into captivity (B.C. 494). The other Greek cities in Asia and the neighbouring islands were treated with the same cruelty. The islands of Chios, Lesbos, and Tenedos were swept of their inhabitants; and the Persian fleet sailed up to the Hellespont and Propontis, carrying with it fire and sword. The Athenian Miltiades only escaped falling into the power of the Persians by a rapid flight to Athens.

The subjugation of Ionia was now complete. This was the third time that the Asiatic Greeks had been conquered by a foreign power: first by the Lydian Croesus;

secondly by the generals of Cyrus; and lastly by those of Darius. It was from the last that they suffered most, and they never fully recovered their former prosperity.

Darius was now at liberty to take vengeance upon the Athenians. He appointed Mardonius to succeed Artaphernes as satrap in western Asia, and he placed under his command a large armament, with injunctions to bring to Susa those Athenians and Eretrians who had insulted the authority of the Great King. Mardonius, after crossing the Hellespont, commenced his march through Thrace and Macedonia, subduing, as he went along, the tribes which had not yet submitted to the Persian power. He ordered the fleet to double the promontory of Mount Athos, and join the land forces at the head of the gulf of Therma; but one of the hurricanes which frequently blow off this dangerous coast overtook the Persian fleet, destroyed 300 vessels and drowned or dashed upon the rocks 20,000 men. Meantime the land forces of Mardonius had suffered so much from an attack made upon them by a Thracian tribe, that he could not proceed farther. He led his army back across the Hellespont, and returned to the Persian court covered with shame and grief (B.C. 492).

The failure of this expedition did not shake the resolution of Darius. He began to make preparations for another attempt on a still larger scale, and meantime sent heralds to most of the Grecian states to demand from each earth and water as the symbol of submission. Such terror had the Persians inspired by their recent conquest of Ionia, that a large number of the Grecian cities at once complied with the demand; but the Athenians cast the herald into a deep pit, and the Spartans threw him into a well bidding him take earth and water from thence.

In the spring of B.C. 490 a large army and fleet were assembled in Cilicia, and the command was given to Datis, a Median, and Artaphernes, son of the satrap of Sardis of that name. Warned by the recent disaster of Mardonius in doubling the promontory of Mount Athos, they resolved to sail straight across the AEgean to Euboea, subduing on their way the Cyclades. These islands yielded a ready submission; and it was not till Datis and Artaphernes reached Euboea that they encountered any resistance. Eretria defended itself gallantly for six days, and repulsed the Persians with loss; but on the seventh the gates were opened to the besiegers by the treachery of two of its leading citizens. The city was razed to the ground, and the inhabitants were put in chains. From Eretria the Persians crossed over to Attica, and landed on the ever memorable plain of Marathon, a spot which had been pointed out to them by the despot Hippias, who accompanied the army.

As soon as the news of the fall of Eretria reached Athens, a courier had been sent to Sparta to solicit assistance. This was promised; but the superstition of the Spartans prevented them from setting out immediately, since it wanted a few days to the full moon, and it was contrary to their religious customs to commence a march during this interval. Meantime the Athenians had marched to Marathon, and were encamped upon the mountains which surrounded the plain. They were commanded, according to the regular custom, by ten generals, one for each tribe, and by the Polemarch, or third Archon, who down to this time continued to be a colleague of the generals. Among these the most distinguished was Miltiades, who, though but lately a tyrant in the Chersonesus, had shown such energy and ability, that the Athenians had elected him one of their commanders upon the approach of the Persian fleet. Upon learning the answer which the courier brought from Sparta, the ten generals were divided in opinion. Five of them were opposed to an immediate engagement with the overwhelming number of Persians, and urged the importance of waiting for the arrival of the Lacedaemonian succours. Miltiades and the remaining four contended that not a moment should be lost in fighting the Persians, not only in order to avail themselves of the present enthusiasm of the people, but still more to prevent treachery from spreading among their ranks. Callimachus, the Polemarch, yielded to the arguments of Miltiades, and gave his vote for the battle. The ten generals commanded their army in rotation, each for one day; but they now agreed to surrender to Miltiades their days of command, in order to invest the whole power in a single person. While the Athenians were preparing for battle, they received unexpected assistance from the little town or Plataea, in Boeotia. Grateful to the Athenians for the assistance which they had rendered them against the Thebans, the whole force of Plataea, amounting to 1000 heavy-armed men, marched to the assistance of their allies and joined them at Marathon. The Athenian army numbered only 10,000 hoplites, or heavy-armed soldiers: there were no archers or cavalry, and only some slaves as light-armed attendants. Of the number of the Persian army we have no trustworthy account, but the lowest estimate makes it consist of 110,000 men.

The plain of Marathon lies on the eastern coast of Attica, at the distance of twenty-two miles from Athens by the shortest road. It is in the form of a crescent, the horns of which consist of two promontories running into the sea, and forming a semicircular bay. This plain is about six miles in length, and in its widest or central part about two in breadth. On the day of battle the Persian army was drawn up along the plain about a mile from the sea, and their fleet was ranged behind them on the beach. The Athenians occupied the rising ground above the plain, and extended from one side of the plain to the other. This arrangement was necessary in order to protect their flanks by the mountains on each side, and to prevent the cavalry from passing round to attack them in rear. But so large a breadth of ground could not be occupied with a small a number of men without weakening some portion of the line. Miltiades, therefore, drew up the troops in the centre in shallow files, and resolved to rely for success upon the stronger and deeper masses of his wings. The right wing, which was the post of honour in a Grecian army, was commanded by the Polemarch Callimachus; the hoplites were arranged in the order of their tribes, so that the members of the same tribe fought by each other's side; and at the extreme left stood the Plataeans.

Miltiades, anxious to come to close quarters as speedily as possible, ordered his soldiers to advance at a running step over the mile of ground which separated them from the foe. Both the Athenian wings were successful, and drove the enemy before them towards the shore and the marshes. But the Athenian centre was broken by the Persians, and compelled to take to flight. Miltiades thereupon recalled his wings from pursuit, and charged the Persian centre. The latter could not withstand this combined attack. The rout now became general along the whole Persian line; and they fled to their ships, pursued by the Athenians.

The Persians lost 6400 men in this memorable engagement: of the Athenians only 192 fell. The aged tyrant Hippias is said to have perished in the battle, and the brave Polemarch Callimachus was also one of the slain. The Persians embarked and sailed away to Asia. Their departure was hailed at Athens with one unanimous burst of heartfelt joy. Marathon became a magic word at Athens. The Athenian people in succeeding ages always looked back upon this day as the most glorious in their annals, and never tired of hearing its praises sounded by their orators and poets. And they had reason to be proud of it. It was the first time that the Greeks had ever defeated the Persians in the field. It was the exploit of the Athenians alone. It had saved not only Athens but all Greece. If the Persians had conquered at Marathon, Greece must, in all likelihood, have become a Persian province; the destinies of the world would have been changed; and oriental despotism might still have brooded over the fairest countries of Europe.

The one hundred and ninety-two Athenians who had perished in the battle were buried on the field, and over their remains a tumulus or mound was erected, which may still be seen about half a mile from the sea.

Shortly after the battle Miltiades requested of the Athenians a fleet of seventy ships, without telling them the object of his expedition, but only promising to enrich the state. Such unbounded confidence did the Athenians repose in the hero of Marathon, that they at once complied with his demand. This confidence Miltiades abused. In order to gratify a private animosity against one of the leading citizens of Paros, he sailed to this island and laid siege to the town. The citizens repelled all his attacks; and having received a dangerous injury on his thigh, he was compelled to raise the siege and return to Athens. Loud was the indignation against Miltiades on his return. He was accused by Xanthippus, the father of Pericles, of having deceived the people, and was brought to trial. His wound had already begun to show symptoms of gangrene. He was carried into court on a couch, and there lay before the assembled judges, while his friends pleaded on his behalf. They could offer no excuse for his recent conduct, but they reminded the Athenians of the services he had rendered, and, begged them to spare the victor of Marathon. The judges were not insensible to this appeal; and instead of condemning him to death as the accuser had demanded, they commuted the penalty to a fine of fifty talents. Miltiades was unable immediately to raise this sum and died soon afterwards of his wound. The fine was subsequently paid by his son Cimon. The melancholy end of Miltiades must not blind us to his offence. He had grossly abused the public confidence, and deserved his punishment. The Athenians did not forget his services at Marathon, and it was their gratitude towards him which alone saved him from death.

Soon after the battle of Marathon a war broke out between Athens and AEgina. This war is of great importance in Grecian history, since to it the Athenians were indebted for their navy, which enabled them to save Greece at Salamis as they had already done at Marathon. AEgina was one of the chief maritime powers in Greece; and accordingly Themistocles urged the Athenians to build and equip a large and powerful fleet, without which it was impossible for them to humble their rival. There was at this time a large surplus in the public treasury, arising from the produce of the silver-mines at Laurium. It had been recently proposed to distribute this surplus among the Athenian citizens; but Themistocles persuaded them to sacrifice their private advantage to the public good, and to appropriate the money to building a fleet of 200 ships.

The two leading citizens of Athens at this period were Themistocles and Aristides. These two eminent men formed a striking contrast to each other. Themistocles possessed abilities of the most extraordinary kind; but they were marred by a want of honesty. Aristides was inferior to Themistocles in ability, but was incomparably superior to him in honesty and integrity. His uprightness and justice were so universally acknowledged that he received the surname of the "Just." Themistocles was the leader of the democratical, and Aristides of the conservative party at Athens. After three or four years of bitter rivalry, the two chiefs appealed to the ostracism, and Aristides was banished (B.C. 483). We are told that an unlettered countryman gave his vote against Aristides at the ostracism, because he was tired of hearing him always called the Just.

CHAPTER VIII.
THE PERSIAN WARS.--THE BATTLES OF THERMOPYLAE, SALAMIS, AND PLATAEA, B.C. 480-479.

The defeat of the Persians at Marathon served only to increase the resentment of Darius. He now resolved to collect the whole forces of his empire, and to lead them in person against Athens. For three years busy preparations were made throughout his vast dominions. In the fourth year his attention was distracted by a revolt of the Egyptians; and before he could reduce them to subjection he was surprised by death, after a reign of 37 years (B.C. 485). Xerxes, the son and successor of Darius, had received the education of an eastern despot, and been surrounded with slaves from his cradle. In person he was the tallest and handsomest man amidst the vast hosts which he led against Greece; but there was nothing in his mind to correspond to this fair exterior. His character was marked by faint-hearted timidity and childish vanity. Xerxes had not inherited his father's animosity against Greece; but he was surrounded by men who urged him to continue the enterprise. Foremost among these was Mardonius, who was eager to retrieve his reputation, and to obtain the conquered country as a satrapy for himself after subduing Egypt (B.C. 484), Xerxes began to make preparations for the invasion of Greece. For four years the din of preparation sounded throughout Asia. Troops were collected from every quarter of the Persian empire, and were ordered to assemble in Cappadocia. As many as forty-six different nations composed the land-force, of various complexions, languages, dresses, and arms. Meantime Xerxes ordered a bridge to be thrown across the Hellespont, that his army might march from Asia into Europe: and he likewise gave directions that a canal should be cut through the isthmus of Mount Athos, in order to avoid the necessity of doubling this dangerous promontory, where the fleet of Mardonius had suffered shipwreck. The making of this canal, which was about a mile and a half long employed a number of men for three years.

In the spring of B.C. 480 Xerxes set out from Sardis with his vast host. Upon reaching Abydos on the Hellespont the army crossed over to Europe by the bridge of boats. Xerxes surveyed the scene from a marble throne. His heart swelled within him at the sight of such a vast assemblage of human beings; but his feelings of pride and pleasure soon gave way to sadness, and he burst into tears at the reflection that in a hundred years not one of them would be alive. Xerxes continued his march through Europe along the coast of Thrace. Upon arriving at the spacious plain of Doriscus, which is traversed by the river Hebrus, he resolved to number his forces. He found that the whole armament, both military and naval, consisted of 2,317,610 men. In his march from Doriscus to Thermopylae he received a still further accession of strength; and accordingly when he reached Thermopylae the land and sea forces amounted to 2,641,610 fighting men. The attendants are said to have been more in number than the fighting men; but if they were only equal, the number of persons who accompanied Xerxes to Thermopylae reaches the astounding figure of 5,283,220! The number is quite incredible; but though the exact number of the invading army cannot be determined, we may safely conclude, from all the circumstances of the case, that it was the largest ever assembled at any period of history.

From Doriscus Xerxes his march along the coast through Thrace and Macedonia. The principal cities through which he passed had to furnish a day's meal for the immense host, and for this purpose had made preparations many months beforehand. The cost of feeding such a multitude brought many cities to the brink of ruin. At Acanthus his fleet sailed through the isthmus of Athos and after doubling the promontories of Sithonia and Pallene joined him at the city of Therma, better known by its later name of Thessalonica. Thence he continued his march through the southern part of Macedonia and Thessaly, meeting with no opposition till he reached the celebrated pass of Thermopylae.

The mighty preparations of Xerxes had been no secret in Greece; and during the preceding winter a congress of the Grecian states had been summoned by the Spartans and Athenians to meet at the isthmus of Corinth. But so great was the terror inspired by the countless hosts of Xerxes that many of the Grecian states at once tendered their submission to him, and others refused to take any part in the congress. The only people, north of the isthmus of Corinth, who remained faithful to the cause of Grecian liberty, were the Athenians and Phocians, and the inhabitants of the small Boeotian towns of Plataea and Thespiae. The other people in northern Greece were either partisans of the Persians, like the Thebans, or were unwilling to make any great sacrifices for the preservation of their independence. In Peloponnesus, the powerful city of Argos and the Achaeans stood aloof. From the more distant members of the Hellenic race no assistance was obtained. Gelon, the ruler of Syracuse, offered to send a powerful armament, provided the command of the allied forces was intrusted to him; but the envoys did not venture to accept a proposal which would have placed both Sparta and Athens under the control of a Sicilian tyrant.

The desertion of the cause of Grecian independence by so many of the Greeks did not shake the resolution of Sparta and of Athens. The Athenians, especially, set a noble example of an enlarged patriotism. They became reconciled to the AEginetans, and thus gained for the common cause the powerful navy of their rival. They readily granted to the Spartans the supreme command of the forces by sea as well as by land, although they furnished two-thirds of the vessels of the entire fleet. Their illustrious citizen Themistocles was the soul of the congress. He sought to enkindle in the other Greeks some portion of the ardour and energy which he had succeeded in breathing into the Athenians.

The Greeks determined to make a stand at the pass of Thermopylae, which forms the entrance from northern into southern Greece. This pass lies between Mount OEta and the sea. It is about a mile in length. At each of its extremities the mountains approach so near the sea as to leave barely room for the passage of a single carriage. The northern, or, to speak more properly, the western Gate, was close to the town of Anthela, where the Amphictyonic council held its autumnal meetings; while the southern, or the eastern Gate, was near the Locrian town of Alpeni. These narrow entrances were called Pylae, or the Gates. The space between the gates was wider and more open, and was distinguished by its hot springs, from which the pass derived the name of Thermopylae, or the "Hot-Gates." The island of Euboea is here separated from the mainland by a narrow strait, which in one part is only two miles and a half in breadth; and accordingly it is easy, by defending this part of the sea with a fleet, to prevent an enemy from landing troops at the southern end of the pass.

The Grecian fleet, under the command of the Spartan Eurybiades, took up its station off that portion of the northern coast of Euboea which faces Magnesia and the entrance to the Thessalian gulf and which was called Artemisium, from a neighbouring temple of Artemis (Diana). It was, however, only a small land-force that was sent to the defence of Thermopylae. When the arrival of Xerxes at Therma became known, the Greeks were upon the point of celebrating the Olympic games, and the festival of the Carnean Apollo, which was observed with great solemnity at Sparta and in other Doric states. The Peloponnesians therefore sent forward only 300 Spartans and 3000 hoplites from other Peloponnesian states, under the command of the Spartan king Leonidas, a force which they thought would be sufficient to maintain the pass till the festivals were over. In his march northwards Leonidas received additions from the Thespians, Phocians, and Locrians, so that he had under his command at Thermopylae about 7000 men.

Meanwhile Xerxes had arrived within sight of Thermopylae. He had heard that a handful of desperate men, commanded by a Spartan, had determined to dispute his passage, but he refused to believe the news. He was still more astonished when a horseman, whom he had sent to reconnoitre, brought back word that he had seen several Spartans outside the wall in front of the pass, some amusing themselves with gymnastic exercises, and others combing their long hair. In great perplexity, he sent for the exiled Spartan king Demaratus, who had accompanied him from Persia, and asked him the meaning of such madness. Demaratus replied, that the Spartans would defend the pass to the death, and that it was their practice to dress their heads with peculiar care when they were going to battle. Later writers relate that Xerxes sent to them to deliver up their arms. Leonidas desired him "to come and take them." One of the Spartans being told that "the Persian host was so prodigious that their arrows would conceal the sun:"--"So much the better" (he replied), "we shall then fight in the shade."

At length, upon the fifth day, Xerxes ordered a chosen body of Medes to advance against the presumptuous foes and bring them into his presence. But their superior numbers were of no avail in such a narrow space, and they were kept at bay by the long spears and steady ranks of the Greeks. After the combat had lasted a long time with heavy loss to the Medes, Xerxes ordered his ten thousand "Immortals," the flower of the Persian army, to advance. But they were as unsuccessful as the Medes. Xerxes beheld the repulse of his troops from a lofty throne which had been provided for him, and was seen to leap thrice from his seat in an agony of fear or rage.

On the following day the attack was renewed, but with no better success: and Xerxes was beginning to despair of forcing his way through the pass, when a Malian, of the name of Ephialtes, betrayed to the Persian king that there was an unfrequented path across Mount OEta, ascending on the northern side of the mountain and descending on the southern side near the termination of the pass. Overjoyed at this discovery, a strong detachment of Persians was ordered to follow the traitor. Meantime Leonidas and his troops had received ample notice of the impending danger. During the night deserters from the enemy had brought him the news; and their intelligence was confirmed by his own scouts on the hills. His resolution was at once taken. As a Spartan he was bound to conquer or to die in the post assigned to him; and he was the more ready to sacrifice his life, since an oracle had declared that either Sparta itself or a Spartan king must perish by the Persian arms. His three hundred comrades were fully equal to the same heroism which actuated their King; and the seven hundred Thespians resolved to share the fate of this gallant band. He allowed the rest of the allies to retire, with the exception of four hundred Boeotians, whom he retained as hostages. Xerxes delayed his attack till the middle of the day, when it was expected that the detachment sent across the mountain would arrive at the rear of the pass. But Leonidas and his comrades, only anxious to sell their lives as dearly as possible, did not wait to receive the attack of the Persians, but advanced into the open space in front of the pass, and charged the enemy with desperate valour. Numbers of the Persians were slain; many were driven into the neighbouring sea; and others again were trampled to death by the vast hosts behind them. As long as the Greeks could maintain their ranks they repelled every attack; but when their spears were broken, and they had only their swords left, the enemy began to press in between them. Leonidas was one of the first that fell, and around his body the battle raged fiercer than ever. The Persians made the greatest efforts to obtain possession of it; but four times they were driven back by the Greeks with great slaughter. At length, thinned in numbers, and exhausted by fatigue and wounds, this noble band retired within the pass, and seated themselves on a hillock. Meanwhile the Persian detachment, which had been sent across the mountains, began to enter the pass from the south. The Spartan heroes were now surrounded on every side, overwhelmed with a shower of missiles, and killed to a man.

On the hillock, where the Greeks made their last stand, a marble lion was set up in honour of Leonidas. Another monument, erected near the spot, contained the memorable inscription:--

"Go, tell the Spartans, thou that passest by,
That here obedient to their laws we lie."

While Leonidas had been fighting at Thermopylae, the Greek fleet had also been engaged with the Persians at Artemisium. The Persian fleet set sail from the gulf of Therma, and arrived in one day at almost the southern corner of Magnesia. In this position they were overtaken by a sudden hurricane, which blew upon the shore with irresistible fury. For three days and three nights the tempest raged without intermission; and when calm at length returned, the shore was seen strewed for many miles with wrecks and corpses. At least four hundred ships of war were destroyed, together with a countless number of transports, stores, and treasures. The Greek fleet had been seized with a panic terror at the approach of the Persians, and retreated to Chalcis in the narrowest part of the Euboean straits; but upon hearing of the disaster of the Persian fleet, they took courage, and sailed back with the utmost speed to their former station at Artemisium. Being now encouraged to attack the enemy, they gained some success. On the following night another terrific storm burst upon the Persians. All night long it blew upon the Thessalian coast at Aphetae, where the Persian ships were stationed, thus causing little inconvenience to the Greeks upon the opposite shore. Notwithstanding these losses, the Persian fleet still had a vast superiority of numbers, and determined to offer battle to the Greeks. Quitting the Thessalian coast, they sailed towards Artemisium in the form of a crescent. The Greeks kept near the shore, to prevent the Persians from bringing their whole fleet into action. The battle raged furiously the whole day, and each side fought with determined valour. Both parties suffered severely; and though the

Persians lost a greater number of ships and men, yet so many of the Greek vessels were disabled that they found it would be impossible to renew the combat. Under these circumstances the Greek commanders saw that it would be necessary to retreat; and their determination was hastened by the news which they now received, that Leonidas and his companions had fallen, and that Xerxes was master of the pass of Thermopylae. Having sailed through the Euboean strait, the fleet doubled the promontory of Sunium, and did not stop till it reached the island of Salamis.

Meanwhile the Peloponnesians had abandoned Attica and the adjoining states to their fate, whilst they strained every nerve to secure themselves by fortifying the isthmus of Corinth. The Athenians, relying upon the march of a Peloponnesian army into Boeotia, had taken no measures for the security of their families and property, and beheld with terror and dismay the barbarian host in full march towards their city. In six days it was calculated Xerxes would be at Athens--a short space to remove the population of a whole city: but fear and necessity work wonders. Before the six days had elapsed, all who were willing to abandon their homes had been safely transported, some to AEgina, and others to Troezen in Peloponnesus; but many could not be induced to proceed farther than Salamis. It was necessary for Themistocles to use all his art and all his eloquence on this occasion. The oracle at Delphi had told the Athenians that "the divine Salamis would make women childless,"--yet, "when all was lost, a wooden wall should still shelter the Athenians." Themistocles told his countrymen that these words clearly indicated a fleet and a naval victory as the only means of safety. Some however gave to the words another meaning; and a few, especially among the aged and the poor, resolved to shut themselves up in the Acropolis, and to fortify its accessible or western front with barricades of timber.

On his march towards Athens, Xerxes sent a detachment of his army to take and plunder Delphi. But this attempt proved unsuccessful. The god of the most renowned oracle of the Grecian world vindicated at once the majesty of his sanctuary and the truth of his predictions. As the Persians climbed the rugged path at the foot of Mount Parnassus, leading up to the shrine, thunder was heard to roll, and two crags, suddenly detaching themselves from the mountain, rolled down upon the Persians, and spread dismay and destruction in their ranks, Seized with a sudden panic, they turned and fled, pursued, as they said, by two warriors of superhuman size and prowess, who had assisted the Delphians in defending their temple.

On arriving before Athens, Xerxes found the Acropolis occupied by a handful of desperate citizens, who made a brave resistance; but they were overpowered and put to the sword. The temples and houses on the Acropolis were pillaged and burnt; and Xerxes thus became undisputed master of Athens.

About the same time the Persian fleet arrived in the bay of Phalerum. Its strength is not accurately known, but it must have exceeded 1000 vessels. The combined Grecian fleet at Salamis consisted of 366 ships, of which 200 were Athenian.

At this critical juncture dissension reigned in the Grecian fleet. In the council of war which had been summoned by Eurybiades the Spartan commander, Themistocles urged the assembled chiefs to remain at Salamis, and give battle to the Persians in the narrow straits, where the superior numbers of the Persians would be of less consequence. The Peloponnesian commanders, on the other hand, were anxious that the fleet should be removed to the isthmus of Corinth, and thus be put in communication with their land-forces. The council came to a vote in favour of retreat; but Themistocles prevailed upon Eurybiades to convene another assembly upon the following day. When the council met, the Peloponnesian commanders loudly expressed their dissatisfaction at seeing a debate re-opened which they had deemed concluded. Adimantus, the Corinthian admiral broke out into open rebukes and menaces. "Themistocles," he exclaimed, "those who rise at the public games before the signal are whipped." "True," replied Themistocles; "but they who lag behind it never win a crown." Another incident in this discussion has been immortalized by Plutarch. Eurybiades, incensed by the language of Themistocles, lifted up his stick to strike him, whereupon the Athenian exclaimed, "Strike, but hear me!" Themistocles repeated his arguments and entreaties; and at length threatened that he and the Athenians would sail away to Italy and there found a new city, if the Peloponnesians still determined to retreat. Eurybiades now gave way and issued orders for the fleet to remain and fight at Salamis; but the Peloponnesians obeyed the order with reluctance. A third council was summoned and Themistocles, perceiving that the decision of the assembly would be against him, determined to effect his object by stratagem. He secretly despatched a trusty slave with a message to Xerxes, representing the dissensions which prevailed in the Grecian fleet, and how easy a matter it would be to surround and vanquish an armament both small and disunited. Xerxes readily adopted the suggestion, and ordered his captains to close up the straits of Salamis at both ends during the night. On the council assembling in the morning, Aristides arrived with the news that the Grecian fleet was completely surrounded by that of the Persians, and that retreat was no longer possible. As the veil of night rolled gradually away, the Persian fleet was discovered stretching as far as the eye could reach along the coast of Attica. The Grecian fleet, being concentrated in the harbour of Salamis, was thus surrounded by the Persians. Xerxes had caused a lofty throne to be erected upon one of the projecting declivities of Mount AEgaleos, opposite the harbour of Salamis, whence he could survey the combat, and stimulate by his presence the courage of his men.

As a battle was now inevitable the Grecian commanders lost no time in making preparations for the encounter. The Greek seamen embarked with alacrity, encouraging one another to deliver their country, their wives, and children, and the temples of their gods, from the grasp of the barbarians. History has preserved to us but few details of the engagement. The Persian fleet, with the exception of some of the Ionic contingents, fought with courage. But the very numbers on which they so confidently relied, proved one of the chief causes of their defeat. Too crowded either to advance or to retreat, their oars broken or impeded by collision with one another, their fleet lay like an inert and lifeless mass upon the water, and fell an easy prey to the Greeks. A single incident will illustrate the terror and confusion which reigned among the Persians. Artemisia, queen of Halicarnassus in Caria, distinguished herself in it by deeds of daring bravery. At length she turned and fled, pursued by an Athenian galley. Full in her course lay the vessel of a Carian prince. Instead of avoiding, she struck and sunk it, sending her countryman and all his crew to the bottom. The captain of the Athenian galley, believing from this act that she was a deserter from the Persian cause, suffered her to escape. Xerxes, who from his lofty throne beheld the feat of the Halicarnassian queen, but who imagined that the sunken ship belonged to the Greeks, was filled with admiration at her courage, and exclaimed--"My men are become women, my women men!"

Two hundred of the Persian ships were destroyed and sunk when night put an end to the engagement. But notwithstanding this loss the fleet was still formidable by its numbers. The Greeks themselves did not regard the victory as decisive, and prepared to renew the combat. But the pusillanimity of Xerxes relieved them from all further anxiety. He became alarmed for his own personal safety; and his whole care was now centred on securing his retreat by land. The best troops were disembarked from the ships, and marched towards the Hellespont, in order to secure the bridge, whilst the fleet itself was ordered to make for Asia. These dispositions of Xerxes were prompted by Mardonius. He represented to his master that the defeat, after all, was but slight; that having attained one of the great objects of the expedition by the capture of Athens, he might now retire with honour, and even with glory; and that for the rest he (Mardonius) would undertake to complete the conquest of Greece with 300,000 men. While the Persian fleet sailed towards Asia, Xerxes set out on his homeward march. In Thessaly Mardonius selected the 300,000 men with whom he proposed to conclude the war; but as autumn was now approaching, he resolved to postpone all further operations till the spring.

After forty-five days' march from Attica, Xerxes again reached the shores of the Hellespont, with a force greatly diminished by famine and pestilence. On the Hellespont he found his fleet, but the bridge had been washed away by storms. Landed on the shores of Asia, the Persian army at length obtained abundance of provisions, and contracted new maladies by the sudden change from privation to excess. Thus terminated this mighty but unsuccessful expedition.

Greece owed its salvation to one man--Themistocles, This was virtually admitted by the leaders of the other Grecian states, when they assembled to assign the prizes of wisdom and conduct. Upon the altar of Poseidon, at the isthmus of Corinth, each chief deposited a ticket inscribed with two names, of those whom he considered entitled to the first and second prizes. But in this adjudication vanity and self-love defeated their own objects. Each commander had put down his own name for the first prize; for the second, a great majority preponderated in favour of Themistocles. From the Spartans, also, Themistocles received the honours due to his merit. A crown of olive was conferred upon him, together with one of the most splendid chariots which the city could produce.

On the very same day on which the Persians were defeated at Salamis the Sicilian Greeks also obtained a victory over the Carthaginians. There is reason to believe that the invasion of Sicily by the Carthaginians was concerted with Xerxes, and that the simultaneous attach on two distinct Grecian peoples, by two immense armaments, was not merely the result of chance. Gelon, the powerful ruler of Syracuse, defeated Hamilcar, the Carthaginian general, with the loss it is said of 150,000 men.

In the spring of B.C. 479 Mardonius prepared to open the campaign. He was not without hopes of inducing the Athenians to join the Persian alliance, and he despatched Alexander, king of Macedon, to conciliate the Athenians, now partially re-established in their dilapidated city. His offers on the part of the Persians were of the most seductive kind; but the Athenians dismissed him with a positive refusal, whilst to the Lacedaemonians they protested that no temptations, however great, should ever induce them to desert the common cause of Greece and freedom. In return for this disinterested conduct all they asked was that a Peloponnesian army should be sent into Boeotia for the defence of the Attic frontier: a request which the Spartan envoys promised to fulfil. No sooner, however, had they returned into their own country than this promise was completely forgotten.

When Mardonius was informed that the Athenians had rejected his proposal, he immediately marched against Athens, accompanied by all his Grecian allies; and in May or June, B.C. 479, about ten months after the retreat of Xerxes, the Persians again occupied that city. With feelings of bitter indignation against their faithless allies, the Athenians saw themselves once more compelled to remove to Salamis. Mardonius took advantage of his situation to endeavour once more to win them to his alliance. Through a Hellespontine Greek, the same favourable conditions were again offered to them, but were again refused. One voice alone, that of the senator Lycidas, broke the unanimity of the assembly. But his opposition cost him his life. He and his family were stoned to death by the excited populace. In this desperate condition the Athenians sent ambassadors to the Spartans to remonstrate against their breach of faith, and to intimate that necessity might at length compel them to listen to the proposals of the enemy. The Spartans became alarmed. That very night 5000 citizens, each attended by seven Helots, were despatched to the frontiers; and these were shortly followed by 5000 Lacedaemonian Perioeci, each attended by one light-armed Helot. Never before had the Spartans sent so large a force into the field. Their example was followed by other Peloponnesian cities; and the Athenian envoys returned to Salamis with the joyful news that a large army was preparing to march against the enemy, under the command of Pausanias, who acted as regent for the infant son of Leonidas.

Mardonius, on learning the approach of the Lacedaemonians, abandoned Attica and crossed into Boeotia. He finally took up a position on the left bank of the Asopus, and not far from the town of Plataea. Here he caused a camp to be constructed of ten furlongs square, and fortified with barricades and towers. Meanwhile the Grecian army continued to receive reinforcements from the different states, and by the time it reached Boeotia, it formed a grand total of about 110,000 men. After several days' manoeuvring a general battle took place near Plataea. The light-armed undisciplined Persians, whose bodies were unprotected by armour, maintained a very unequal combat against the serried ranks, the long spears, and the mailed bodies of the Spartan phalanx. Mardonius, at the head of his body-guard of 1000 picked men, and conspicuous by his white charger, was among the foremost in the fight, till struck down by the hand of a Spartan. The fall of their general was the signal for flight to the Persians, already wearied and disheartened by the fruitless contest; nor did they once stop till they lad again crossed the Asopus and reached their fortified camp. The glory of having defeated the Persians at Plataea rests with the Lacedaemonians, since the Athenians were engaged in another part of the field with the Thebans. After repulsing the Thebans, the Athenians joined the Lacedaemonians, who had pursued the Persians as far as their fortified camp. Upon the arrival of the Athenians the barricades were stormed and carried, after a gallant resistance on the part of the Persians. The camp became a scene of the most horrible carnage. The Persian loss was immense, while that of the Greeks seems not to have exceeded 1300 or 1400 men.

It remained to bury the dead and divide the booty, and so great was the task that ten days were consumed in it. The booty was ample and magnificent. Gold and silver coined, as well as in plate and trinkets, rich vests and carpets, ornamented arms, horses, camels--in a word, all the magnificence of Eastern luxury. The failure of the Persian expedition was completed by the destruction of their naval armament. Laotychides, the Spartan admiral, having sailed across the AEgean, found the Persian fleet at Mycale a promontory of Asia Minor near Miletus. Their former reverses seem completely to have discouraged the Persians from hazarding another naval engagement. The ships were hauled ashore and surrounded with a rampart, whilst an army of 60,000 Persians lined the coast for their defence. The Greeks landed on the very day on which the battle of Plataea was fought. A supernatural presentiment of that decisive victory, conveyed by a herald's staff which floated over the AEgean from the shores of Greece, is said to have pervaded the Grecian ranks at Mycale as they marched to the attack. The Persians did not long resist: they turned their backs and fled to their fortifications, pursued by the Greeks, who entered them almost simultaneously. A large number of the Persians perished; and the victory was rendered still more decisive by the burning of the fleet.

The Grecian fleet now sailed towards the Hellespont with the view of destroying the bridge; but hearing that it no longer existed, Leotychides departed homewards with the Peloponnesian vessels. Xanthippus however, the Athenian commander, seized the opportunity to recover from the Persians the Thracian Chersonese, which had long been an Athenian possession; and proceeded to blockade Sestos, the key of the strait. This city surrendered in the autumn, after a protracted siege, whereupon the Athenians returned home, carrying with them the cables of the bridge across the Hellespont, which were afterwards preserved in the Acropolis as a trophy.

CHAPTER IX.
FROM THE END OF THE PERSIAN WARS TO THE BEGINNING OF THE PELOPONNESIAN WAR, B.C. 479-431.

The Athenians, on their return to Attica, after the defeat of the Persians, found their city ruined and their country desolate. They began to rebuild their city on a larger scale than before, and to fortify it with a wall. Those allies to whom the increasing maritime power of Athens was an object of suspicion, and especially the AEginetans, to whom it was more particularly formidable, beheld her rising fortifications with dismay. They endeavoured to inspire the Lacedaemonians with their fears, and urged them to arrest the work. But though Sparta shared the jealousy of the allies, she could not with any decency interfere by force to prevent a friendly city from exercising a right inherent in all independent states. She assumed therefore the hypocritical garb of an adviser and counsellor. Concealing her jealousy under the pretence of zeal for the common interests of Greece, she represented to the Athenians that, in the event of another Persian invasion, fortified towns would serve the enemy for camps and strongholds, as Thebes had done in the last war; and proposed that the Athenians should not only desist from completing their own fortifications, but help to demolish those which already existed in other towns.

The object of the proposal was too transparent to deceive so acute a statesman as Themistocles. Athens was not yet, however, in a condition to incur the danger of openly rejecting it; and he therefore advised the Athenians to dismiss the Spartan envoys with the assurance that they would send ambassadors to Sparta to explain their views. He then caused himself to be appointed one of these ambassadors;

and setting off straightway for Sparta, directed his colleagues to linger behind as long as possible. At Sparta, the absence of his colleagues, at which he affected to be surprised, afforded him an excuse for not demanding an audience of the ephors. During the interval thus gained, the whole population of Athens, of both sexes and every age, worked day and night at the walls, which, when the other ambassadors at length arrived at Sparta, had attained a height sufficient to afford a tolerable defence. Meanwhile the suspicions of the Spartans had been more than once aroused by messages from the AEginetans respecting the progress of the walls. Themistocles, however, positively denied their statements; and urged the Spartans to send messengers of their own to Athens in order to learn the true state of affairs, at the same time instructing the Athenians to detain them as hostages for the safety of himself and colleagues. When there was no longer any motive for concealment, Themistocles openly avowed the progress of the works, and his intention of securing the independence of Athens, and enabling her to act for herself. The walls being now too far advanced to be easily taken, the Spartans found themselves compelled to acquiesce, and the works were completed without further hindrance.

Having thus secured the city from all danger of an immediate attack, Themistocles pursued his favourite project of rendering Athens the greatest maritime and commercial power of Greece. He erected a town round the harbour of Piraeus, distant between four and five miles from Athens, and enclosed it with a wall as large in extent as the city itself, but of vastly greater height and thickness. Meanwhile an event occurred which secured more firmly than ever the maritime supremacy of Athens, by transferring to her the command of the allied fleet.

In the year after the battle of Plataea a fleet had been fitted out and placed under the command of the Spartan regent, Pausanias, in order to carry on the war against the Persians. After delivering most of the Grecian towns in Cyprus from the Persians, this armament sailed up the Bosporus and laid siege to Byzantium, which was garrisoned by a large Persian force. The town surrendered after a protracted siege; but it was during this expedition that the conduct of the Spartan commander struck a fatal blow at the interests of his country.

The immense booty, as well as the renown, which Pausanias had acquired at Plataea, had filled him with pride and ambition. After the capture of Byzantium he despatched a letter to Xerxes, offering to marry the king's daughter, and to bring

Sparta and the rest of Greece under his dominion. Xerxes was highly delighted with this letter, and sent a reply in which he urged Pausanias to pursue his project night and day, and promised to supply him with all the money and troops that might be needful for its execution. But the childish vanity of Pausanias betrayed his plot before it was ripe for execution. Elated by the confidence of Xerxes, and by the money with which he was lavishly supplied, he acted as if he had already married the Great King's daughter. He assumed the Persian dress; he made a progress through Thrace, attended by Persian and Egyptian guards; and copied, in the luxury of his table and the dissoluteness of his manners, the example of his adopted country. Above all, he offended the allies by his haughty reserve and imperiousness. His designs were now too manifest to escape attention. His proceedings reached the ears of the Spartans, who sent out Dorcis to supersede him. Disgusted by the insolence of Pausanias, the Ionians serving in the combined Grecian fleet addressed themselves to Aristides, whose manners formed a striking contrast to those of the Spartan leader, and begged him to assume the command. This request was made precisely at the time when Pausanias was recalled; and accordingly, when Dorcis arrived, he found Aristides in command of the combined fleet (B.C. 478).

This event was not a mere empty question about a point of honour. It was a real revolution, terminated by a solemn league, of which Athens was to be the head. Aristides took the lead in the matter, for which his proverbial justice and probity eminently qualified him. The league obtained the name of "the Confederacy of Delos," from its being arranged that deputies of the allies belonging to it should meet periodically for deliberation in the temple of Apollo and Artemis (Diana) in that island. Each state was assessed in a certain contribution, either of money or ships, as proposed by the Athenians and ratified by the synod. The assessment was intrusted to Aristides, whose impartiality was universally applauded. Of the details, however, we only know that the first assessment amounted to 460 talents (about 106,000L sterling), that certain officers called Hellenotamiae were appointed by the Athenians to collect and administer the contributions, and that Delos was the treasury.

Such was the origin of the Confederacy of Delos. Soon after its formation Aristides was succeeded in the command of the combined fleet by Cimon, the son of Miltiades.

Pausanias, on his return to Sparta, seems to have been acquitted of any definite charges; but he continued his correspondence with Persia, and an accident at length afforded convincing proofs of his guilt. A favourite slave, to whom he had intrusted a letter to the Persian satrap at Sardis, observed with dismay that none of the messengers employed in this service had ever returned. Moved by these fears, he broke the seal and read the letter, and finding his suspicions of the fate that awaited him confirmed, he carried the document to the ephors. But in ancient states the testimony of a slave was always regarded with suspicion. The ephors refused to believe the evidence offered to them unless confirmed by their own ears. For this purpose they directed him to plant himself as a suppliant in a sacred grove near Cape Taenarus, in a hut behind which two of their body might conceal themselves. Pausanias, as they had expected, anxious at the step taken by his slave, hastened to the spot to question him about it. The conversation which ensued, and which was overheard by the ephors, rendered the guilt of Pausanias no longer doubtful. They now determined to arrest him on his return to Sparta. They met him in the street near the temple of Athena Chalcioecus (of the Brazen House), when Pausanias, either alarmed by his guilty conscience, or put on his guard by a secret signal from one of the ephors, turned and fled to the temple, where he took refuge in a small chamber belonging to the building. From this sanctuary it was unlawful to drag him; but the ephors caused the doors to be built up and the roof to be removed, and his own mother is said to have placed the first stone at the doors. When at the point of death from starvation, he was carried from the sanctuary before he polluted it with his corpse. Such was the end of the victor of Plataea. After his death proofs were discovered among his papers that Themistocles was implicated in his guilt. But in order to follow the fortunes of the Athenian statesman, it is necessary to take a glance at the internal history of Athens.

The ancient rivalry between Themistocles and Aristides had been in a good degree extinguished by the danger which threatened their common country during the Persian wars. Aristides had since abandoned his former prejudices, and was willing to conform to many of the democratical innovations of his rival. The effect of this was to produce, soon after their return to Attica, a still further modification of the constitution of Clisthenes. The Thetes the lowest of the four classes of Athenian citizens, were declared eligible for the magistracy, from which they had been excluded by the laws of Solon. Thus not only the archonship, but consequently the Council of Areopagus, was thrown open to them; and, strange to say, this reform was proposed by Aristides himself.

Nevertheless party spirit still ran high at Athens. Cimon and Alcmaeon were violent opponents of Themistocles, and of their party Aristides was still the head. The popularity of Aristides was never greater than at the present time, owing not only to the more liberal spirit which he exhibited, but also to his great services in establishing the Confederacy of Delos. Themistocles had offended the Athenians by his ostentation and vanity. He was continually boasting of his services to the state; but worse than all this, his conduct was stained with positive guilt. Whilst, at the head of an Athenian squadron, he was sailing among the Greek islands for the ostensible purpose of executing justice, there is little room to doubt that he corrupted its very source by accepting large sums of money from the cities which he visited. Party spirit at length reached such a height that it was found necessary to resort to ostracism, and Themistocles was condemned to a temporary banishment (B.C. 471). He retired to Argos, where he was residing when the Spartans called upon the Athenians to prosecute their great statesman before a synod of the allies assembled at Sparta, on the ground of treasonable correspondence with Persia. Accordingly joint envoys were sent from Athens and Sparta to arrest him (B.C. 466). Themistocles avoided the impending danger by flying from Argos to Corcyra. The Corcyraeans, however, not daring to shelter him, he passed over to the continent; where, being still pursued, he was forced to seek refuge at the court of Admetus, king of the Molossians, though the latter was his personal enemy. Fortunately, Admetus happened to be from home. The forlorn condition of Themistocles excited the compassion of the wife of the Molossian king, who placed her child in his arms, and bade him seat himself on the hearth as a suppliant. As soon as the king arrived, Themistocles explained his peril, and adjured him by the sacred laws of hospitality not to take vengeance upon a fallen foe. Admetus accepted his appeal, and raised him from the hearth; he refused to deliver him up to his pursuers, and at last only dismissed him on his own expressed desire to proceed to Persia. After many perils, Themistocles succeeded in reaching in safety the coast of Asia. Artaxerxes, the son of Xerxes, was now upon the throne of Persia, and to him Themistocles hastened to announce himself. The king was delighted at his arrival, and treated him with the greatest distinction. In a year's time, Themistocles, having acquired a sufficient knowledge of the Persian language to be able to converse in it, entertained Artaxerxes with magnificent schemes for the subjugation of Greece. Artaxerxes loaded him with presents, gave him a Persian wife, and appointed Magnesia, a town not far from the Ionian coast, as his place of residence. After living there some time he was carried off by disease at the age of sixty-five, without having realised, or apparently attempted, any of those plans with which he had dazzled the Persian monarch. Rumour ascribed his death to poison, which he took of his own accord, from a consciousness of his inability to perform his promises; but this report, which was current in the time of Thucydides, is rejected by that historian.

Aristides died about four years after the banishment of Themistocles. The common accounts of his poverty are probably exaggerated, and seem to have been founded on the circumstances of a public funeral, and of handsome donations made to his three children by the state. But whatever his property may have been, it is at least certain that he did not acquire or increase it by unlawful means; and not even calumny has ventured to assail his well-earned title of THE JUST.

On the death of Aristides, Cimon became the undisputed leader of the conservative party at Athens. Cimon was generous, affable, magnificent; and, notwithstanding his political views, of exceedingly popular manners. He had inherited the military genius of his father, and was undoubtedly the greatest commander of his time. He employed the vast wealth acquired in his expeditions in adorning Athens and gratifying his fellow-citizens. It has been already mentioned that he succeeded Aristides in the command of the allied fleet. His first exploits were the capture of Eion on the Strymon, and the reduction of the island of Scyros (B.C. 476). A few years afterwards we find the first symptoms of discontent among the members of the Confederacy of Delos. Naxos, one of the confederate islands, and the largest of the Cyclades, revolted in B.C. 466, probably from a feeling of the growing oppressiveness of the Athenian headship. It was immediately invested by the confederate fleet, reduced, and made tributary to Athens. This was another step towards dominion gained by the Athenians, whose pretensions were assisted by the imprudence of the allies. Many of the smaller states belonging to the confederacy, wearied with perpetual hostilities, commuted for a money payment the ships which they were bound to supply; and thus, by depriving themselves of a navy, lost the only means by which they could assert their independence.

The same year was marked by a memorable action against the Persians. Cimon at the head of 200 Athenian triremes, and 100 furnished by the allies, proceeded to the coast of Asia Minor. The Persians had assembled a large fleet and army at the mouth of the river Eurymedon in Pamphylia. After speedily defeating the fleet, Cimon landed his men and marched against the Persian army which was drawn up on the shore to protect the fleet. The land-force fought with bravery, but was at length put to the rout.

The island of Thasos was the next member of the confederacy against which the Athenians directed their arms. After a siege of more than two years that island surrendered, when its fortifications were razed, and it was condemned to pay tribute (B.C. 463).

The expedition to Thasos was attended with a circumstance which first gives token of the coming hostilities between Sparta and Athens. At an early period of the blockade the Thasians secretly applied to the Lacedaemonians to make a diversion in their favour by invading Attica: and though the Lacedaemonians were still ostensibly allied with Athens, they were base enough to comply with this request. Their treachery, however, was prevented by a terrible calamity which befel themselves. In the year B.C. 461 their capital was visited by an earthquake which laid it in ruins and killed 20,000 of the citizens. But this was only part of the calamity. The earthquake was immediately followed by a revolt of the Helots, who were always ready to avail themselves of the weakness of their tyrants. Being joined by the Messenians, they fortified themselves in Mount Ithome in Messenia. Hence this revolt is sometimes called the Third Messenian War (B.C. 464). after two or three years spent in a vain attempt to dislodge them from this position, the Lacedaemonians found themselves obliged to call in the assistance of their allies, and, among the rest, of the Athenians. It was with great difficulty that Cimon persuaded the Athenians to comply with this request; but he was at length despatched to Laconia with a force of 4000 hoplites. The aid of the Athenians had been requested by the Lacedaemonians on account of their acknowledged superiority in the art of attacking fortified places. As, however, Cimon did not succeed in dislodging the Helots from Ithome the Lacedaemonians, probably from a consciousness of their own treachery in the affair of Thasos, suspected that the Athenians were playing them false, and abruptly dismissed them, saying that they had no longer any occasion for their services. This rude dismissal gave great offence at Athens, and annihilated for a time the political influence of Cimon. The democratical party had from the first opposed the expedition; and it afforded them a great triumph to be able to point to Cimon returning not only unsuccessful but insulted. That party was now led by Pericles. A sort of hereditary feud existed between Pericles and Cimon; for it was Xanthippus, the father of Pericles, who had impeached Miltiades, the father of Cimon. The character of Pericles was almost the reverse of Cimon's. Although the leader of the popular party, his manners were reserved. He appeared but little in society, and only in public upon great occasions. His mind had received the highest polish which that period was capable of giving. He constantly conversed with Anaxagoras, Protagoras, Zeno, and other eminent philosophers. To oratory in particular he had devoted much attention, as an indispensable instrument for swaying the public assemblies of Athens.

Pericles seized the occasion presented by the ill success of Cimon, both to ruin that leader and to strike a fatal blow at the aristocratical party. He deprived the Areopagus of its chief functions, and left it a mere shadow of its former influence and power. He rendered the election to magistracies dependent simply upon lot, so that every citizen however poor, had an equal chance of obtaining the honours of the state. Other changes which accompanied this revolution--for such it must be called--were the institution of paid DICASTERIES or jury-courts, and the almost entire abrogation of the judicial power of the Senate of Five Hundred. It cannot be supposed that such fundamental changes were effected without violent party strife. The poet AEschylus, in the tragedy of the EUMENIDIES, in vain exerted all the powers of his genius in support of the aristocratical party and of the tottering Areopagus; his exertions on this occasion resulted only in his own flight from Athens. The same fate attended Cimon himself; and he was condemned by ostracism (B.C. 461) to a ten years' banishment. Nay, party violence even went the length of assassination. Ephialtes, who had taken the lead in the attacks upon the Areopagus, fell beneath the dagger of a Boeotian, hired by the conservative party to dispatch him.

It was from this period (B.C. 461) that the long administration of Pericles may be said to have commenced. The effects of his accession to power soon became visible in the foreign relations of Athens. Pericles had succeeded to the political principles of Themistocles, and his aim was to render Athens the leading power of Greece. The Confederacy of Delos had already secured her maritime ascendency; Pericles directed his policy to the extension of her influence in continental Greece. She formed an alliance with the Thessalians, Argos, and Megara. The possession of Megara was of great importance, as it enabled the Athenians to arrest the progress of an invading army from Peloponnesus, AEgina, so long the maritime rival of Athens, was subdued and made tributary. The Athenians marched with rapid steps to the dominion of Greece. Shortly afterwards the battle of OEnophyta (B.C. 456), in which the Athenians defeated the Boeotians, gave Athens the command of Thebes, and of all the other Boeotian towns. From the gulf of Corinth to the straits of Thermopylae Athenian influence was now predominant. During these events the Athenians had continued to prosecute the war against Persia. In the year B.C. 460 they sent a powerful fleet to Egypt to assist Inarus, who had revolted against Persia; but this expedition proved a complete failure, for at the end of six years the revolt was put down by the Persians, and the Athenian fleet destroyed (B.C. 455). At a later period (B.C. 449) Cimon, who had been recalled from exile, sailed to Cyprus with a fleet of 200 ships. He undertook the siege of Citium in that island; but died during the progress of it, either from disease or from the effects of a wound. Shortly afterwards a pacification was concluded with Persia, which is sometimes, but erroneously, called "the peace of Cimon." It is stated that by this compact the Persian monarch agreed not to tax or molest the Greek colonies on the coast of Asia Minor, nor to send any vessels of war westward of Phaselis in Lycia, or within the Cyanean rocks at the junction of the Euxine with the Thracian Bosporus; the Athenians on their side undertaking to leave the Persians in undisturbed possession of Cyprus and Egypt. During the progress of these events, the states which formed the Confederacy of Delos, with the exception of Chios, Lesbos, and Samos, had gradually become, instead of the active allies of Athens, her disarmed and passive tributaries. Even the custody of the fund had been transferred from Delos to Athens. The purpose for which the confederacy had been originally organised disappeared with the Persian peace; yet what may now be called Imperial Athens continued, for her own ends, to exercise her prerogatives as head of the league. Her alliances, as we have seen, had likewise been extended in continental Greece, where they embraced Megara, Boeotia, Phocis, Locris, together with Troezen and Achaia in Peloponnesus. Such was the position of Athens in the year 448 B.C., the period of her greatest power and prosperity. From this time her empire began to decline; whilst Sparta, and other watchful and jealous enemies, stood ever ready to strike a blow.

In the following year (B.C. 447) a revolution in Boeotia deprived Athens of her ascendency in that country. With an overweening contempt of their enemies, a small band of 1000 Athenian hoplites, chiefly composed of youthful volunteers belonging to the best Athenian families, together with a few auxiliaries, marched under the command of Tolmides to put down the revolt, in direct opposition to the advice of Pericles, who adjured them to wait and collect a more numerous force. The enterprise proved disastrous in the extreme. Tolmides was defeated and slain near Chaeronea, a large number of the hoplites also fell in the engagement, while a still larger number were taken prisoners. This last circumstance proved fatal to the interests of Athens in Boeotia. In order to recover these prisoners, she agreed to evacuate Boeotia, and to permit the re-establishment of the aristocracies which she had formerly overthrown. But the Athenian reverses did not end here. The expulsion of the partisans of Athens from the government of Phocis and Locris, and the revolt of Euboea and Megara, were announced in quick succession. The youthful Pleistoanax, king of Sparta, actually penetrated, with an army of Lacedaemonians and Peloponnesian allies, as far as the neighbourhood of Eleusis; and the capital itself, it is said, was saved only by Pericles having bribed the Spartan monarch. Pericles reconquered Euboea; but this was the only possession which the Athenians succeeded in recovering. Their empire on land had vanished more speedily than it had been acquired; and they were therefore induced to conclude, at the beginning of B.C. 445, a THIRTY YEARS' TRUCE with Sparta and her allies, by which they consented to abandon all the acquisitions which they had made in Peloponnesus, and to leave Megara to be included among the Peloponnesian allies of Sparta.

From the Thirty Years' Truce to the commencement of the Peloponnesian war, few political events of any importance occurred. During these fourteen years (B.C. 445-431) Pericles continued to enjoy the sole direction of affairs. His views were of the most lofty kind. Athens was to become the capital of Greece, and the centre of art and refinement. In her external appearance the city was to be rendered worthy of the high position to which she aspired, by the beauty and splendour of her public buildings, by her works of art in sculpture, architecture, and painting, and by the pomp and magnificence of her religious festivals. All these objects Athens was enabled to attain in an incredibly short space of time, through the genius and energy of her citizens and the vast resources at her command. No state has ever exhibited so much intellectual activity and so great a progress in art as was displayed by Athens in the period which elapsed between the Thirty Years' Truce and the breaking out of the Peloponnesian war. She was the seat and centre of Grecian literature. The three great tragic poets of Greece were natives of Attica. AEschylus, the earliest of the three, had recently died in Sicily; but Sophocles was now at the full height of his reputation, and Euripides was rapidly rising into notice. Aristophanes, the greatest of the Grecian comic poets, was also born in Attica, and exhibited plays soon after the beginning of the Peloponnesian war. Herodotus, the Father of History, though a native of Halicarnassus in Asia Minor, resided some time at Athens, and accompanied a colony which the Athenians sent to Thurii in Italy. Thucydides, the greatest of Greek historians, was an Athenian, and was a young man at this period.

Colonization, for which the genius and inclination of the Athenians had always been suited, was another method adopted by Pericles for extending the influence and empire of Athens. The settlements made under his auspices were of two kinds CLERUCHIES, and regular colonies. The former mode was exclusively Athenian. It consisted in the allotment of land in conquered or subject countries to certain bodies of Athenians who continued to retain all their original rights of citizenship. This circumstance, as well as the convenience of entering upon land already in a state of cultivation instead of having to reclaim it from the rude condition of nature, seems to have rendered such a mode of settlement much preferred by the Athenians. The earliest instance which we find of it is in the year B.C. 506, when four thousand Athenians entered upon the domains of the Chalcidian knights (see Ch.5). But it was under Pericles that this system was most extensively adopted. During his administration 1000 Athenian citizens were settled in the Thracian Chersonese, 500 in Naxos, and 250 in Andros. The islands of Lemnos, Imbros, and Scyros, as well as a large tract in the north of Euboea, were also completely occupied by Athenian proprietors.

The most important colonies settled by Pericles were those of Thurii and Amphipolis. Since the destruction of Sybaris by the Crotoniates, in B.C. 509, the former inhabitants had lived dispersed in the adjoining territory along the gulf of

Tarentum, In B.C. 443 Pericles sent out a colony to found Thurii, near the site of the ancient Sybaris. The colony of Amphipolis was founded some years later (B.C. 437), under the conduct of Agnon.

But Pericles, notwithstanding his influence and power, had still many bitter and active enemies, who assailed him through his private connections, and even endeavoured to wound his honour by a charge of peculation. Pericles, after divorcing a wife with whom he had lived unhappily, took his mistress Aspasia to his house, and dwelt with her till his death on terms of the greatest affection. She was distinguished not only for her beauty, but also for her learning and accomplishments. Her intimacy with Anaxagoras, the celebrated Ionic philosopher, was made a handle for wounding Pericles in his tenderest relations. Paganism, notwithstanding its licence, was capable of producing bigots: and even at Athens the man who ventured to dispute the existence of a hundred gods with morals and passions somewhat worse than those of ordinary human nature, did so at the risk of his life. Anaxagoras was indicted for impiety. Aspasia was included in the same charge, and dragged before the courts of justice. Anaxagoras prudently fled from Athens, and thus probably avoided a fate which in consequence of a similar accusation afterwards overtook Socrates. Pericles himself pleaded the cause of Aspasia. He was indeed indirectly implicated in the indictment; but he felt no concern except for his beloved Aspasia, and on this occasion the cold and somewhat haughty statesman, whom the most violent storms of the assembly could not deprive of his self-possession, was for once seen to weep. His appeal to the jury was successful, but another trial still awaited him. An indictment was preferred against his friend, the great sculptor Phidias, for embezzlement of the gold intended to adorn the celebrated ivory statue of Athena; and according to some, Pericles himself was included in the charge of peculation. Whether Pericles was ever actually tried on this accusation is uncertain; but at all events, if he was, there can be no doubt that he was honourably acquitted. The gold employed in the statue had been fixed in such a manner that it could be detached and weighed, and Pericles challenged his accusers to the proof. But Phidias did not escape so fortunately. There were other circumstances which rendered him unpopular, and amongst them the fact that he had introduced portraits both of himself and Pericles in the sculptures which adorned the frieze of the Parthenon. Phidias died in prison before the day of trial.

The Athenian empire, since the conclusion of the Thirty Years' Truce, had again become exclusively maritime. Yet even among the subjects and allies united with Athens by the Confederacy of Delos, her sway was borne with growing discontent. One of the chief causes of this dissatisfaction was the amount of the tribute exacted by the Athenians, as well as their misapplication of the proceeds. In the time of Aristides and Cimon, when an active war was carrying on against the Persians, the sum annually collected amounted to 460 talents. In the time of Pericles, although that war had been brought to a close, the tribute had nevertheless increased to the annual sum of 600 talents. Another grievance was the transference to Athens of all lawsuits, at least of all public suits; for on this subject we are unable to draw the line distinctly. In criminal cases, at all events, the allies seem to have been deprived of the power to inflict capital punishment. Besides all these causes of complaint, the allies had often to endure the oppressions and exactions of Athenian officers, both military and naval, as well us of the rich and powerful Athenian citizens settled among them.

In B.C. 440 Samos, one of the free independent allies already mentioned, revolted from Athens; but even this island was no match for the Athenian power. Pericles, who sailed against the Samians in person, defeated their fleet in several engagements, and forced the city to capitulate. The Samians were compelled to raze their fortifications, to surrender their fleet, to give hostages for their future conduct, and to pay the expenses of the war.

The triumphs and the power of Athens were regarded with fear and jealousy by her rivals; and the quarrel between Corinth and Corcyra lighted the spark which was to produce the conflagration. On the coast of Illyria near the site of the modern Durazzo, the Corcyraeans had founded the city of Epidamnus. Corcyra (now Corfu) was itself a colony of Corinth; and though long at enmity with its mother country, was forced, according to the time-hallowed custom of the Greeks in such matters, to select the founder of Epidamnus from the Corinthians. Accordingly Corinth became the metropolis of Epidamnus as well as of Corcyra. At the time of which we speak, the Epidamnians, being hard pressed by the Illyrians, led by some oligarchical exiles of their own city, applied to Corcyra for assistance, which the Corcyraeans, being connected with the Epidamnian oligarchy, refused. The Epidamnians then sought help from the Corinthians, who undertook to assist them.

The Corcyraeans, highly resenting this interference, attacked the Corinthian fleet off Cape Actium, and gained a signal victory (B.C. 435).

Deeply humbled by this defeat, the Corinthians spent the two following years in active preparations for retrieving it. The Corcyraeans, who had not enrolled themselves either in the Lacedaemonian or Athenian alliance, and therefore stood alone, were greatly alarmed at these preparations. They now resolved to remedy this deficiency; and as Corinth belonged to the Lacedaemonian alliance, the Corcyraeans had no option, and were obliged to apply to Athens. The majority of the Athenians were ready to comply with their request; but in order to avoid an open infringement of the Thirty Years' Truce, it was resolved to conclude only a defensive alliance with Corcyra: that is, to defend the Corcyraeans in case their territories were actually invaded by the Corinthians, but beyond that not to lend them any active assistance. A small Athenian squadron of only 10 triremes was despatched to the assistance of the Corcyraeans. Soon after their arrival a battle ensued off the coast of Epirus, between the Corinthian and Corcyraean fleets. After a hard-fought day, victory finally declared in favour of the Corinthians. The Athenians now abandoned their neutrality, and did all in their power to save the dying Corcyraeans from their pursuers. This action took place early in the morning; and the Corinthians prepared to renew the attack in the afternoon, when they saw in the distance 20 Athenian vessels, which they believed to be the advanced guard of a still larger fleet. They accordingly sailed away to the coast of Epirus; but finding that the Athenians did not mean to undertake offensive operations against them, they departed homewards with their whole fleet. These events took place in the year B.C. 432.

The Corinthians were naturally incensed at the conduct of Athens; and it is not surprising that they should have watched for an opportunity of revenge. This was soon afforded them by the enmity of the Macedonian prince Perdiccas towards the Athenians. He incited her tributaries upon the coast of Macedonia to revolt, including Potidaea, a town seated on the isthmus of Pallene. Potidaea, though now a tributary of Athens, was originally a colony of the Corinthians, and received from them certain annual magistrates. Being urged as well by the Corinthians as by Perdiccas, the Potidaeans openly raised the standard of revolt (B.C. 432). A powerful Athenian armament was despatched to the coast of Macedonia and laid siege to

Potidaea.

Meanwhile the Lacedaemonians, urged on all sides by the complaints of their allies against Athens, summoned a general meeting of the Peloponnesian confederacy at Sparta. The Corinthians took the most prominent part in the debate; but other members of the confederacy had also heavy grievances to allege against Athens. Foremost among these were the Megarians, who complained that their commerce had been ruined by a recent decree of the Athenians which excluded them from every port within the Athenian jurisdiction. It was generally felt that the time had now arrived for checking the power of Athens. Influenced by these feelings, the Lacedaemonians decided upon war; and the congress passed a resolution to the same effect, thus binding the whole Peloponnesian confederacy to the same policy. This important resolution was adopted towards the close of B.C. 432, or early in the following year. Before any actual declaration of war, hostilities were begun in the spring of B.C. 431 by a treacherous attack of the Thebans upon Plataea. Though Boeotians by descent, the Plataeans did not belong to the Boeotian league, but had long been in close alliance with the Athenians. Hence they were regarded with hatred and jealousy by the Thebans, which sentiments were also shared by a small oligarchical faction in Plataea itself. The Plataean oligarchs secretly admitted a body of 300 Thebans into the town at night; but the attempt proved a failure; the citizens flew to arms, and in the morning all the Thebans were either slain or taken prisoner.

CHAPTER X.
ATHENS IN THE TIME OF PERICLES.

[Note: The figures referred to in a few places in this chapter have had to be omitted from the etext.]

At the commencement of the Peloponnesian war Athens was at the height of its glory under the brilliant administration of Pericles. We may therefore here pause to take a brief survey of the city and of its most important buildings. Athens is situated about three miles from the sea-coast, in the central plain of Attica. In this plain rise several eminences. Of these the most prominent is a lofty insulated mountain, with a conical peaked summit, now called the Hill of St. George, and which bore in ancient times the name of LYCABETTUS. This mountain, which was not included within the ancient walls, lies to the northeast of Athens, and forms the most striking feature in the environs of the city. It is to Athens what Vesuvius is to Naples, or Arthur's Seat to Edinburgh. South-west of Lycabettus there are four hills of moderate height, all of which formed part of the city. Of these the nearest to Lycabettus and at the distance of a mile from the latter, was the ACROPOLIS, or citadel of Athens, a square craggy rock rising abruptly about 150 feet, with a flat summit of about 1000 feet long from east to west, by 500 feet broad from north to south. Immediately west of the Acropolis is a second hill of irregular form, the AREOPAGUS. To the south-west there rises a third hill, the PNYX, on which the assemblies of the citizens were held; and to the south of the latter is a fourth hill, known as the MUSEUM. On the eastern and western sides of the city there run two small streams, which are nearly exhausted before they reach the sea, by the heats of summer and by the channels for artificial irrigation. That on the east is the Ilissus, which flowed through the southern quarter of the city: that on the west is the Cephissus. South of the city was seen the Saronic gulf, with the harbours of Athens.

Athens is said to have derived its name from the prominence given to the worship of Athena by its king Erechtheus. The inhabitants were previously called Cranai and Cecropidae, from Cecrops, who according to tradition, was the original founder of the city. This at first occupied only the hill or rock which afterwards became the ACROPOLIS; but gradually the buildings began to spread over the ground at the southern foot of this hill. It was not till the time of Pisistratus and his sons (B.C. 560-514) that the city began to assume any degree of splendour. The most remarkable building of these despots was the gigantic temple of the Olympian Zeus, which, however, was not finished till many centuries later. In B.C. 500 the theatre of Dionysus was commenced on the south-eastern slope of the Acropolis, but was not completed till B.C. 340; though it must have been used for the representation of plays long before that period.

Xerxes reduced the ancient city almost to a heap of ashes. After the departure of the Persians, its reconstruction on a much larger scale was commenced under the superintendence of Themistocles, whose first care was to provide for its safety by the erection of walls. The Acropolis now formed the centre of the city, round which the new walls described an irregular circle of about 60 stadia or 7 1/2 miles in circumference. The space thus enclosed formed the ASTY, or city, properly so called. But the views of Themistocles were not confined to the mere defence of Athens: he contemplated making her a great naval power, and for this purpose adequate docks and arsenals were required. Previously the Athenians had used as their only harbour the open roadstead of PHALERUM on the eastern side of the Phaleric bay, where the sea-shore is nearest to Athens. But Themistocles transferred the naval station of the Athenians to the peninsula of Piraeus, which is distant about 4 1/2 miles from Athens, and contains three natural harbours,--a large one on the western side, called simply Piraeus or The Harbour, and two smaller ones an the eastern side, called respectively ZEA and MUNYCHIA, the latter being nearest to the city. It was not till the administration of Pericles that the walls were built which connected Athens with her ports. These were at first the outer or northern Long Wall, which ran from Athens to Piraeus, and the Phaleric wall connecting the city with Phalerum. These were commenced in B.C. 457, and finished in the following year. It was soon found, however, that the space thus enclosed was too vast to be easily defended; and as the port of Phalerum was small and insignificant in comparison with the Piraeus, and soon ceased to be used by the Athenian ships of war, its wall was abandoned and probably allowed to fall into decay. Its place was supplied by another Long wall, which was built parallel to the first at a distance of only 550 feet, thus rendering both capable of being defended by the same body of men. Their height in all probability was not less than 60 feet. In process of time the space between the two Long Walls was occupied on each side by houses.

It will be seen from the preceding description that Athens, in its larger acceptation, and including its port, consisted of two circular cities, the Asty and Piraeus, each of about 7 1/2 miles in circumference, and joined together by a broad street of between four and five miles long.

Such was the outward and material form of that city, which during the period between the Persian and Peloponnesian wars reached the highest pitch of military, artistic, and literary glory. The latter portion of this period, or that comprised under the ascendency of Pericles, exhibits Athenian art in its highest state of perfection, and is therefore by way of excellence commonly designated as the age of Pericles. The great sculptor of this period--perhaps the greatest the world has ever seen--was Phidias, to whom Pericles intrusted the superintendence of all the works executed in his administration.

The first public monuments that arose after the Persian wars were erected under the auspices of Cimon, who was, like Pericles, a lover and patron of the arts. The principal of these were the small Ionic temple of Nike Apteros (Wingless Victory), and the Theseum, or temple of Theseus. The temple of Nike Apteros was only 27 feet in length by 18 in breadth, and was erected on the Acropolis in commemoration of Cimon's victory at the Eurymedon. A view of it is given at the beginning of this chapter, and its position on the Acropolis, on one side of the Propylaea, is seen in the drawings on p. 91, as well as on the Frontispiece of the work.

The Theseum is situated on a height to the north of the Areopagus, and was built to receive the bones of Theseus, which Cimon brought from Scyros in B.C. 469. It was probably finished about 465, and is the best preserved of all the monuments of ancient Athens. It was at once a tomb and temple, and possessed the privileges of an asylum. It is of the Doric order, 164 feet in length by 45 feet broad, and surrounded with columns.

But it was the Acropolis which was the chief centre of the architectural splendour of Athens. After the Persian wars the Acropolis had ceased to be inhabited, and was appropriated to the worship of Athena and to the other guardian deities of the city. It was covered with the temples of gods and heroes; and thus its platform presented not only a sanctuary, but a museum, containing the finest productions of the architect and the sculptor, in which the whiteness of the marble was relieved by brilliant colours, and rendered still more dazzling by the transparent clearness of the Athenian atmosphere. It was surrounded with walls, and the surface seems to have been divided into terraces communicating with one another by steps. The only approach to it was from the Agora on its western side at the top of a magnificent flight of marble steps, 70 feet broad, stood the Propylaea, constructed under the auspices of Pericles, and which served as a suitable entrance to the exquisite works within. The Propylaea were themselves one of the masterpieces of Athenian art. They were entirely of Pentelic marble, and covered the whole of the western end of the Acropolis, having a breadth of 168 feet. The central portion of them consisted of two porticoes, of which the western one faced the city, and the eastern one the interior of the Acropolis, each consisting of a front of six fluted Doric columns. This central part of the building was 58 feet in breadth, but the remaining breadth of the rock at this point was covered by two wings, which projected 26 feet in front of the western portico. Each of these wings was in the form of a Doric temple. The northern one, or that on the left of a person ascending the Acropolis, was called the PINACOTHECA, from its walls being covered with paintings. The southern wing consisted only of a porch or open gallery. Immediately before its western front stood the little temple of Nike Apteros already mentioned.

On passing through the Propylaea all the glories of the Acropolis became visible. The chief building was the Parthenon (I.E. House of the Virgin), the most perfect production of Grecian architecture. It derived its name from its being the temple of Athena Parthenos, or Athena the Virgin, the invincible goddess of war. It was also called HECATOMPEDON, from its breadth of 100 feet. It was built under the administration of Pericles, and was completed in B.C. 438. The Parthenon stood on the highest part of the Acropolis near its centre, and probably occupied the site of an earlier temple destroyed by the Persians. It was entirely of Pentelic marble, on a rustic basement of ordinary limestone, and its architecture, which was of the Doric order, was of the purest kind. Its dimensions were about 228 feet in length, 101 feet in breadth, and 66 feet in height to the top of the pediment. It consisted of a cella, surrounded by a peristyle. The cella was divided into two chambers of unequal size, the eastern one of which was about 98 feet long, and the western one about 43 feet. The ceiling of both these chambers was supported by rows of columns. The whole building was adorned with the most exquisite sculptures, executed by various artists under the direction of Phidias. These consisted of, 1. The sculptures in the tympana of the pediments (I.E. the inner portion of the triangular gable ends of the roof above the two porticoes), each of which was filled with about 24 colossal figures. The group in the eastern or principal front represented the birth of Athena from the head of Zeus, and the western the contest between Athena and Poseidon (Neptune) for the land of Attica. 2. The metopes between the triglyphs in the frieze of the entablature (I.E. the upper of the two portions into which the space between the columns and the roof is divided) were filled with sculptures in high relief, representing a variety of subjects relating to Athena herself, or to the indigenous heroes of Attica. Each tablet was 4 feet 3 inches square. Those on the south side related to the battle of the Athenians with the Centaurs. One of the metopes is figured below. 3. The frieze which ran along outside the wall of the cella, and within the external columns which surround the building, at the same height and parallel with the metopes, was sculptured with a representation of the Panathenaic festival in very low relief. This frieze was 3 feet 4 inches in height, and 520 feet in length. A small portion of the frieze is also figured below. A large number of the slabs of the frieze, together with sixteen metopes from the south side, and several of the statues of the pediments, were brought to England by Lord Elgin, of whom they were purchased by the nation and deposited in the British Museum.

   But the chief wonder of the Parthenon was the colossal statue of the Virgin Goddess executed by Phidias himself, which stood in the eastern or principal chamber of the cella. It was of the sort called CHRYSELEPHANTINE, a kind of work said to have been invented by Phidias in which ivory was substituted for marble in those parts which were uncovered, while the place of the real drapery was supplied with robes and other ornaments of solid gold. Its height, including the base, was nearly 40 feet. It represented the goddess standing, clothed with a tunic reaching to the ankles, with a spear in her left hand, and an image of Victory in her right.

The Acropolis was adorned with another colossal figure of Athena, in bronze, also the work of Phidias. It stood in the open air, nearly opposite the Propylaea, and was one of the first objects seen after passing through the gates of the latter. With its pedestal it must have stood about 70 feet high, and consequently towered above the roof of the Parthenon, so that the point of its spear and the crest of its helmet were visible off the promontory of Sunium to ships approaching Athens. It was called the "Athena Promachus," because it represented the goddess armed, and in the very attitude of battle.

The only other monument on the summit of the Acropolis which it is necessary to describe is the Erechtheum, or temple of Erechtheus. The traditions respecting Erechtheus vary, but according to one set of them he was identical with the god Poseidon. He was worshipped in his temple under the name of Poseidon Erechtheus, and from the earliest times was associated with Athena as one of the two protecting deities of Athens. The original Erechtheum was burnt by the Persians, but the new temple was erected on the ancient site. This could not have been otherwise; for on this spot was the sacred olive-tree which Athena evoked from the earth in her contest with Poseidon, and also the well of salt-water which Poseidon produced by a stroke of his trident, the impression of which was seen upon the rock. The building was also called the temple of Athena Polias, because it contained a separate sanctuary of the goddess, as well as her most ancient statue. The building of the new Erechtheum was not commenced till the Parthenon and Propylaea were finished, and probably not before the year preceding the breaking out of the Peloponnesian war. Its progress was no doubt delayed by that event, and it was probably not completed before 393 B.C. When finished it presented one of the finest models of the Ionic order, as the Parthenon was of the Doric, It stood to the north of the latter building and close to the northern wall of the Acropolis. The form of the Erechtheum differed from every known example of a Grecian temple. Usually a Grecian temple was an oblong figure with a portico at each extremity. The Erechtheum, on the contrary, though oblong in shape and having a portico at the eastern or principal front, had none at its western end, where, however, a portico projected north and south from either side, thus forming a kind of transept. This irregularity seems to have been chiefly owing to the necessity of preserving the different sanctuaries and religious objects belonging to the ancient temple. A view of it is given opposite. The roof of the southern portico, as shown in the view, was supported by six Caryatides.

Such were the principal objects which adorned the Acropolis at the time of which we are now speaking. Their general appearance will be best gathered from the engraving on the Frontispiece.

Before quitting the city of Athens, there are two or three other objects of interest which must be briefly described. First, the Dionysiac theatre, which occupied the slope at the south-eastern extremity of the Acropolis. The middle of it was excavated out of the rock, and the rows of seats ascended in curves one above another, the diameter increasing with the height. It was no doubt sufficiently large to accommodate the whole body of Athenian citizens, as well as the strangers who flocked to Athens during the Dionysiac festival, but its dimensions cannot now be accurately ascertained. It had no roof, but the spectators were probably protected from the sun by an awning, and from their elevated seats they had a distinct view of the sea, and of the peaked hills of Salamis in the horizon. Above them rose the Parthenon and the other buildings of the Acropolis, so that they sat under the shadow of the ancestral gods of the country.

The Areopagus, or Hill of Ares (Mars), was a rocky height opposite the western end of the Acropolis, from which it was separated only by some hollow ground. It derived its name from the tradition that Ares (Mars) was brought to trial here before the assembled gods, by Poseidon (Neptune), for murdering Halirrhothius the son of the latter. It was here that the Council of Areopagus met, frequently called the Upper Council, to distinguish it from the Council of Five Hundred, which assembled in the valley below. The Areopagites sat as judges in the open air, and two blocks of stone are still to be seen, probably those which were occupied respectively by the accuser and the accused. The Areopagus was the spot where the Apostle Paul preached to the men of Athens.

The Pnyx, or place for holding the public assemblies of the Athenians, stood on the side of a low rocky hill, at the distance of about a quarter of a mile from the Areopagus. Projecting from the hill and hewn out of it, still stands a solid rectangular block, called the Bema or pulpit, from whence the orators addressed the multitude in the area before them. The position of the Bema commanded a view of the Propylaea and the other magnificent edifices of the Acropolis, while beneath it was the city itself studded with monuments of Athenian glory. The Athenian orators frequently roused the national feelings of their audience by pointing to the Propylaea and to the other splendid buildings before them. Between the Pnyx on the west, the Areopagus on the north, and the Acropolis on the east, and closely adjoining the base of these hills, stood the Agora (or market-place). In a direction from north-west to south-east a street called the Ceramicus ran diagonally through the Agora, entering it through the valley between the Pnyx and the Areopagus. The street was named after a district of the city, which was divided into two parts, the Inner and Outer Ceramicus. The former lay within the city walls, and included the Agora. The Outer Ceramicus, which formed a handsome suburb on the north-west of the city, was the burial-place of all persons honoured with a public funeral. Through it ran the road to the gymnasium and gardens of the Academy which were situated about a mile from the walls. The Academy was the place where Plato and his disciples taught. On each side of this road were monuments to illustrious Athenians, especially those who had fallen in battle.

East of the city, and outside the walls, was the Lyceum, a gymnasium dedicated to Apollo Lyceus, and celebrated as the place in which Aristotle taught.

CHAPTER XI.
THE PELOPONNESIAN WAR.--FIRST PERIOD, FROM THE COMMENCEMENT OF THE WAR TO THE PEACE OF NICIAS, B.C. 431-421.

War was now fairly kindled. All Greece looked on in suspense as its two leading cities were about to engage in a strife of which no man could forsee the end; but the youth, with which both Athens and Peloponnesus then abounded, having had no experience of the bitter calamities of war, rushed into it with ardour. It was a war of principles and races. Athens was a champion of democracy, Sparta of aristocracy; Athens represented the Ionic tribes, Sparta the Dorian; the former were fond of novelty, the latter were conservative and stationary; Athens had the command of the sea, Sparta was stronger upon land. On the side of Sparta was ranged the whole of Peloponnesus, except Argos and Achaia, together with the Megarians, Boeotians, Phocians, Opuntian Locrians, Ambraciots, Leucadians, and Anactorians. The allies of Athens, with the exception of the Thessalians, Acarnanians, Messenians at Naupactus, and Plataeans, were all insular, and consisted of the Chians, Lesbians, Corcyraeans, and Zacynthians, and shortly afterwards of the Cephallenians, To these must be added her tributary towns on the coast of Thrace and Asia Minor, together with all the islands north of Crete, except Melos and Thera.

The Peloponnesians commenced the war by an invasion of Attica, with a large army, under the command of the Spartan King Archidamus (B.C. 431). Pericles had instructed the inhabitants of Attica to secure themselves and their property within the walls of Athens. They obeyed his injunctions with reluctance, for the Attic population had from the earliest times been strongly attached to a rural life.

But the circumstances admitted of no alternative. Archidamus advanced as far as Acharnae, a flourishing Attic borough situated only about seven miles from Athens. Here he encamped on a rising ground within sight of the metropolis, and began to lay waste the country around, expecting probably by that means to provoke the Athenians to battle. But in this he was disappointed. Notwithstanding the murmurs and clamours of the citizens Pericles remained firm, and steadily refused to venture an engagement in the open held. The Peloponnesians retired from Attica after still further ravaging the country; and the Athenians retaliated by making descents upon various parts of the coasts of Peloponnesus, and ravaging the territory of Megara.

Such were the results of the first campaign. From the method in which the war was conducted it had become pretty evident that it would prove of long duration; and the Athenians now proceeded to provide for this contingency. It was agreed that a reserve fund of 1000 talents should be set apart, which was not to be touched in any other case than an attack upon Athens by sea. Any citizen who proposed to make a different use of the fund incurred thereby the punishment of death. With the same view it was resolved to reserve every year 100 of their best triremes, fully manned and equipped.

Towards the winter Pericles delivered, from a lofty platform erected in the Ceramicus, the funeral oration of those who had fallen in the war. This speech, or at all events the substance of it, has been preserved by Thucydides, who may possibly have heard it pronounced. It is a valuable monument of eloquence and patriotism, and particularly interesting for the sketch which it contains of Athenian manners as well as of the Athenian constitution.

In the following year (B.C. 430) the Peloponnesians, under Archidamus, renewed their invasion of Attica. At the same time the Athenians were attacked by a more insidious and a more formidable enemy. The plague broke out in the crowded city. This terrible disorder, which was supposed to have originated in AEthiopia, had already desolated Asia and many of the countries around the Mediterranean. A great proportion of those who were seized perished in from seven to nine days. It frequently attacked the mental faculties, and left even those who recovered from it so entirely deprived of memory that they could recognise neither themselves nor others. The disorder being new, the physicians could find no remedy in the resources of their art. Despair now began to take possession of the Athenians. Some suspected that the Peloponnesians had poisoned the wells; others attributed the pestilence to the anger of Apollo. A dreadful state of moral dissolution followed. The sick were seized with unconquerable despondency; whilst a great part of the population who had hitherto escaped the disorder, expecting soon to be attacked in turn, abandoned themselves to all manner of excess, debauchery, and crime. The numbers carried off by the pestilence can hardly be estimated at less than a fourth of the whole population.

Oppressed at once by war and pestilence, their lands desolated, their homes filled with mourning, it is not surprising that the Athenians were seized with rage and despair, or that they vented their anger on Pericles, whom they deemed the author of their misfortunes. But that statesman still adhered to his plans with unshaken firmness. Though the Lacedaemonians were in Attica, though the plague had already seized on Athens, he was vigorously pushing his schemes of offensive operations. A foreign expedition might not only divert the popular mind but would prove beneficial by relieving the crowded city of part of its population; and accordingly a fleet was fitted out, of which Pericles himself took the command, and which committed devastations upon various parts of the Peloponnesian coast. But, upon returning from this expedition, Pericles found the public feeling more exasperated than before. Envoys had even been despatched to Sparta to sue for peace, but had been dismissed without a hearing; a disappointment which had rendered the populace still more furious. Pericles now found it necessary to call a public assembly in order to vindicate his conduct, and to encourage the desponding citizens to persevere. But though he succeeded in persuading them to prosecute the war with vigour; they still continued to nourish their feelings of hatred against the great statesman. His political enemies, of whom Cleon was the chief, took advantage of this state of the public mind to bring against him a charge of peculation. The main object of this accusation was to incapacitate him for the office of Strategus, or general. [The Strategi, or Generals, were ten in number, elected annually, and were intrusted not only with the command on military expeditions, but with the superintendence of all warlike preparations, and with the regulation of all matters in any way connected with the war department of the state.] He was brought before the dicastery on this charge, and sentenced to pay a considerable fine; but eventually a strong reaction occurred in his favour. He was re-elected general, and apparently regained all the influence he had ever possessed.

But he was not destined long to enjoy this return of popularity. His life was now closing in, and its end was clouded by a long train of domestic misfortunes. The epidemic deprived him not only of many personal and political friends, but also of several near relations, amongst whom were his sister and his two legitimate sons Xanthippus and Paralus. The death of the latter was a severe blow to him. During the funeral ceremonies, as he placed a garland on the body of this his favourite son, he was completely overpowered by his feelings and wept aloud. His ancient house was now left without an heir. By Aspasia, however, he had an illegitimate son who bore his own name, and whom the Athenians now legitimised and thus alleviated, as far as lay in their power, the misfortunes of their great leader.

After this period it was with difficulty that Pericles was persuaded by his friends to take any active part in public affairs; nor did he survive more than a twelvemonth. An attack of the prevailing epidemic was succeeded by a low and lingering fever, which undermined both his strength of body and vigour of intellect. As Pericles lay apparently unconscious on his death-bed, the friends who stood around it were engaged in recalling his exploits. The dying man interrupted them by remarking: "What you praise in me is partly the result of good fortune, and at all events common to me with many other commanders. What I chiefly pride myself upon you have not noticed--no Athenian ever wore mourning through me."

The enormous influence which Pericles exercised for so long a period over an ingenious but fickle people like the Athenians, is an unquestionable proof of his intellectual superiority. This hold on the public affection is to be attributed to a great extent to his extraordinary eloquence. Cicero regards him as the first example of an almost perfect orator, at once delighting the Athenians with his copiousness and grace, and overawing them by the force and cogency of his diction and arguments. He seems, indeed, to have singularly combined the power of persuasion with that more rapid and abrupt style of oratory which takes an audience by storm and defies all resistance. As the accomplished man of genius and the liberal patron of literature and art, Pericles is worthy of the highest admiration. By these qualities he has justly given name to the most brilliant intellectual epoch that the world has ever seen. But on this point we have already touched, and shall have occasion to refer hereafter in the sketch of Grecian literature.

In the third year of the war (B.C. 429) Archidamus directed his whole force against the ill-fated town of Plataea. The siege that ensued is one of the most memorable in the annals of Grecian warfare. Plataea was but a small city, and its garrison consisted of only 400 citizens and 80 Athenians, together with 110 women to manage their household affairs. Yet this small force set at defiance the whole army of the Peloponnesians. The latter, being repulsed in all their attempts to take the place by storm, resolved to turn the siege into a blockade, and reduce the city by famine. The Plataeans endured a blockade of two years, during which the Athenians attempted nothing for their relief. In the second year, however, about half the garrison effected their escape; but the rest were obliged to surrender shortly afterwards (B.C. 427). The whole garrison, consisting of 200 Plataeans and 25 Athenians, were now arraigned before five judges sent from Sparta. Their indictment was framed in a way which precluded the possibility of escape. They were simply asked "Whether, during the present war, they had rendered any assistance to the Lacedaemonians and their allies?" Each man was called up separately before the judgment-seat, and the same question having been put to him and of course answered in the negative, he was immediately led away to execution. The town of Plataea was transferred to the Thebans, who a few months afterwards levelled all the private buildings to the ground. Thus was Plataea blotted out from the map of Greece (B.C. 427). In recording the fall of Plataea we have anticipated the order of chronology.

The most important event in the fourth year of the war (B.C. 428) was the revolt of Mytilene; the capital of Lesbos, and of the greater part of that island. The Athenians sent out a fleet which blockaded Mytilene both by sea and land, The Peloponnesians promised their assistance; but from various causes their fleet was unable to reach the place. Meanwhile the provisions of the town were exhausted, and it was therefore resolved, as a last desperate expedient, to make a sally, and endeavour to raise the blockade. With this view even the men of the lower classes were armed with the full armour of the hoplites. But this step produced a very different result from what had been expected or intended. The great mass of the Mytileneans regarded their own oligarchical government with suspicion and now threatened that, unless their demands were complied with, they would surrender the city to the Athenians. In this desperate emergency the Mytilenean government perceived that their only chance of safety lay in anticipating the people in this step. They accordingly opened a negotiation with Paches, the Athenian commander, and a capitulation was agreed upon by which the city was to be surrendered and the fate of its inhabitants to be decided by the Athenian Assembly.

At Athens the disposal of the prisoners caused great debate. It was on this occasion that the leather-seller Cleon first comes prominently forward in Athenian affairs. If we may trust the picture drawn by the comic poet Aristophanes, Cleon was a perfect model of a low-born demagogue; a noisy brawler, insolent in his gestures, corrupt and venal in his principles. Much allowance must no doubt be made for comic licence and exaggeration in this portrait, but even a caricature must have some grounds of truth for its basis. It was this man who took the lead in the debate respecting the disposal of the Mytileneans, and made the savage and horrible proposal to put to death the whole male population of Mytilene of military age, and to sell the women and children into slavery. This motion he succeeded in carrying and a trireme was immediately despatched to Mytilene, conveying orders to Paches to carry the bloody decree into execution. This barbarous decree made no discrimination between the innocent and the guilty; and on the morrow so general a feeling prevailed of the horrible injustice that had been committed, that the magistrates acceded to the prayer of the Mytilenean envoys and called a fresh assembly. Notwithstanding the violent opposition of Creon, the majority of the assembly reversed their former decree and resolved that the Mytileneans already in custody should be put upon their trial, but that the remainder of the population should be spared. A second trireme was immediately despatched to Mytilene, with orders to Paches to arrest the execution. The utmost diligence was needful. The former trireme had a start of four-and-twenty hours, and nothing but exertions almost superhuman would enable the second to reach Mytilene early enough to avert the tragical catastrophe, The oarsmen were allowed by turns only short intervals of rest, and took their food, consisting of barley-meal steeped in wine and oil, as they sat at the oar. Happily the weather proved favourable; and the crew, who had been promised large rewards in case they arrived in time, exerted themselves to deliver the reprieve, whilst the crew of the preceding vessel had conveyed the order for execution with slowness and reluctance. Yet even so the countermand came only just in time. The mandate was already in the hands of Paches, who was taking measures for its execution. The fortifications of Mytilene were razed, and her fleet delivered up to the Athenians.

The fate of the Plataeans and Mytileneans affords a fearful illustration of the manners of the age; but these horrors soon found a parallel in Corcyra. A fearful struggle took place in this island between the aristocratical and democratical parties. The people at length obtained the mastery, and the vengeance which they took on their opponents was fearful. The most sacred sanctuaries afforded no protection; the nearest ties of blood and kindred were sacrificed to civil hatred. In one case a father slew even his own son. These scenes of horror lasted for seven days, during which death in every conceivable form was busily at work.

The seventh year of the war (B.C. 425) was marked by an important event. An Athenian fleet was detained by bad weather at Pylus in Messenia, on the modern bay of Navarino. Demosthenes, an active Athenian officer, who was on board the fleet, thought it an eligible spot on which to establish some of the Messenians from Naupactus, since it was a strong position, from which they might annoy the Lacedaemonians, and excite revolt among their Helot kinsmen. As the bad weather continued for some time, the soldiers on board amused themselves, under the directions of Demosthenes, in constructing a sort of rude fortification. The nature of the ground was favourable for the work, and in five or six days a wall was throws up sufficient for the purposes of defence. Demosthenes undertook to garrison the place; and five ships and 200 hoplites were left behind with him.

This insult to the Lacedaemonian territory caused great alarm and indignation at Sparta. The Peloponnesian fleet was ordered to Pylus; and the Lacedaemonian commander, on arriving with the fleet, immediately occupied the small uninhabited and densely wooded island of Sphacteria, which, with the exception of two narrow channels on the north and south, almost blocked up the entrance of the bay. Between the island and the mainland was a spacious basin, in which the fleet took up its station. The Lacedaemonians lost no time in attacking the fortress; but notwithstanding their repeated attempts they were unable to effect a landing.

Whilst they were preparing for another assault, they were surprised by the appearance of the Athenian fleet. They had strangely neglected to secure the entrances into the bay: and, when the Athenian ships came sailing through both the undefended channels, many of their triremes were still moored, and part of their crews ashore. The battle which ensued was desperate. Both sides fought with extraordinary valour; but victory at length declared for the Athenians. Five Peloponnesian ships were captured; the rest were saved only by running them ashore, where they were protected by the Lacedaemonian army.

The Athenians, thus masters of the sea, were enabled to blockade the island of Sphacteria, in which the flower of the Lacedaemonian army was shut up, many of them native Spartans of the highest families. In so grave an emergency messengers were sent to Sparta for advice. The Ephors themselves immediately repaired to the spot; and so desponding was their view of the matter, that they saw no issue from it but a peace. They therefore proposed and obtained an armistice for the purpose of opening negotiations at Athens. But the Athenians, at the instigation of Cleon, insisted upon the most extravagant demands, and hostilities were accordingly resumed. They were not however attended with any decisive result. The blockade of Sphacteria began to grow tedious and harassing. The force upon it continually received supplies of provisions either from swimmers, who towed skins filled with linseed and poppy-seed mixed with honey, or from Helots, who, induced by the promise of large rewards, eluded the blockading squadron during dark and stormy nights, and landed cargoes on the back of the island. The summer, moreover, was fast wearing away, and the storms of winter might probably necessitate the raising of the blockade altogether. Under these circumstances, Demosthenes began to contemplate a descent upon the island; with which view he sent a message to Athens to explain the unfavourable state of the blockade, and to request further assistance.

These tidings were very distasteful to the Athenians, who had looked upon Sphacteria as their certain prey. They began to regret having let slip the favourable opportunity for making a peace, and to vent their displeasure upon Cleon, the director of their conduct on that occasion. But Cleon put on a face of brass. He abused the Strategi. His political opponent, Nicias, was then one of those officers, a man of quiet disposition and moderate abilities, but thoroughly honest and incorruptible. Him Cleon now singled out for his vituperation, and, pointing at him with his finger, exclaimed--"It would be easy enough to take the island if our generals were MEN. If I were General, I would do it at once!" This burst of the tanner made the assembly laugh. He was saluted with cries of "Why don't you go, then?" and Nicias, thinking probably to catch his opponent in his own trap, seconded the voice of the assembly by offering to place at his disposal whatever force he might deem necessary for the enterprise. Cleon at first endeavoured to avoid the dangerous honour thus thrust upon him. But the more he drew back the louder were the assembly in calling upon him to accept the office; and as Nicias seriously repeated his proposition, he adopted with a good grace what there was no longer any possibility of evading, and asserted that he would take Sphacteria within twenty days, and either kill all the Lacedaemonians upon it, or bring them prisoners to Athens.

Never did general set out upon an enterprise under circumstances more singular; but, what was still more extraordinary, fortune enabled him to make his promise good. In fact, as we have seen, Demosthenes had already resolved on attacking the island; and when Cleon arrived at Pylus he found everything prepared for the assault. Accident favoured the enterprise. A fire kindled by some Athenian sailors, who had landed for the purpose of cooking their dinner, caught and destroyed the woods with which the island was overgrown, and thus deprived the Lacedaemonians of one of their principal defences. Nevertheless such was the awe inspired by the reputation of the Spartan army that Demosthenes considered it necessary to land about 10,000 soldiers of different descriptions, although the Lacedaemonian force consisted of only about 420 men. But this small force for a long while kept their assailants at bay; till some Messenians, stealing round by the sea-shore, over crags and cliffs which the Lacedaemonians had deemed impracticable, suddenly appeared on the high ground which overhung their rear. They now began to give way, and would soon have been all slain; but Cleon and Demosthenes, being anxious to carry them prisoners to Athens, sent a herald to summon them to surrender. The latter, in token of compliance, dropped their shields, and waved their hands above their heads. They requested, however, permission to communicate with their countrymen on the mainland; who, after two or three communications, sent them a final message--"to take counsel for themselves, but to do nothing disgraceful." The survivors then surrendered. They were 292 in number, 120 of whom were native Spartans belonging to the first families. By this surrender the prestige of the Spartan arms was in a great degree destroyed. The Spartans were not, indeed, deemed invincible; but their previous feats, especially at Thermopylae, had inspired the notion that they would rather die than yield; an opinion which could now no longer be entertained.

Cleon had thus performed his promise. On the day after the victory he and Demosthenes started with the prisoners for Athens, where they arrived within 20 days from the time of Cleon's departure. Altogether, this affair was one of the most favourable for the Athenians that had occurred during the war. The prisoners would serve not only for a guarantee against future invasions, which might be averted by threatening to put them to death, but also as a means for extorting advantageous conditions whenever a peace should be concluded. Nay, the victory itself was of considerable importance, since it enabled the Athenians to place Pylus in a better posture of defence, and, by garrisoning it with Messenians from Naupactus, to create a stronghold whence Laconia might be overrun and ravaged at pleasure. The Lacedaemonians themselves were so sensible of these things, that they sent repeated messages to Athens to propose a peace, but which the Athenians altogether disregarded.

The eighth year of the war (B.C. 424) opened with brilliant prospects for the Athenians. Elate with their continued good fortune, they aimed at nothing less than the recovery of all the possessions which they had held before the Thirty Years' Truce. For this purpose they planned an expedition against Boeotia. But their good fortune had now reached its culminatiug point. They were defeated by the Boeotians with great loss at the battle of Delium, which was the greatest and most decisive engagement fought during the first period of the war an interesting feature of the battle is that both Socrates and his pupil Alcibiades were engaged in it, the former among the hoplites, the latter in the cavalry. Socrates distinguished himself by his bravery, and was one of those who, instead of throwing down their arms, kept together in a compact body, and repulsed the attacks of the pursuing horse. His retreat was also protected by Alcibiades.

This disastrous battle was speedily followed by the overthrow of the Athenian empire in Thrace. At the request of Perdiccas, King of Macedonia, and of the Chalcidian towns, who had sued for help against the Athenians, Brasidas was sent by the Lacedaemonian government into Macedonia, at the head of a small body of troops. On his arrival in Macedonia he proclaimed that he was come to deliver the Grecian cities from the tyrannous yoke of Athens. His bravery, his kind and conciliating demeanour, his probity, moderation, and good faith, soon gained him the respect and love of the allies of Athens in that quarter. Acanthus and Stagirus hastened to open their gates to him; and early in the ensuing winter, by means of forced marches, he suddenly and unexpectedly appeared before the important Athenian colony of Amphipolis on the Strymon. In that town the Athenian party sent a message for assistance to Thucydides, the historian, who was then general in those parts. Thucydides hastened with seven ships from Thasos, and succeeded in securing Eion at the mouth of the Strymon; but Amphipolis, which lay a little higher up the river, allured by the favourable terms offered, had already surrendered to Brasidas. For his want of vigilance on this occasion, Thucydides was, on the motion of Cleon, sentenced to banishment, and spent the following twenty years of his life in exile. Torone, Scione, and other towns also revolted from Athens.

In the following year (B.C. 422) Cleon was sent to Macedonia to recover the Athenian dependencies, and especially Amphipolis. He encamped on a rising ground on the eastern side of the town. Having deserted the peaceful art of dressing hides for the more hazardous trade of war, in which he was almost totally inexperienced, and having now no Demosthenes to direct his movements, Cleon was thrown completely off his guard by a very ordinary stratagem on the part of Brasidas, who contrived to give the town quite a deserted and peaceful appearance. Cleon suffered his troops to fall into disorder, till he was suddenly surprised by the astounding news that Brasidas was preparing for a sally. Cleon at once resolved to retreat. But his skill was equal to his valour. He conducted his retreat in the most disorderly manner. His left wing had already filed off and his centre with straggling ranks was in the act of following, when Brasidas ordered the gates of the town to be flung open, and, rushing out at the head of only 150 chosen soldiers, charged the retreating columns in flank. They were immediately routed; but Brasidas received a mortal wound and was carried off the field. Though his men were forming on the hill, Cleon fled as fast as he could on the approach of the enemy, but was pursued and slain by a Thracian peltast. In spite, however, of the disgraceful flight of their general, the right wing maintained their ground for a considerable time, till some cavalry and peltasts issuing from Amphipolis attacked them in flank and rear, and compelled them to fly. On assembling again at Eion it was found that half the Athenian hoplites had been slain. Brasidas was carried into Amphipolis, and lived long enough to receive the tidings of his victory. He was interred within the walls with great military pomp in the centre of what thenceforth became the chief agora; he was proclaimed oecist, or founder of the town; and was worshipped as a hero with annual games and sacrifices.

By the death of Brasidas and Cleon the two chief obstacles to a peace were removed; for the former loved war for the sake of its glory, the latter for the handle which it afforded for agitation and for attacking his political opponents. The Athenian Nicias, and the Spartan king Pleistoanax, zealously forwarded the negotiations, and in the spring of the year B.C. 421 a peace for 50 years, commonly called the PEACE OF NICIAS, was concluded on the basis of a mutual restitution of prisoners and places captured during the war.

CHAPTER XII.
THE PELOPONNESIAN WAR.--SECOND PERIOD, FROM THE PEACE OF NICIAS TO THE DEFEAT OF THE ATHENIANS IN SICILY, B.C. 421-413.

Several of the allies of Sparta were dissatisfied with the peace which she had concluded; and soon afterwards some of them determined to revive the ancient pretensions of Argos, and to make her the head of a new confederacy, which should include all Greece, with the exception of Sparta and Athens. The movement was begun by the Corinthians, and the league was soon joined by the Eleans, the Mantineans, and the Chalcidians.

Between Sparta and Athens themselves matters were far from being on a satisfactory footing. Sparta confessed her inability to compel the Boeotians and Corinthians to accede to the peace, or even to restore the town of Amphipolis. Athens consequently refused to evacuate Pylus, though she removed the Helots and Messenians from it. In the negotiations which ensued respecting the surrender of Pylus, Alcibiades took a prominent part. This extraordinary man had already obtained immense influence at Athens. Young, rich, handsome, profligate, and clever, Alcibiades was the very model of an Athenian man of fashion. In lineage he was a striking contrast to the plebeian orators of the day. He traced his paternal descent from Ajax, whilst on his mother's side he claimed relationship with the Alcmaeonidae and consequently with Pericles. On the death of his father Clinias Pericles had become his guardian. From early youth the conduct of Alcibiades was marked by violence, recklessness, and vanity. He delighted in astonishing the more sober portion of the citizens by his capricious and extravagant feats. He was utterly destitute of morality, whether public or private. But his vices were partly redeemed by some brilliant qualities. He possessed both boldness of design and vigour of action; and, though scarcely more than thirty at the time of which we are now speaking, he had already on several occasions distinguished himself by his bravery. His more serious studies were made subservient to the purposes of his ambition, for which some skill as an orator was necessary. In order to attain it he frequented the schools of the sophists, and exercised himself in the dialectics of Prodicus, Protagoras, and above all of Socrates.

Such was the man who now opposed the application of the Lacedaemonian ambassadors. Their reception had been so favourable, that Alcibiades alarmed at the prospect of their success, resorted to a trick in order to defeat it. He called upon the Lacedaemonian envoys, one of whom happened to be his personal friend; and he advised them not to tell the Assembly that they were furnished with full powers, as in that case the people would bully them into extravagant concessions, but rather to say that they were merely come to discuss and report. He promised, if they did so, to speak in their favour, and induce the Assembly to grant the restitution of Pylus, to which he himself had hitherto been the chief obstacle. Accordingly on the next day, when the ambassadors were introduced into the Assembly, Alcibiades, assuming his blandest tone and most winning smile, asked them on what footing they came and what were their powers. In reply to these questions, the ambassadors, who only a day or two before had told Nicias and the Senate that they were come as plenipotentiaries, now publicly declared, in the face of the Assembly, that they were not authorized to conclude, but only to negotiate and discuss. At this announcement, those who had heard their previous declaration could scarcely believe their ears. A universal burst of indignation broke forth at this exhibition of Spartan duplicity; whilst, to wind up the scene, Alcibiades, affecting to be more surprised than any, distinguished himself by being the loudest and bitterest in his invectives against the perfidy of the Lacedaemonians.

Shortly afterwards Alcibiades procured the completion of a treaty of alliance for 100 years with Argos, Elis, and Mantinea (B.C. 420). Thus were the Grecian states involved in a complicity of separate and often apparently opposite alliances. It was evident that allies so heterogeneous could not long hold together; nevertheless, nominally at least, peace was at first observed.

In the July which followed the treaty with Argos, the Olympic games, which recurred every fourth year, were to be celebrated. The Athenians had been shut out by the war from the two previous celebrations; and curiosity was excited throughout Greece to see what figure Athens would make at this great Pan-Hellenic festival. War, it was surmised, must have exhausted her resources, and would thus prevent her from appearing with becoming splendour. But from this reproach she was rescued by the wealth and vanity, if not by the patriotism, of Alcibiades. By his care, the Athenian deputies exhibited the richest display of golden ewers, censers, and other plate to be used in the public sacrifice and procession; whilst for the games he entered in his own name no fewer than the unheard-of number of seven four-horsed chariots, of which one gained the first, and another the second prize. Alcibiades was consequently twice crowned with the olive, and twice proclaimed victor by the herald.

The growing ambition and success of Alcibiades prompted him to carry his schemes against Sparta into the very heart of Peloponnesus, without, however, openly violating the peace.

The Lacedaemonians now found it necessary to act with more vigour; and accordingly in B.C. 418 they assembled a very large army, under the command of the Spartan king, Agis. A decisive battle was fought near Mantinea, in which Agis gained a brilliant victory over the Argives and their allies. This battle and that of Delium were the two most important engagements that had yet been fought in the Peloponnesian war. Although the Athenians had fought on the side of the Argives at Mantinea, the peace between Sparta and Athens continued to be nominally observed.

In B.C. 416 the Athenians attacked and conquered Melos, which island and Thera were the only islands in the AEgean not subject to the Athenian supremacy. The Melians having rejected all the Athenian overtures for a voluntary submission, their capital was blockaded by sea and land, and after a siege of some months surrendered. On the proposal, as it appears, of Alcibiades, all the adult males were put to death, the women and children sold into slavery, and the island colonized afresh by 500 Athenians. This horrible proceeding was the more indefensible, as the Athenians, having attacked the Melians in full peace, could not pretend that they were justified by the custom of war in slaying the prisoners. It was the crowning act of insolence and cruelty displayed during their empire, which from this period began rapidly to decline.

The event destined to produce that catastrophe--the intervention of the Athenians in the affairs of Sicily--was already in progress. A quarrel had broken out between Egesta and Selinus, both which cities were seated near the western extremity of Sicily; and Selinus, having obtained the aid of Syracuse, was pressing very hard upon the Egestaeans. The latter appealed to the interests of the Athenians rather than to their sympathies. They represented how great a blow it would be to Athens if the Dorians became predominant in Sicily, and joined the Peloponnesian confederacy; and they undertook, if the Athenians would send an armament to their assistance, to provide the necessary funds for the prosecution of the war. Their most powerful advocate was Alcibiades, whose ambitious views are said to have extended even to the conquest of Carthage. The quieter and more prudent Nicias and his party threw their weight into the opposite scale. But the Athenian assembly, dazzled by the idea of so splendid an enterprise, decided on despatching a large fleet under Nicias, Alcibiades, and Lamachus, with the design of assisting Egesta, and of establishing the influence of Athens throughout Sicily, by whatever means might be found practicable.

For the next three months the preparations for the undertaking were pressed on with the greatest ardour. Young and old, rich and poor, all vied with one another to obtain a share in the expedition. Five years of comparative peace had accumulated a fresh supply both of men and money; and the merchants of Athens embarked in the enterprise as in a trading expedition. It was only a few of the wisest heads that escaped the general fever of excitement, The expedition was on the point of sailing, when a sudden and mysterious event converted all these exulting feelings into gloomy foreboding.

At every door in Athens, at the corners of streets, in the market place, before temples, gymnasia, and other public places, stood Hermae, or statues of the god Hermes, consisting of a bust of that deity surmounting a quadrangular pillar of marble about the height of the human figure. When the Athenians rose one morning towards the end of May, 415 B.C., it was found that all these figures had been mutilated during the night, and reduced by unknown hands to a shapeless mass. The act inspired political, as well as religious, alarm. It seemed to indicate a widespread conspiracy, for so sudden and general a mutilation must have been the work of many hands. The sacrilege might only be a preliminary attempt of some powerful citizen to seize the despotisn, and suspicion pointed its finger at Alcibiades. Active measures were taken and large rewards offered for the discovery of the perpetrators. A public board was appointed to examine witnesses, which did not, indeed, succeed in eliciting any facts bearing on the actual subject of inquiry, but which obtained evidence respecting similar acts of impiety committed at previous times in drunken frolics. In these Alcibiades himself was implicated; and though the fleet was on the very eve of departure, a citizen rose in the assembly and accused Alcibiades of having profaned the Eleusinian mysteries by giving a representation of them in a private house, producing in evidence the testimony of a slave. Alcibiades denied the accusation, and implored the people to have it investigated at once. His enemies, however, had sufficient influence to get the inquiry postponed till his return; thus keeping the charge hanging over his head, and gaining time to poison the public mind against him.

The Athenian fleet, consisting of 100 triremes, and having on board 1500 chosen Athenian hoplites, as well as auxiliaries, at length set sail, and proceeded to Corcyra, where it was joined by the other allies in the month of July, 415 B.C. Upon arriving at Rhegium the generals received the discouraging news that Egesta was unable to contribute more than thirty talents. A council of war was now held; and it was finally resolved to gain as many allies as they could among the Greek cities in Sicily, and, having thus ascertained what assistance they could rely upon, to attack Syracuse and Selinus.

Naxos joined the Athenians, and shortly afterwards they obtained possession by surprise of the important city of Catana, which was now made the head-quarters of the armament. Here an unwelcome message greeted Alcibiades. After his departure from Athens, Thessalus, the son of Cimon, preferred an indictment against him in consequence of his profanation of the Eleusinian mysteries. The Salaminian, or state, trireme was despatched to Sicily, carrying the decree of the assembly for Alcibiades to come home and take his trial. The commander of the Salaminia was, however, instructed not to seize his person, but to allow him to sail in his own trireme. Alcibiades availed himself of this privilege to effect his escape. When the ships arrived at Thurii in Italy, he absconded, and contrived to elude the search that was made after him, Nevertheless, though absent, he was arraigned at Athens, and condemned to death; his property was confiscated; and the Eumolpidae, who presided ever the celebration of the Eleusinian mysteries, pronounced upon him the curses of the gods. On hearing of his sentence Alcibiades is said to have exclaimed, "I will show them that I am still alive."

Three months had now been frittered away in Sicily, during which the Athenians had done little or nothing, if we except the acquisition of Naxos and Catana. Nicias now resolved to make an attempt upon Syracuse. By a false message that the Catanaeans were ready to assist in expelling the Athenians, he induced the Syracusans to proceed thither in great force, and he availed himself of their absence to sail with his whole fleet into the Great Harbour of Syracuse, where he landed near the mouth of the Anapus. The Syracusans, when they found that they had been deceived at Catana, marched back and offered Nicias battle in his new position. The latter accepted it, and gained the victory; after which he retired to Catana, and subsequently to Naxos into winter quarters.

The Syracusans employed the winter in preparations for defence. They also despatched envoys to Corinth and Sparta to solicit assistance, in the latter of which towns they found an unexpected advocate. Alcibiades, having crossed from Thurii to Cyllene in Peloponnesus, received a special invitation to proceed to Sparta. Here he revealed all the plans of Athens, and exhorted the Lacedaemonians to frustrate them. For this purpose he advised them to send an army into Sicily, under the command of a Spartan general, and, by way of causing a diversion, to establish a fortified post at Decelea in the Attic territory. The Spartans fell in with these views, and resolved to send a force to the assistance of Syracuse in the spring, under the command of Gylippus.

Nicias, having received reinforcements from Athens, recommenced hostilities as soon as the season allowed of it, and resolved on besieging Syracuse. That town consisted of two parts--the inner and the outer city. The former of these--the original settlement was comprised in the island of Ortygia; the latter afterwards known by the name of Achradina, covered the high ground of the peninsula north of Ortygia, and was completely separate from the inner city. The island of Ortygia, to which the modern city is now confined, is of an oblong shape, about two miles in circumference, lying between the Great Harbour on the west, and the Little Harbour on the east, and separated from the mainland by a narrow channel. The Great

Harbour is a splendid bay, about five miles in circumference, and the Little Harbour was spacious enough to receive a large fleet of ships of war. The outer city was surrounded on the north and east by the sea and by sea-walls which rendered an assault on that side almost impracticable. On the land side it was defended by a wall, and partly also by the nature of the ground, which in some part was very steep. West and north-west of the wall of the outer city stood two unfortified suburbs, which were at a later time included within the walls of Syracuse under the names of Tyche and Neapolis. Between these two suburbs the ground rose in a gentle acclivity to the summit of the ranges of hills called Epipolae.

It was from the high ground of Epipolae that Syracuse was most exposed to attack. Nicias landed at Leon, a place upon the bay of Thapsus, at the distance of only six or seven stadia from Epipolae, took possession of Epipolae, and erected on the summit a fort called Labdalum. Then coming farther down the hill towards Syracuse, he built another fort of a circular form and of considerable size at a place called Syke. From the latter point he commenced his line of circumvallation, one wall extending southwards from Syke to the Great Harbour, and the other wall running northwards to the outer sea. The Athenians succeeded in completing the circumvallation towards the south, but in one of their many engagements with the Syracusans they lost the gallant Lamachus. At the same time, the Athenian fleet entered the Great Harbour, where it was henceforth permanently established. The northern wall was never completed, and through the passage thus left open the besieged continued to obtain provisions. Nicias, who, by the death of Lamachus, had become sole commander, seemed now on the point of succeeding. The Syracusans were so sensible of their inferiority in the field that they no longer ventured to show themselves outside the walls. They began to contemplate surrender, and even sent messages to Nicias to treat of the terms. This caused the Athenian commander to indulge in a false confidence of success, and consequent apathy; and the army having lost the active and energetic Lamachus, operations were no longer carried on with the requisite activity.

It was in this state of affairs that the Spartan commander, Gylippus, passed over into Italy with a little squadron of four ships, with the view merely of preserving the Greek cities in that country, supposing that Syracuse, and, with her, the other Greek cities in Sicily, were irretrievably lost. At Tarentum he learned to his great surprise and satisfaction that the Athenian wall of circumvallation at Syracuse had not yet been completed on the northern side. He now sailed through the straits of Messana, which were left completely unguarded, and arrived safely at Himera on the north coast of Sicily. Here he announced himself as the forerunner of larger succours, and began to levy an army which the magic of the Spartan name soon enabled him to effect; and in a few days he was in a condition to march towards Syracuse with about 3000 men. The Syracusans now dismissed all thoughts of surrender, and went out boldly to meet Gylippus, who marched into Syracuse over the heights of Epipolae, which the supineness of Nicias had left unguarded. Upon arriving in the city, Gylippus sent a message to the Athenians allowing them a five days' truce to collect their effects and evacuate the island. Nicias returned no answer to this insulting proposal; but the operations of Gylippus soon showed that the tide of affairs was really turned. His first exploit was to capture the Athenian fort at Labdalum, which made him master of Epipolae. He next commenced constructing a counter-wall to intersect the Athenian lines on the northern side. This turn of affairs induced those Sicilian cities which had hitherto hesitated to embrace the side of Syracuse. Gylippus was also reinforced by the arrival of thirty triremes from Corinth, Leucas, and Ambracia. Nicias now felt that the attempt to blockade Syracuse with his present force was hopeless. He therefore resolved to occupy the headland of Plemmyrium, the southernmost point of the entrance to the Great Harbour, which would be a convenient station for watching the enemy, as well as for facilitating the introduction of supplies. Here he accordingly erected three forts and formed a naval station. Some slight affairs occurred in which the balance of advantage was in favour of the Syracusans. By their change of station the Athenians were now a besieged rather than a besieging force. Their triremes were becoming leaky, and their soldiers and sailors were constantly deserting. Nicias himself had fallen into a bad state of health; and in this discouraging posture of affairs he wrote to Athens requesting to be recalled, and insisting strongly on the necessity of sending reinforcements.

The Athenians refused to recall Nicias, but they determined on sending a large reinforcement to Sicily, under the joint command of Demosthenes and Eurymedon. The news of these fresh and extensive preparations incited the Lacedaemonians to more vigorous action. The peace, if such it can be called, was now openly broken;

and in the spring of 413 B.C. the Lacedaemonians, under King Agis, invaded Attica itself, and, following the advice of Alcibiades, established themselves permanently at Decelia, a place situated on the ridge of Mount Parnes about 14 miles north of Athens, and commanding the Athenian plain. The city was thus placed in a state of siege. Scarcity began to be felt within the walls; the revenues were falling off, whilst on the other hand expenses were increasing.

Meanwhile in Sicily the Syracusans had gained such confidence that they even ventured on a naval engagement with the Athenians. In the first battle the Athenians were victorious, but the second battle, which lasted two days, ended in their defeat. They were now obliged to haul up their ships in the innermost part of the Great Harbour, under the lines of their fortified camp. A still more serious disaster than the loss of the battle was the loss of their naval reputation. It was evident that the Athenians had ceased to be invincible on the sea; and the Syracusans no longer despaired of overcoming them on their own element.

Such was the state of affairs when, to the astonishment of the Syracusans, a fresh Athenian fleet of 75 triremes, under Demosthenes and Eurymedon, entered the Great Harbour with all the pomp and circumstance of war. It had on board a force of 5000 hoplites, of whom about a quarter were Athenians, and a great number of light-armed troops. The active and enterprising character of Demosthenes led him to adopt more vigorous measures than those which had been hitherto pursued. He saw at once that whilst Epipolae remained in the possession of the Syracusans there was no hope of taking their city, and he therefore directed all his efforts to the recapture of that position. But his attempts were unavailing. He was defeated not only in an open assault upon the Syracusan wall, but in a nocturnal attempt to carry it by surprise. These reverses were aggravated by the breaking out of sickness among the troops. Demosthenes now proposed to return home and assist in expelling the Lacedaemonians from Attica, instead of pursuing an enterprise which seemed to be hopeless. But Nicias, who feared to return to Athens with the stigma of failure, refused to give his consent to this step. Demosthenes then urged Nicias at least to sail immediately out of the Great Harbour, and take up their position either at Thapsus or Catana, where they could obtain abundant supplies of provisions, and would have an open sea for the manoeuvres of their fleet. But even to this proposal Nicias would not consent; and the army and navy remained in their former position. Soon afterwards, however, Gylippus received such large reinforcements, that Nicias found it necessary to adopt the advice of his colleague. Preparations were secretly made for their departure, the enemy appear to have had no suspicion of their intention and they were on the point of quitting their ill-fated quarters on the following morning, when on the very night before (27 Aug. 413 B.C.) an eclipse of the moon took place. The soothsayers who were consulted said that the army must wait thrice nine days, a full circle of the moon, before it could quit its present position; and the devout and superstitious Nicias forthwith resolved to abide by this decision.

Meanwhile the intention of the Athenians became known to the Syracusans, who determined to strike a blow before their enemy escaped. They accordingly attacked the Athenian station both by sea and land. On land the attack of Gylippus was repulsed; but at sea the Athenian fleet was completely defeated, and Eurymedon, who commanded the right division, was slain The spirits of the Symcusans rose with their victories; and though they would formerly have been content with the mere retreat of the Athenians, they now resolved on effecting their utter destruction. With this view they blocked up the entrance of the Great Harbour with a line of vessels moored across it. All hope seemed now to be cut off from the Athenians, unless they could succeed in forcing this line and thus effecting their escape. The Athenian fleet still numbered 110 triremes, which Nicias furnished with grappling-irons, in order to bring the enemy to close quarters, and then caused a large proportion of his land-force to embark.

Never perhaps was a battle fought under circumstances of such intense interest, or witnessed by so many spectators vitally concerned in the result. The basin of the Great Harbour, about 5 miles in circumference, in which nearly 200 ships, each with crews of more than 200 men, were about to engage, was lined with spectators. The Syracusan fleet was the first to leave the shore. A considerable portion was detached to guard the barrier at the mouth of the harbour. Hither the first and most impetuous attack of the Athenians was directed, who sought to break through the narrow opening which had been left for the passage of merchant vessels. Their onset was repulsed, and the battle then became general. The shouts of the combatants, and the crash of the iron heads of the vessels as they were driven together, resounded over the water, and were answered on shore by the cheers or wailings of the spectators as their friends were victorious or vanquished. For a long time the battle was maintained with heroic courage and dubious result. At length, as the Athenian vessels began to yield and make back towards the shore, a universal shriek of horror and despair arose from the Athenian army, whilst shouts of joy and victory were raised from the pursuing vessels, and were echoed back from the Syracusans on land. As the Athenian vessels neared the shore their crews leaped out, and made for the camp, whilst the boldest of the land army rushed forward to protect the ships from being seized by the enemy. The Athenians succeeded in saving only 60 ships, or about half their fleet. The Syracusan fleet, however, had been reduced to 50 ships; and on the same afternoon, Nicias and Demosthenes, as a last hope of escape, exhorted their men to make another attempt to break the enemy's line, and force their way out of the harbour. But the courage of the crews was so completely damped that they positively refused to re-embark.

The Athenian army still numbered 40,000 men; and as all chance of escape by sea was now hopeless, it was resolved to retreat by land to some friendly city, and there defend themselves against the attacks of the Syracusans. As the soldiers turned to quit that fatal encampment, the sense of their own woes was for a moment suspended by the sight of their unburied comrades, who seemed to reproach them with the neglect of a sacred duty; but still more by the wailings and entreaties of the wounded, who clung around their knees, and implored not to be abandoned to certain destruction. Amid this scene of universal woe and dejection, a fresh and unwonted spirit of energy and heroism seemed to be infused into Nicias. Though suffering under an incurable complaint, he was everywhere seen marshalling his troops and encouraging them by his exhortations. The march was directed towards the territory of the Sicels in the interior of the island. The army was formed into a hollow square with the baggage in the middle; Nicias leading the van, and Demosthenes bringing up the rear. The road ascended by a sort of ravine over a steep hill called the Acraean cliff on which the Syracusans had fortified themselves. After spending two days in vain attempts to force this position, Nicias and Demosthenes resolved during the night to strike off to the left towards the sea. But they were overtaken, surrounded by superior forces, and compelled to surrender at discretion. Out of the 40,000 who started from the camp only 10,000 at the utmost were left at the end of the sixth day's march, the rest had either deserted or been slain.

The prisoners were sent to work in the stone-quarries of Achradina and Epipolae. Here they were crowded together without any shelter, and with scarcely provisions enough to sustain life. The numerous bodies of those who died were left to putrify where they had fallen, till at length the place became such an intolerable centre of stench and infection that, at the end of seventy days, the Syracusans, for their own comfort and safety, were obliged to remove the survivors, who were sold as slaves. Nicias and Demosthenes were condemned to death in spite of all the efforts of Gylippus and Hermocrates to save them.

Such was the end of two of the largest and best appointed armaments that had ever gone forth from Athens. Nicias, as we have seen, was from the first opposed to the expedition in which they were employed, as pregnant with the most dangerous consequences to Athens; and, though it must be admitted that in this respect his views were sound, it cannot at the same time be concealed that his own want of energy, and his incompetence as a general, were the chief causes of the failure of the undertaking. His mistakes involved the fall of Demosthenes, an officer of far greater resolution and ability than himself, and who, had his counsels been followed, would in all probability have conducted the enterprise to a safe termination, though there was no longer room to hope for success.

CHAPTER XIII.
THE PELOPONNESIAN WAR.--THIRD PERIOD, FROM THE SICILIAN EXPEDITION TO THE END OF THE WAR, B.C. 413-404.

The destruction of the Sicilian armament was a fatal blow to the power of Athens. It is astonishing that she was able to protract the war so long with diminished strength and resources. Her situation inspired her enemies with new vigour; states hitherto neutral declared against her; her subject-allies prepared to throw off the yoke; even the Persian satraps and the court of Susa bestirred themselves against her. The first blow to her empire was struck by the wealthy and populous island of Chios. This again was the work of Alcibiades, the implacable enemy of his native land, at whose advice a Lacedaemonian fleet was sent to the assistance of the Chians. Their example was followed by all the other Athenian allies in Asia, with the exception of Samos, in which the democratical party gained the upper hand. In the midst of this general defection the Athenians did not give way to despair. Pericles had set apart a reserve of 1000 talents to meet the contingency of an actual invasion. This still remained untouched, and now by an unanimous vote the penalty of death, which forbad its appropriation to any other purpose, was abolished, and the fund applied in fitting out a fleet against Chios. Samos became the head-quarters of the fleet, and the base of their operations during the remainder of the war.

After a time the tide of success began to turn in favour of the Athenians. They recovered Lesbos and Clazomenae, defeated the Chians, and laid waste their territory. They also gained a victory over the Peloponnesians at Miletus; while the Peloponnesian fleet had lost the assistance of Tissaphernes, the Persian satrap, through the intrigues of Alcibiades. In the course of a few months Alcibiades had completely forfeited the confidence of the Lacedaemonians. The Spartan king Agis, whose wife he had seduced, was his personal enemy; and after the defeat of the Peloponnesians at Miletus, Agis denounced him as a traitor, and persuaded the new Ephors to send out instructions to put him to death. Of this, however, he was informed time enough to make his escape to Tissaphernes at Magnesia. Here he ingratiated himself into the confidence of the satrap, and persuaded him that it was not for the interest of Persia that either of the Grecian parties should be successful, but rather that they should wear each other out in their mutual struggles, when Persia would in the end succeed in expelling both. This advice was adopted by the satrap; and in order to carry it into execution, steps were taken to secure the inactivity of the Peloponnesian armament, which, if vigorously employed, was powerful enough to put a speedy end to the war. In order to secure his return to Athens, Alcibiades now endeavoured to persuade Tissaphernes that it was more for the Persian interest to conclude a league with Athens than with Sparta; but the only part of his advice which the satrap seems to have sincerely adopted was that of playing off one party against the other. About this, however, Alcibiades did not at all concern himself. It was enough for his views, which had merely the selfish aim of his own restoration to Athens, if he could make it appear that he possessed sufficient influence with Tissaphernes to procure his assistance for the Athenians. He therefore began to communicate with the Athenian generals at Samos, and held out the hope of a Persian alliance as the price of his restoration to his country. But as he both hated and feared the Athenian democracy, he coupled his offer with the condition that a revolution should be effected at Athens, and an oligarchy established. The Athenian generals greedily caught at the proposal; and though the great mass of the soldiery were violently opposed to it, they were silenced, if not satisfied, when told that Athens could be saved only by means of Persia. The oligarchical conspirators formed themselves into a confederacy, and Pisander was sent to Athens to lay the proposal before the Athenian assembly. It met, as it might be supposed, with the most determined opposition. The single but unanswerable reply of Pisander was, the necessities of the republic; and at length a reluctant vote for a change of constitution was extorted from the people. Pisander and ten others were despatched to treat with Alcibiades and Tissaphernes.

Upon their arrival in Ionia they informed Alcibiades that measures had been taken for establishing an oligarchical form of government at Athens, and required him to fulfil his part of the engagement by procuring the aid and alliance of Persia. But Alcibiades knew that he had undertaken what he could not perform, and he now resolved to escape from the dilemma by one of his habitual artifices. He received the Athenian deputation in the presence of Tissaphernes himself, and made such extravagant demands on behalf of the satrap that Pisander and his colleagues indignantly broke off the conference.

Notwithstanding the conduct of Alcibiades the oligarchical conspirators proceeded with the revolution at Athens, in which they had gone too far to recede. Pisander, with five of the envoys, returned to Athens to complete the work they had begun.

Pisander proposed in the assembly, and carried a resolution, that a committee of ten should be appointed to prepare a new constitution, which was to be submitted to the approbation of the people. But when the day appointed for that purpose arrived, the assembly was not convened in the Pnyx, but in the temple of Poseidon at Colonus, a village upwards of a mile from Athens. Here the conspirators could plant their own partisans, and were less liable to be overawed by superior numbers. Pisander obtained the assent of the meeting to the following revolutionary changes:--1. The abolition of all the existing magistracies; 2. The cessation of all payments for the discharge of civil functions; 3. The appointment of a committee of five persons, who were to name ninety-five more; each of the hundred thus constituted to choose three persons; the body of Four Hundred thus formed to be an irresponsible government, holding its sittings in the senate house. The four hundred were to convene a select body of five thousand citizens whenever they thought proper. Nobody knew who these five thousand were, but they answered two purposes, namely, to give an air of greater popularity to the government, as well as to overawe the people by an exaggerated notion of its strength.

Thus perished the Athenian democracy, after an existence of nearly a century since its establishment by Clisthenes The revolution was begun from despair of the foreign relations of Athens, and from the hope of assistance from Persia; but it was carried out through the machinations of the conspirators after that delusion had ceased.

At Samos the Athenian army refused to recognise the new government. At the instance of Thrasybulus and Thrasyllus a meeting was called in which the soldiers pledged themselves to maintain the democracy, to continue the war against Peloponnesus, and to put down the usurpers at Athens. The soldiers, laying aside for a while their military character, constituted themselves into an assembly of the people, deposed several of their officers, and appointed others whom they could better trust. Thrasybulus proposed the recall of Alcibiades, notwithstanding his connection with the oligarchical conspiracy, because it was believed that he was now able and willing to aid the democratic cause with the gold and forces of Persia. After considerable opposition the proposal was agreed to; Alcibiades was brought to Samos and introduced to the assembly, where by his magnificent promises, and extravagant boasts respecting his influence with Tissaphernes, he once more succeeded in deceiving the Athenians. The accomplished traitor was elected one of the generals, and, in pursuance of his artful policy, began to pass backwards and forwards between Samos and Magnesia, with the view of inspiring both the satrap and the Athenians with a reciprocal idea of his influence with either, and of instilling distrust of Tissaphernes into the minds of the Peloponnesians.

At the first news of the re-establishment of democracy at Samos, distrust and discord had broken out among the Four Hundred. Antiphon and Phrynichus, at the head of the extreme section of the oligarchical party, were for admitting a Lacedaemonian garrison. But others, discontented with their share of power, began to affect more popular sentiments, among whom were Theramenes and Aristocrates. Meantime Euboea, supported by the Lacedaemonians and Boeotians, revolted from Athens. The loss of this island seemed a death-blow. The Lacedaemonians might now easily blockade the ports of Athens and starve her into surrender; whilst the partisans of the Four Hundred would doubtless co-operate with the enemy. But from this fate they were saved by the characteristic slowness of the Lacedaemonians, who confined themselves to securing the conquest of Euboea. Thus left unmolested, the Athenians convened an assembly in the Pnyx. Votes were passed for deposing the Four Hundred, and placing the government in the hands of the 5000, of whom every citizen who could furnish a panoply might be a member. In short, the old constitution was restored, except that the franchise was restricted to 5000 citizens, and payment for the discharge of civil functions abolished. In subsequent assemblies, the Archons, the Senate, and other institutions were revived; and a vote was passed to recall Alcibiades and some of his friends. The number of the 5000 was never exactly observed, and was soon enlarged into universal citizenship. Thus the Four Hundred were overthrown after a reign of four months, B.C. 411.

While these things were going on at Athens, the war was prosecuted with vigour on the coast of Asia Minor. Mindarus, who now commanded the Peloponnesian fleet, disgusted at length by the often-broken promises of Tissaphernes, and the scanty and irregular pay which he furnished, set sail from Miletus and proceeded to the Hellespont, with the intention of assisting the satrap Pharnabazus, and of effecting, if possible, the revolt of the Athenian dependencies in that quarter. Hither he was pursued by the Athenian fleet under Thrasyllus. In a few days an engagement ensued (in August, 411 B.C.), in the famous straits between Sestos and Abydos, in which the Athenians, though with a smaller force, gained the victory and erected a trophy on the promontory of Cynossema, near the tomb and chapel of the Trojan queen Hecuba. The Athenians followed up their victory by the reduction of Cyzicus, which had revolted from them. A month or two afterwards another obstinate engagement took place between the Peloponnesian and Athenian fleets ness Abydos, which lasted a whole day, and was at length decided in favour of the Athenians by the arrival of Alcibiades with his squadron of eighteen ships from Samos.

Shortly after the battle Tissaphernes arrived at the Hellespont with the view of conciliating the offended Peloponnesians. He was not only jealous of the assistance which the latter were now rendering to Pharnabarzus, but it is also evident that his temporizing policy had displeased the Persian court. This appears from his conduct on the present occasion, as well as from the subsequent appointment of Cyrus to the supreme command on the Asiatic coast as we shall presently have to relate. When Alcibiades, who imagined that Tissaphernes was still favourable to the Athenian cause waited on him with the customary presents, he was arrested by order of the satrap, and sent in custody to Sardis. At the end of a month, however, he contrived to escape to Clazomenae, and again joined the Athenian fleet early in the spring of 410 B.C. Mindaras, with the assistance of Pharnabazas on the land side, was now engaged in the siege of Cyzicus, which the Athenian admirals determined to relieve. Here a battle ensued, in which Mindarus was slain, the Lacedaemonians and

Persians routed, and almost the whole Peloponnesian fleet captured. The severity of this blow was pictured in the laconic epistle in which Hippocrates, the second in command, [Called Epistoteus or "Secretary" in the Lacedaemonian fleet. The commander of the fleet had the title of NAVARCHUS.] announced it to the Ephors: "Our good luck is gone; Mindarus is slain; the men are starving; we know not what to do."

The results of this victory were most important. Perinthus and Selymbria, as well as Cyzicus, were recovered; and the Athenians, once more masters of the Propontis, fortified the town of Chrysopolis, over against Byzantium, at the entrance of the Bosporus; re-established their toll of ten per cent, on all vessels passing from the Euxine; and left a squadron to guard the strait and collect the dues. So great was the discouragement of the Lacedaemonians at the loss of their fleet that the Ephor Endius proceeded to Athens to treat for peace on the basis of both parties standing just as they were. The Athenian assembly was at this time led by the demagogue Cleophon, a lamp-maker, known to us by the later comedies of Aristophanes. Cleophon appears to have been a man of considerable ability; but the late victories had inspired him with too sanguine hopes and he advised the Athenians to reject the terms proposed by Endius. Athens thus throw away the golden opportunity of recruiting her shattered forces of which she stood so much in need; and to this unfortunate advice must be ascribed the calamities which subsequently overtook her.

The possession of the Bosporus reopened to the Athenians the trade of the Euxine. From his lofty fortress at Decelea the Spartan king Agris could descry the corn-ships from the Euxine sailing into the Harbour of the Piraeus, and felt how fruitless it was to occupy the fields of Attica whilst such abundant supplies of provisions were continually finding their way to the city.

In B.C. 408 the important towns of Chalcedon, Selymbria, and Byzantium fell into the hands of the Athenians, thus leaving them undisputed masters of the Propontis.

These great achievements of Alcibiades naturally paved the way for his return to Athens. In the spring of 407 B.C. he proceeded with the fleet to Samos, and from thence sailed to Piraeus. His reception was far more favourable than he had ventured to anticipate. The whole population of Athens flocked down to Piraeus to welcome him, and escorted him to the city. He seemed to be in the present juncture the only man capable of restoring the grandeur and the empire of Athens: he was accordingly named general with unlimited powers, and a force of 100 triremes, 1500 hoplites, and 150 cavalry placed at his disposal. Before his departure he took an opportunity to atone for the impiety of which he had been suspected. Although his armament was in perfect readiness, he delayed its sailing till after the celebration of the Eleusinian mysteries at the beginning of September. For seven years the customary procession across the Thriasian plain had been suspended, owing to the occupation of Decelea by the enemy, which compelled the sacred troop to proceed by sea. Alcibiades now escorted them on their progress and return with his forces, and thus succeeded in reconciling himself with the offended goddesses and with their holy priests, the Eumolpidae.

Meanwhile a great change had been going on in the state of affairs in the East. We have already seen that the Great King was displeased with the vacillating policy of Tissaphernes, and had determined to adopt more energetic measures against the Athenians. During the absence of Alcibiades, Cyrus, the younger son of Darius, a prince of a bold and enterprising spirit, and animated with a lively hatred of Athens, had arrived at the coast for the purpose of carrying out the altered policy of the Persian court; and with that view he had been invested with the satrapies of Lydia, the Greater Phrygia, and Cappadocia. The arrival of Cyrus opens the last phase of the Peloponnesian war. Another event, in the highest degree unfavourable to the Athenian cause, was the accession of Lysander, as NAVARCHUS, to the command of the Peloponnesian fleet. Lysander was the third of the remarkable men whom Sparta produced during the war. In ability, energy, and success he may be compared with Brasidas and Gylippus, though immeasurably inferior to the former in every moral quality. He was born of poor parents, and was by descent one of those Lacedaemonians who could never enjoy the full rights of Spartan citizenship. His ambition was boundless, and he was wholly unscrupulous about the means which he employed to gratify it. In pursuit of his objects he hesitated at neither deceit, nor perjury, nor cruelty, and he is reported to have laid it down as one of his maxims in life to avail himself of the fox's skin where the lion's failed.

Lysander had taken up his station at Ephesus, with the Lacedaemonian fleet of 70 triremes; and when Cyrus arrived at Sardis, in the spring of 407 B.C., he hastened to pay his court to the young prince, and was received with every mark of favour.

A vigorous line of action was resolved on. Cyrus at once offered 500 talents, and affirmed that, if more were needed, he was prepared even to coin into money the very throne of gold and silver on which he sat. In a banquet which ensued Cyrus drank to the health of Lysander, and desired him to name any wish which he could gratify. Lysander immediately requested an addition of an obolus to the daily pay of the seamen. Cyrus was surprised at so disinterested a demand, and from that day conceived a high degree of respect and confidence for the Spartan commander. Lysander on his return to Ephesus employed himself in refitting his fleet, and in organising clubs in the Spartan interest in the cities of Asia.

Alcibiades set sail from Athens in September. Being ill provided with funds for carrying on the war, he was driven to make predatory excursions for the purpose of raising money. During his absence he intrusted the bulk of the fleet at Samos to his pilot, Antiochus, with strict injunctions not to venture on an action. Notwithstanding these orders, however, Antiochus sailed out and brought the Peloponnesian fleet to an engagement off Notium, in which the Athenians were defeated with the loss of 15 ships, and Antiochus himself was slain. Among the Athenian armament itself great dissatisfaction was growing up against Alcibiades. Though at the head of a splendid force, he had in three months time accomplished literally nothing. His debaucheries and dissolute conduct on shore were charged against him, as well as his selecting for confidential posts not the men best fitted for them, but those who, like Antiochus were the boon companions and the chosen associates of his revels. These accusations forwarded to Athens, and fomented by his secret enemies, soon produced an entire revulsion in the public feeling towards Alcibiades. The Athenians voted that he should be dismissed from his command, and they appointed in his place ten new generals, with Conon at their head.

The year of Lysander's command expired about the same time as the appointment of Conon to the Athenian fleet. Through the intrigues of Lysander, his successor Callicratidas was received with dissatisfaction both by the Lacedaemonian seamen and by Cyrus. Loud complaints were raised of the impolicy of an annual change of commanders. Lysander threw all sorts of difficulties into the way of his successor, to whom he handed over an empty chest, having first repaid to Cyrus all the money in his possession under the pretence that it was a private loan. The straightforward conduct of Callicratidas, however, who summoned the Lacedaemonian commanders, and after a dignified remonstrance, plainly put the question whether he should return home or remain, silenced all opposition. But he was sorely embarrassed for funds. Cyrus treated him with haughtiness; and when he waited on that prince at Sardis, he was dismissed not only without money, but even without an audience. Callicratidas, however, had too much energy to be daunted by such obstacles. Sailing with his fleet from Ephesus to Miletus, he laid before the assembly of that city, in a spirited address, all the ill they had suffered at the hands of the Persians, and exhorted them to bestir themselves and dispense with the Persian alliance. He succeeded in persuading the Milesians to make him a large grant of money, whilst the leading men even came forward with private subscriptions. By means of this assistance he was enabled to add 50 triremes to the 90 delivered to him by Lysander; and the Chians further provided him with ten days' pay for the seamen.

The fleet of Callicratidas was now double that of Conon. The latter was compelled to run before the superior force of Callicratidas. Both fleets entered the harbour of Mytilene at the same time, where a battle ensued in which Conon lost 30 ships, but he saved the remaining 40 by hauling them ashore under the walls of the town. Callicratidas then blockaded Mytilene both by sea and land; but Conon contrived to despatch a trireme to Athens with the news of his desperate position.

As soon as the Athenians received intelligence of the blockade of Mytilene; vast efforts were made for its relief; and we learn with surprise that in thirty days a fleet of 110 triremes was equipped and despatched from Piraeus. The armament assembled at Samos, where it was reinforced by scattered Athenian ships, and by contingents from the allies, to the extent of 40 vessels. The whole fleet of 150 sail then proceeded to the small islands of Arginusae, near the coast of Asia, and facing Malea, the south-eastern cape of Lesbos. Callicratidas, who went out to meet them, took up his station at the latter point, leaving a squadron of 50 ships to maintain the blockade of Mytilene. He had thus only 120 ships to oppose to the 150 of the Athenians, and his pilot advised him to retire before the superior force of the enemy. But Callicratidas replied that he would not disgrace himself by flight, and that if he should perish Sparta would not feel his loss. The battle was long and obstinate. All order was speedily lost, and the ships fought singly with one another, In one of these contests, Callicratidas, who stood on the prow of his vessel ready to board the enemy, was thrown overboard by the shock of the vessels as they met, and perished. At length victory began to declare for the Athenians. The Lacedaemonians, after losing 77 vessels, retreated with the remainder to Chios and Phocaea. The loss of the Athenians was 25 vessels.

The battle of Arginusae led to a deplorable event, which has for ever sullied the pages of Athenian history. At least a dozen Athenian vessels were left floating about in a disabled condition after the battle; but, owing to a violent storm that ensued, no attempt was made to rescue the survivors, or to collect the bodies of the dead for burial. Eight of the ten generals were summoned home to answer for this conduct; Conon, by his situation at Mytilene, was of course exculpated, and Archestratus had died. Six of the generals obeyed the summons, and were denounced in the Assembly by Theramenes, formerly one of the Four Hundred, for neglect of duty. The generals replied that they had commissioned Theramenes himself and Thrasybulus, each of whom commanded a trireme in the engagement, to undertake the duty, and had assigned 48 ships to them for that purpose. This, however, was denied by Theramenes. There are discrepancies in the evidence, and we have no materials for deciding positively which statement was true; but probability inclines to the side of the generals. Public feeling, however, ran very strongly against them, and was increased by an incident which occurred during their trial. After a day's debate the question was adjourned; and in the interval the festival of the APATURIA was celebrated, in which, according to annual custom, the citizens met together according to their families and phratries. Those who had perished at Arginusae were naturally missed on such an occasion; and the usually cheerful character of the festival was deformed and rendered melancholy by the relatives of the deceased appearing in black clothes and with shaven heads. The passions of the people were violently roused. At the next meeting of the Assembly, Callixenus, a senator, proposed that the people should at once proceed to pass its verdict on the generals, though they had been only partially heard in their defence; and, moreover, that they should all be included in one sentence, though it was contrary to a rule of Attic law, known as the psephisma of Canonus, to indict citizens otherwise than individually. The Prytanes, or senators of the presiding tribe, at first refused to put the question to the Assembly in this illegal way; but their opposition was at length overawed by clamour and violence. There was, however, one honourable exception. The philosopher Socrates, who was one of the Prytanes, refused to withdraw his protest. But his opposition was disregarded, and the proposal of Callixenus was carried, The generals were condemned, delivered over to the Eleven for execution, and compelled to drink the fatal hemlock. Among them was Pericles, the son of the celebrated statesman.

In the following year (B.C. 405), through the influence of Cyrus and the other allies of Sparta, Lysander again obtained the command of the Peloponnesian fleet, though nominally under Aracus as admiral; since it was contrary to Spartan usage that the same man should be twice NAVARCHUS. His return to power was marked by more vigorous measures. He sailed to the Hellespont, and laid siege to Lampsacus. The Athenian fleet arrived too late to save the town, but they proceeded up the strait and took post at AEgospotami, or the "Goat's River;" a place which had nothing to recommend it, except its vicinity to Lampsacus, from which it was separated by a channel somewhat less than two miles broad. It was a mere desolate beach, without houses or inhabitants, so that all the supplies had to be fetched from Sestos, or from the surrounding country, and the seamen were compelled to leave their ships in order to obtain their meals. Under these circumstances the Athenians were very desirous of bringing Lysander to an engagement. But the Spartan commander, who was in a strong position, and abundantly furnished with provisions, was in no hurry to run any risks. In vain did the Athenians sail over several days in succession to offer him battle; they always found his ships ready manned, and drawn up in too strong a position to warrant an attack; nor could they by all their manoeuvres succeed in enticing him out to combat. This cowardice, as they deemed it, on the part of the Lacedaemonians, begat a corresponding negligence on theirs; discipline was neglected and the men allowed to straggle almost at will. It was in vain that Alcibiades, who since his dismissal resided in a fortress in that neighbourhood, remonstrated with the Athenian generals on the exposed nature of the station they had chosen, and advised them to proceed to Sestos. His counsels were received with taunts and insults. At length, on the fifth day, Lysander, having watched an opportunity when the Athenian seamen had gone on shore and were dispersed over the country, rowed swiftly across the strait with all his ships. He found the Athenian fleet, with the exception of 10 or 12 vessels, totally unprepared, and he captured nearly the whole of it, without having occasion to strike a single blow. Of the 180 ships which composed the fleet, only the trireme of Conon himself, the Paralus, and 8 or 10 other vessels succeeded in escaping. Conon was afraid to return to Athens after so signal a disaster, and took refuge with Evagoras, prince of Salamis in Cyprus.

By this momentous victory (September, B.C. 405) the Peloponnesian war was virtually brought to an end. Lysander, secure of an easy triumph, was in no haste to gather it by force. The command of the Euxine enabled him to control the supplies of Athens; and sooner or later, a few weeks of famine must decide her fall. He now sailed forth to take possession of the Athenian towns, which fell one after another into his power as soon as he appeared before them. About November he arrived at AEgina, with an overwhelming fleet of 150 triremes, and proceeded to devastate Salamis and blockade Piraeus. At the same time the whole Peloponnesian army was marched into Attica and encamped in the precincts of the Academus, at the very gates of Athens. Famine soon began to be felt within the walls, and at the end of three months it became so dreadful, that the Athenians saw themselves compelled to submit to the terms of the conqueror. These terms were: That the long walls and the fortifications of Piraeus should be demolished; that the Athenians should give up all their foreign possessions, and confine themselves to their own territory; that they should surrender all their ships of war; that they should readmit all their exiles; and that they should become allies of Sparta.

It was about the middle or end of March, B.C. 404, that Lysander sailed into Piraeus, and took formal possession of Athens; the war, in singular conformity with the prophecies current at the beginning of it, having lasted for a period of thrice nine, or 27 years. The insolence of the victors added another blow to the feelings of the conquered. The work of destruction, at which Lysander presided, was converted into a sort of festival. Female flute-players and wreathed dancers inaugurated the demolition of the strong and proud bulwarks of Athens; and as the massive walls fell piece by piece exclamations arose from the ranks of the Peloponnesians that freedom had at length begun to dawn upon Greece.

CHAPTER XIV
THE THIRTY TYRANTS, AND THE DEATH OF SOCRATES, B.C. 404-399.

The fall of Athens brought back a host of exiles, all of them the enemies of her democratical constitution. Of these these most distinguished was Critias, a man of wealth and family, the uncle of Plato, and once the intimate friend of Socrates, distinguished both for his literary and political talents, but of unmeasured ambition and unscrupulous conscience. Critias and his companions soon found a party with which they could co-operate; and supported by Lysander they proposed in the assembly that a committee of thirty should be named to draw up laws for the future government of the city, and to undertake its temporary administration. Among the most prominent of the thirty names were those of Critias and Theramenes. The proposal was of course carried. Lysander himself addressed the Assembly, and contemptuously told them that they had better take thought for their personal safety, which now lay at his mercy, than for their political constitution. The committee thus appointed soon obtained the title of the Thirty Tyrants, the name by which they have become known in all subsequent time. After naming an entirely new Senate, and appointing fresh magistrates, they proceeded to exterminate their most obnoxious opponents. But Critias, and the more violent party among them, still called for more blood; and with the view of obtaining it, procured a Spartan garrison, under the harmost Callibius, to be installed in the Acropolis. Besides this force, they had an organized band of assassins at their disposal. Blood now flowed on all sides. Many of the leading men of Athens fell, others took to flight.

Thus the reign of terror was completely established. In the bosom of the Thirty, however, there was a party, headed by Theramenes, who disapproved of these proceedings. But his moderation cost him his life. One day as he entered the Senate-house, Critias rose and denounced him as a public enemy, and ordered him to be carried off to instant death. Upon hearing these words Theramenes sprang for refuge to the altar in the Senate-house; but he was dragged away by Satyrus, the cruel and unscrupulous head of the "Eleven," a body of officers who carried into execution the penal sentence of the law. Being conveyed to prison, he was compelled to drink the fatal hemlock. The constancy of his end might have adorned a better life after swallowing the draught, he jerked on the floor a drop which remained in the cup, according to the custom of the game called COTTABOS, exclaiming, "This to the health of the GENTLE Critias!"

Alcibiades had been included by the Thirty in the list of exiles; but the fate which now overtook him seems to have sprung from the fears of the Lacedaemonians, or perhaps from the personal hatred of Agis. After the battle of Ægospotami, Pharnabazus permitted the Athenian exile to live in Phrygia, and assigned him a revenue for his maintenance. But a despatch came out from Sparta, to Lysander, directing that Alcibiades should be put to death. Lysander communicated the order to Pharnabazus, who arranged for carrying it into execution. The house of Alcibiades was surrounded with a band of assassins, and set on fire. He rushed out with drawn sword upon his assailants, who shrank from the attack, but who slew him from a distance with their javelins and arrows. Timandra, a female with whom he lived, performed towards his body the last offices of duty and affection. Thus perished miserably, in the vigour of his age, one of the most remarkable, but not one of the greatest, characters in Grecian history. With qualities which, properly applied, might have rendered him the greatest benefactor of Athens, he contrived to attain the infamous distinction of being that citizen who had inflicted upon her the most signal amount of damage.

Meantime an altered state of feeling was springing up in Greece. Athens had ceased to be an object of fear or jealousy, and those feelings began now to be directed towards Sparta. Lysander had risen to a height of unparalleled power. He was in a manner idolized. Poets showered their praises on him, and even altars were raised in his honour by the Asiatic Greeks. In the name of Sparta he exercised almost uncontrolled authority in the cities he had reduced, including Athens itself.

But it was soon discovered that, instead of the freedom promised by the Spartans, only another empire had been established, whilst Lysander was even meditating to extort from the subject cities a yearly tribute of one thousand talents. And all these oppressions were rendered still more intolerable by the overweening pride and harshness of Lysander's demeanour.

Even in Sparta itself the conduct of Lysander was beginning to inspire disgust and jealousy. Pausanias, son of Plistoanax, who was now king with Agis, as well as the new Ephors appointed in September, B.C. 404, disapproved of his proceedings. The Thebans and Corinthians themselves were beginning to sympathise with Athens, and to regard the Thirty as mere instruments for supporting the Spartan dominion; whilst Sparta in her turn looked upon them as the tools of Lysander's ambition. Many of the Athenian exiles had found refuge in Boeotia: and one of them Thrasybulus, with the aid of Ismenias and other Theban citizens, starting from Thebes at the head of a small band of exiles, seized the fortress of Phyle in the passes of Mount Parnes and on the direct road to Athens. The Thirty marched out to attack Thrasybulus, at the head of the Lacedaemonian garrison and a strong Athenian force. But their attack was repulsed with considerable loss.

Shortly afterwards Thrasybulus marched from Phyle to Piraeus which was now an open town, and seized upon it without opposition. When the whole force of the Thirty, including the Lacedaemonians, marched on the following day to attack him, he retired to the hill of Munychia, the citadel of Piraeus, the only approach to which was by a steep ascent. Here he drew up his hoplites in files of ten deep, posting behind them his slingers and dartmen. He exhorted his men to stand patiently till the enemy came within reach of the missiles. At the first discharge the assailing column seemed to waver; and Thrasybulus, taking advantage of their confusion, charged down the hill, and completely routed them, killing seventy, among whom was Critias himself. The loss of their leader had thrown the majority into the hands of the party formerly led by Theramenes, who resolved to depose the Thirty and constitute a new oligarchy of Ten. Some of the Thirty were re-elected into this body; but the more violent colleagues of Critias were deposed and retired for safety to Eleusis. The new government of the Ten sent to Sparta to solicit further aid; and a similar application was made at the same time from the section of the Thirty at Eleusis. Their request was complied with; and Lysander once more entered Athens at the head of a Lacedaemonian force. Fortunately, however, the jealousy of the Lacedaemonians towards Lysander led them at this critical juncture to supersede him in the command. King Pausanias was appointed to conduct an army into Attica, and when he encamped in the Academus he was joined by Lysander and his forces. It was known at Athens that the views of Pausanias were unfavourable to the proceedings of Lysander; and the presence of the Spartan king elicited a vehement reaction against the oligarchy, which fear had hitherto suppressed. All parties sent envoys to Sparta. The Ephors and the Lacedaemonian Assembly referred the question to a committee of fifteen, of whom Pausanias was one. The decision of this board was: That the exiles in Piraeus should be readmitted to Athens, and that there should be an amnesty for all that had passed, except as regarded the Thirty and the Ten.

When these terms were settled and sworn to, the Peloponnesians quitted Attica; and Thrasybulus and the exiles, marching in solemn procession from Piraeus to Athens, ascended to the Acropolis and offered up a solemn sacrifice and thanksgiving. An assembly of the people was then held, and after Thrasybulus had addressed an animated reproof to the oligarchical party, the democracy was unanimously restored. This important counter-revolution took place in the spring of 403 B.C. The archons, the senate of 500, the public assembly, and the dicasteries seem to have been reconstituted in the same form as before the capture of the city.

Thus was terminated, after a sway of eight months, the despotism of the Thirty. The year which contained their rule was not named after the archon, but was termed "the year of anarchy." The first archon drawn after their fall was Euclides, who gave his name to a year ever afterwards memorable among the Athenians.

For the next few years the only memorable event in the history of Athens is the death of Socrates. This celebrated philosopher was born in the year 468 B.C., in the immediate neighbourhood of Athens. His father, Sophroniscus, was a sculptor, and Socrates was brought up to, and for some time practised, the same profession. He was married to Xanthippe, by whom he had three sons; but her bad temper has rendered her name proverbial for a conjugal scold. His physical constitution was healthy, robust, and wonderfully enduring. Indifferent alike to heat and cold the same scanty and homely clothing sufficed him both in summer and winter; and even in the campaign of Potidaea, amidst the snows of a Thracian winter, he went barefooted. But though thus gifted with strength of body and of mind, he was far from being endowed with personal beauty. His thick lips, flat nose, and prominent eyes, gave him the appearance of a Silenus, or satyr. He served with credit as an hoplite at Potidaea (B.C. 432), Delium (B.C. 424), and Amphipolis (B.C. 422); but it was not till late in life, in the year 406 B.C., that he filled any political office. He was one of the Prytanes when, after the battle of Arginusae, Callixenus submitted his proposition respecting the six generals to the public Assembly, and his refusal on that occasion to put an unconstitutional question to the vote has been already recorded. He had a strong persuasion that he was intrusted with a divine mission, and he believed himself to be attended by a daemon, or genius, whose admonitions he frequently heard, not, however, in the way of excitement, but of restraint. He never WROTE anything, but he made oral instruction the great business of his life. Early in the morning he frequented the public walks, the gymnasia, and the schools; whence he adjourned to the market-place at its most crowded hours, and thus spent the whole day in conversing with young and old, rich and poor,--with all in short who felt any desire for his instructions.

That a reformer and destroyer, like Socrates, of ancient prejudices and fallacies which passed current under the name of wisdom should have raised up a host of enemies is only what might be expected; but in his case this feeling was increased by the manner in which he fulfilled his mission. The oracle of Delphi, in response to a question put by his friend Chaerephon, had affirmed that no man was wiser than Socrates. No one was more perplexed at this declaration than Socrates himself, since he was conscious of possessing no wisdom at all. However, he determined to test the accuracy of the priestess, for, though he had little wisdom, others might have still less. He therefore selected an eminent politician who enjoyed a high reputation for wisdom, and soon elicited by his scrutinising method of cross-examination, that this statesman's reputed wisdom was no wisdom at all. But of this he could not convince the subject of his examination; whence Socrates concluded that he was wiser than this politician, inasmuch as he was conscious of his own ignorance, and therefore exempt from the error of believing himself wise when in reality he was not so. The same experiment was tried with the same result on various classes of men; on poets, mechanics, and especially on the rhetors and sophists, the chief of all the pretenders to wisdom.

The first indication of the unpopularity which he had incurred is the attack made upon him by Aristophanes in the 'Clouds' in the year 423 B.C. That attack, however, seems to have evaporated with the laugh, and for many years Socrates continued his teaching without molestation. It was not till B.C. 399 that the indictment was preferred against him which cost him his life. In that year, Meletus, a leather-seller, seconded by Anytus, a poet, and Lycon, a rhetor, accused him of impiety in not worshipping the gods of the city, and in introducing new deities, and also of being a corrupter of youth. With respect to the latter charge, his former intimacy with Alcibiades and Critias may have, weighed against him. Socrates made no preparations for his defence, and seems, indeed, not to have desired an acquittal. But although he addressed the dicasts in a bold uncompromising tone, he was condemned only by a small majority of five or six in a court composed of between five and six hundred dicasts. After the verdict was pronounced, he was entitled, according to the practice of the Athenian courts, to make some counter-proposition in place of the penalty of death, which the accusers had demanded, and if he had done so with any show of submission it is probable that the sentence would have been mitigated. But his tone after the verdict was higher than before. Instead of a fine, he asserted that he ought to be maintained in the Prytaneum at the public expense, as a public benefactor. This seems to have enraged the dicasts and he was condemned to death.

It happened that the vessel which proceeded to Delos on the annual deputation to the festival had sailed the day before his condemnation; and during its absence it was unlawful to put any one to death. Socrates was thus kept in prison during thirty days, till the return of the vessel. He spent the interval in philosophical conversations with his friends. Crito, one of these, arranged a scheme for his escape by bribing the gaoler; but Socrates, as might be expected from the tone of his defence, resolutely refused to save his life by a breach of the law. His last discourse, on the day of his death, turned on the immortality of the soul. With a firm and cheerful countenance he drank the cup of hemlock amidst his sorrowing and weeping friends. His last words were addressed to Crito:--"Crito, we owe a cock to AEsculapius; discharge the debt, and by no means omit it."

Thus perished the greatest and most original of the Grecian philosophers, whose uninspired wisdom made the nearest approach to the divine morality of the

Gospel. His teaching forms an epoch in the history of philosophy. From his school sprang Plato, the founder of the Academic philosophy; Euclides, the founder of the Megaric school; Aristippus, the founder of the Cyrenaic school; and many other philosophers of eminence.

CHAPTER XV.
THE EXPEDITION OF THE GREEKS UNDER CYRUS, AND RETREAT OF THE TEN THOUSAND, B.C. 401-400.

The assistance which Cyrus had rendered to the Lacedaemonians in the Peloponnesian war led to a remarkable episode in Grecian history. This was the celebrated expedition of Cyrus against his brother Artaxerxes, in which the superiority of Grecian to Asiatic soldiers was so strikingly shown.

The death of Darius Nothus, king of Persia, took place B.C. 404, shortly before the battle of AEgospotami. Cyrus, who was present at his father's death, was charged by Tissaphernes with plotting against his elder brother Artaxerxes, who succeeded to the throne. The accusation was believed by Artaxerxes, who seized his brother, and would have put him to death, but for the intercession of their mother, Parysatis, who persuaded him not only to spare Cyrus but to confirm him in his former government. Cyrus returned to Sardis burning with revenge, and fully resolved to make an effort to dethrone his brother.

From his intercourse with the Greeks Cyrus had become aware of their superiority to the Asiatics, and of their usefulness in such an enterprise as he now contemplated. The peace which followed the capture of Athens seemed favourable to his projects. Many Greeks, bred up in the practice of war during the long struggle between that city and Sparta, were now deprived of their employment, whilst many more had been driven into exile by the establishment of the Spartan oligarchies in the various conquered cities. Under the pretence of a private war with the satrap, Tissaphernes, Cyrus enlisted large numbers of them in his service. The Greek in whom he placed most confidence was Clearchus, a Lacedaemonian, and formerly harmost of Byzantium, who had been condemned to death by the Spartan authorities for disobedience to their orders.

It was not, however, till the beginning of the year B.C. 401 that the enterprise of Cyrus was ripe for execution. The Greek levies were then withdrawn from the various towns in which they were distributed, and concentrated in Sardis, to the number of about 8000; and in March or April of this year Cyrus marched from Sardis with them, and with an army of 100,000 Asiatics. The object of the expedition was proclaimed to be an attack upon the mountain-freebooters of Pisidia; its real destination was a secret to every one except Cyrus himself and Clearchus. Among the Greek soldiers was Xenophon, an Athenian knight, to whom we owe a narrative of the expedition. He went as a volunteer, at the invitation of his friend Proxenus, a Boeotian, and one of the generals of Cyrus.

The march of Cyrus was directed through Lydia and Phrygia. After passing Colossae he arrived at Colaenae, where he was joined by more Greek troops, the number of whom now amounted to 11,000 hoplites and 2000 peltasts. The line of march, which had been hitherto straight upon Pisidia, was now directed north wards. Cyrus passed in succession the Phrygian towns of Peltae, Ceramon Agora, the Plain of Cayster, Thymbrium, Tyriaeum, and Iconium, the last city in Phrygia. Thence he proceeded through Lycaonia to Dana, and across Mount Taurus into Cilicia.

On arriving at Tarsus, a city on the coast of Cilicia, the Greeks plainly saw that they had been deceived, and that the expedition was designed against the Persian king. Seized with alarm at the prospect of so long a march, they sent a deputation to Cyrus to ask him what his real intentions were. Cyrus replied that his design was to march against his enemy, Abrocomas, satrap of Syria, who was encamped on the banks of the Euphrates. The Greeks, though they still suspected a delusion, contented themselves with this answer in the face of their present difficulties, especially as Cyrus promised to raise their pay from one Daric to one Daric and a half a month. The whole army then marched forwards to Issus, the last town in Cilicia, seated on the gulf of the same name. Here they met the fleet, which brought them a reinforcement of 1100 Greek soldiers, thus raising the Grecian force to about 14,000 men.

Abrocomas, who commanded for the Great King in Syria and Phoenicia, alarmed at the rapid progress of Cyrus, fled before him with all his army, reported as 300,000 strong; abandoning the impregnable pass situated one day's march from Issus, and known as the Gates of Cilicia and Syria. Marching in safety through this pass, the army next reached Myriandrus, a seaport of Phoenicia. From this place Cyrus struck off into the interior, over Mount Amanus. Twelve days' march brought him to Thapsacus on the Euphrates, where for the first time he formally notified to the army that he was marching to Babylon against his brother Artaxerxes, The water happened to be very low, scarcely reaching to the breast; and Abrocomas made no attempt to dispute the passage. The army now entered upon the desert, where the Greeks were struck with the novel sights which met their view, and at once amused and exhausted themselves in the chase of the wild ass and the antelope, or in the vain pursuit of the scudding ostrich. After several days of toilsome march the army at length reached Pylae, the entrance into the cultivated plains of Babylonia, where they halted a few days to refresh themselves.

Soon after leaving that place symptoms became perceptible of a vast hostile force moving in their front. The exaggerated reports of deserters stated it at 1,200,000 men; its real strength was about 900,000. In a characteristic address Cyrus exhorted the Greeks to take no heed of the multitude of their enemies; they would find in them, he affirmed nothing but numbers and noise, and, if they could bring themselves to despise these, they would soon find of what worthless stuff the natives were composed. The army then marched cautiously forwards, in order of battle, along the left bank of the Euphrates. They soon came upon a huge trench, 30 feet broad and 18 deep, which Artaxerxes had caused to be dug across the plain for a length of about 42 English miles, reaching from the Euphrates to the wall of Media. Between it and the river was left only a narrow passage about 20 feet broad; yet Cyrus and his army found with surprise that this pass was left entirely undefended. This circumstance inspired them with a contempt of the enemy, and induced them to proceed in careless array; but on the next day but one after passing the trench, on arriving at a place called Cunaxa, they were surprised with the intelligence that Artaxerxes was approaching with all his forces. Cyrus immediately drew up his army in order of battle. The Greeks were posted on the right, whilst Cyrus himself, surrounded by a picked body-guard of 600 Persian cuirassiers, took up his station in the centre. When the enemy were about half a mile distant, the Greeks engaged them with the usual war-shout. The Persians did not await their onset, but turned and fled. Tissaphernes and his cavalry alone offered any resistance; the remainder of the Persian left was routed without a blow. As Cyrus was contemplating the easy victory of the Greeks, his followers surrounded him, and already saluted him with the title of king. But the centre and right of Artaxerxes still remained unbroken; and that monarch, unaware of the defeat of his left wing, ordered the right to wheel and encompass the army of Cyrus. No sooner did Cyrus perceive this movement than with his body-guard he impetuously charged the enemy's centre, where Artaxerxes himself stood, surrounded with 6000 horse. The latter were routed and dispersed, and were followed so eagerly by the guards of Cyrus, that he was left almost alone with the select few called his "Table Companions." In this situation he caught sight of his brother Artaxerxes, whose person was revealed by the flight of his troops, when, maddened at once by rage and ambition, he shouted out, "I see the man!" and rushed at him with his handful of companions. Hurling his javelin at his brother, he wounded him in the breast, but was himself speedily overborne by superior numbers and slain on the spot.

Meanwhile Clearchus had pursued the flying enemy upwards of three miles; but hearing that the king's troops were victorious on the left and centre, he retraced his steps, again routing the Persians who endeavoured to intercept him. When the Greeks regained their camp they found that it had been completely plundered, and were consequently obliged to go supperless to rest. It was not till the following day that they learned the death of Cyrus; tidings which converted their triumph into sorrow and dismay. They were desirous that Ariaeus who now commanded the army of Cyrus, should lay claim to the Persian crown, and offered to support his pretensions; but Ariaeus answered that the Persian grandees would not tolerate such a claim; that he intended immediately to retreat; and that, if the Greeks wished to accompany him, they must join him during the following night. This was accordingly done; when oaths of reciprocal fidelity were interchanged between the Grecian generals and Ariaeus, and sanctified by a solemn sacrifice.

On the following day a message arrived from the Persian King, with a proposal to treat for peace on equal terms. Clearchus affected to treat the offer with great indifference, and made it an opportunity for procuring provisions. "Tell your king," said he to the envoys, "that we must first fight; for we have had no breakfast, nor will any man presume to talk to the Greeks about a truce without first providing for them a breakfast." This was agreed to, and guides were sent to conduct the Greeks to some villages where they might obtain food. Here they received a visit from Tissaphernes, who pretended much friendship towards them, and said that ha had come from the Great King to inquire the reason of their expedition. Clearchus replied--what was indeed true of the greater part of the army--that they had not come hither with any design to attack the king, but had been enticed forwards by Cyrus under false pretences; that their only desire at present was to return home; but that, if any obstacle was offered, they were prepared to repel hostilities. In a day or two Tissaphernes returned and with some parade stated that he had with great difficulty obtained permission to SAVE the Greek army; that he was ready to conduct them in person into Greece; and to supply them with provisions, for which, however, they were to pay. An agreement was accordingly entered into to this effect; and after many days delay they commenced the homeward march. After marching three days they passed through the wall of Media, which was 100 feet high and 20 feet broad. Two days more brought them to the Tigris, which they crossed on the following morning by a bridge of boats. They then marched northward, arriving in four days at the river Physcus and a large city called Opis. Six days' further march through a deserted part of Media brought them to some villages belonging to queen Parysatis, which, out of enmity to her as the patron of Cyrus, Tissaphernes abandoned to be plundered by the Greeks. From thence they proceeded in five days to the river Zabatus, or Greater Zab, having previously crossed the Lesser Zab, which Xenophon neglects to mention. In the first of these five days they saw on the opposite side of the Tigris a large city called Caenae, the inhabitants of which brought over provisions to them. At the Greater Zab they halted three days. Mistrust, and even slight hostilities, had been already manifested between the Greeks and Persians, but they now became so serious that Clearchus demanded an interview with Tissaphernes. The latter protested the greatest fidelity and friendship towards the Greeks, and promised to deliver to the Greek generals, on the following day, the calumniators who had set the two armies at variance. But when Clearchus, with four other generals, accompanied by some lochages or captains, and 200 soldiers, entered the Persian camp, according to appointment; the captains and soldiers were immediately cut down; whilst the five generals were seized, put into irons, and sent to the Persian court. After a short imprisonment, four of them were beheaded; the fifth, Menon, who pretended that he had betrayed his colleagues into the hands of Tissaphernes, was at first spared; but after a year's detention was put to death with tortures.

Apprehension and dismay reigned among the Greeks. Their situation was, indeed, appalling. They were considerably more than a thousand miles from home, in a hostile and unknown country, hemmed in on all sides by impassable rivers and mountains, without generals, without guides, without provisions. Xenophon was the first to rouse the captains to the necessity for taking immediate precautions. Though young, he possessed as an Athenian citizen some claim to distinction; and his animated address showed him fitted for command. He was saluted general on the spot; and in a subsequent assembly was, with four others, formally elected to that office.

The Greeks, having first destroyed their superfluous baggage, crossed the Greater Zab, and pursued their march on the other bank. They passed by the ruined cities of Larissa and Mespila on the Tigris, in the neighbourhood of the ancient Nineveh. The march from Mespila to the mountainous country of the Carduchi occupied several days in which the Greeks suffered much from the attacks of the enemy.

Their future route was now a matter of serious perplexity. On their left lay the Tigris, so deep that they could not fathom it with their spears; while in their front rose the steep and lofty mountains of the Carduchi, which came so near the river as hardly to leave a passage for its waters. As all other roads seemed barred, they formed the resolution of striking into these mountains, on the farther side of which lay Armenia, where both the Tigris and the Euphrates might be forded near their sources. After a difficult and dangerous march of seven days, during which their sufferings were far greater than any they had experienced from the Persians the army at length emerged into Armenia. It was now the month of December, and Armenia was cold and exposed, being a table-land raised high above the level of the sea. Whilst halting near some well-supplied villages, the Greeks were overtaken by two deep falls of snow, which almost buried them in their open bivouacs. Hence a five days' march brought them to the eastern branch of the Euphrates. Crossing the river, they proceeded on the other side of it over plains covered with a deep snow, and in the face of a biting north wind. Here many of the slaves and beasts of burthen, and even a few of the soldiers, fell victims to the cold. Some had their feet frost-bitten; some were blinded by the snow; whilst others, exhausted with cold and hunger, sunk down and died. On the eighth day they proceeded on their way, ascending the banks of the Phasis, not the celebrated river of that name, but probably the one usually called Araxes.

From thence they fought their way through the country of the Taochi and Chalybes. They next reached the country of the Scythini, in whose territory they found abundance in a large and populous city called Gymnias. The chief of this place having engaged to conduct them within sight of the Euxine, they proceeded for five days under his guidance; when, after ascending a mountain, the sea suddenly burst on the view of the vanguard. The men proclaimed their joy by loud shouts of "The sea! the sea!" The rest of the army hurried to the summit, and gave vent to their joy and exultation in tears and mutual embraces. A few days' march through the country of the Macrones and Colchians at length brought them to the objects for which they had so often pined, and which many at one time had never hoped to see again--a Grecian city and the sea. By the inhabitants of Trapezus or Trebizond, on the Euxine, where they had now arrived, they were hospitably received, and, being cantoned in some Colchian villages near the town, refreshed themselves after the hardships they had undergone by a repose of thirty days.

The most difficult part of the return of the Ten Thousand was now accomplished, and it is unnecessary to trace the remainder of their route. After many adventures they succeeded in reaching Byzantium, and they subsequently engaged to serve the Lacedaemonians in a war which Sparta had just declared against the satraps Tissaphernes and Pharnabazus.

In the spring of B.C. 399, Thimbron, the Lacedaemonian commander, arrived at Pergamus, and the remainder of the Ten Thousand Greeks became incorporated with his army. Xenophon now returned to Athens, where he must have arrived shortly after the execution of his master Socrates. Disgusted probably by that event, he rejoined his old comrades in Asia, and subsequently returned to Greece along with Agesilaus.

CHAPTER XVI.
THE SUPREMACY OF SPARTA, B.C. 404-371.

After the fall of Athens, Sparta stood without a rival in Greece. In the various cities which had belonged to the Athenian empire Lysander established an oligarchical Council of Ten, called a DECARCHY or Decemvirate, subject to the control of a Spartan HARMOST or governor. The Decarchies, however, remained only a short time in power, since the Spartan government regarded them with jealousy as the partisans of Lysander; but harmosts continued to be placed in every state subject to their empire. The government of the harmosts was corrupt and oppressive; no justice could be obtained against them by an appeal to the Spartan authorities at home; and the Grecian cities soon had cause to regret the milder and more equitable sway of Athens.

On the death of Agis in B.C. 398, his half-brother Agesilaus was appointed King, to the exclusion of Leotychides, the son of Agis. This was mainly effected by the powerful influence of Lysander, who erroneously considered Agesilaus to be of a yielding and manageable disposition and hoped by a skilful use of those qualities to extend his own influence, and under the name of another to be in reality king himself.

Agesilaus was now forty years of age, and esteemed a model of those virtues more peculiarly deemed Spartan. He was obedient to the constituted authorities, emulous to excel, courageous, energetic, capable of bearing all sorts of hardship and fatigue, simple and frugal in his mode of life. To these severer qualities he added the popular attractions of an agreeable countenance and pleasing address. His personal defects at first stood in the way of his promotion. He was not only low in stature, but also lame of one leg; and there was an ancient oracle which warned the Spartans to beware of "a lame reign." The ingenuity of Lysander, assisted probably by the popular qualities of Agesilaus, contrived to overcome this objection by interpreting a lame reign to mean not any bodily defect in the king, but the reign of one who was not a genuine descendant of Hercules. Once possessed of power, Agesilaus supplied any defect in his title by the prudence and policy of his conduct; and, by the marked deference which he paid both to the Ephors and the senators, he succeeded in gaining for himself more real power than had been enjoyed by any of his predecessors.

The affairs of Asia Minor soon began to draw the attention of Agesilaus to that quarter. The assistance lent to Cyrus by the Spartans was no secret at the Persian court; and Tissaphernes, who had been rewarded for his fidelity with the satrapy of Cyrus in addition to his own, no sooner returned to his government than he attacked the Ionian cities, then under the protection of Sparta. A considerable Lacedaemonian force under Thimbron was despatched to their assistance, and which, as related in the preceding chapter, was joined by the remnant of the Greeks who had served under Cyrus. Thimbron, however, proved so inefficient a commander, that he was superseded at the end of 399 or beginning of 398 B.C., and Dercyllidas appointed in his place. But though at first successful against Pharnabazus in AEolis, Dercyllidas was subsequently surprised in Caria in such an unfavourable position that he would have suffered severely but for the timidity of Tissaphernes, who was afraid to venture upon an action. Under these circumstances an armistice was agreed to for the purpose of treating for a peace (397 B.C.).

Pharnabazus availed himself of this armistice to make active preparations for a renewal of the war. He obtained large reinforcements of Persian troops, and began to organize a fleet in Phoenicia and Cilicia. This was intrusted to the Athenian admiral Conon, of whom we now first hear again after a lapse of seven years since his defeat at AEgospotami. After that disastrous battle Conon fled with nine triremes to Cyprus, where he was now living under the protection of Evagoras, prince of Salamis.

It was the news of these extensive preparations that induced Agesilaus, on the suggestion of Lysander, to volunteer his services against the Persians. He proposed to take with him only 30 full Spartan citizens, or peers, to act as a sort of council, together with 2000 Neodamodes, or enfranchised Helots, and 6000 hoplites of the allies. Lysander intended to be the leader of the 30 Spartans, and expected through them to be the virtual commander of the expedition of which Agesilaus was nominally the head.

Since the time of Agamemnon no Grecian king had led an army into Asia; and Agesilaus studiously availed himself of the prestige of that precedent in order to attract recruits to his standard. The Spartan kings claimed to inherit the sceptre of Agamemnon; and to render the parallel more complete, Agesilaus proceeded with a division of his fleet to Aulis, intending there to imitate the memorable sacrifice of the Homeric hero. But as he had neglected to ask the permission of the Thebans, and conducted the sacrifice and solemnities by means of his own prophets and ministers, and in a manner at variance with the usual rites of the temple, the Thebans were offended, and expelled him by armed force:--an insult which he never forgave.

It was in 396 B.C. that Agesilaus arrived at Ephesus and took the command in Asia. He demanded of the Persians the complete independence of the Greek cities in Asia; and in order that there might be time to communicate with the Persian court, the armistice was renewed for three months. During this interval of repose, Lysander, by his arrogance and pretensions, offended both Agesilaus and the Thirty Spartans. Agesilaus, determined to uphold his dignity, subjected Lysander to so many humiliations that he was at last fain to request his dismissal from Ephesus, and was accordingly sent to the Hellespont, where he did good service to the Spartan interests.

Meanwhile Tissaphernes, having received large reinforcements, sent a message to Agesilaus before the armistice had expired, ordering him to quit Asia. Agesilaus immediately made preparations as if he would attack Tissaphernes in Caria; but having thus put the enemy on a false scent, he suddenly turned northwards into Phrygia, the satrapy of Pharnabazus, and marched without opposition to the neighbourhood of Dascylium, the residence of the satrap himself. Here, however, he was repulsed by the Persian cavalry. He now proceeded into winter quarters at Ephesus, where he employed himself in organizing a body of cavalry to compete with the Persians. During the winter the army was brought into excellent condition; and Agesilaus gave out early in the spring of 395 B.C. that he should march direct upon Sardis. Tissaphernes suspecting another feint, now dispersed his cavalry in the plain of the Maeander. But this time Agesilaus marched as he had announced, and in three days arrived unopposed on the banks of the Pactolus, before the Persian cavalry could be recalled. When they at last came up, the newly raised Grecian horse, assisted by the peltasts, and some of the younger and more active hoplites, soon succeeded in putting them to flight. Many of the Persians were drowned in the Pactolus, and their camp, containing much booty and several camels, was taken.

Agesilaus now pushed his ravages up to the very gates of Sardis, the residence of Tissaphernes. But the career of that timid and treacherous satrap was drawing to a close. The queen-mother, Parysatis, who had succeeded in regaining her influence over Artaxerxes, caused an order to be sent down from Susa for his execution; in pursuance of which he was seized in a bath at Colossae, and beheaded. Tithraustes, who had been intrusted with the execution of this order, succeeded Tissaphernes in the satrapy, and immediately reopened negotiations with Agesilaus. An armistice of six months was concluded; and meanwhile Tithraustes, by a subsidy of 30 talents, induced Agesilaus to move out of his satrapy into that of Pharnabazus.

During this march into Phrygia Agesilaus received a new commission from home, appointing him the head of the naval as well as of the land force--two commands never before united in a single Spartan. He named his brother-in-law, Pisander, commander of the fleet. But in the following year (B.C. 394), whilst he was preparing an expedition on a grand scale into the interior of Asia Minor, he was suddenly recalled home to avert the dangers which threatened his native country.

The jealousy and ill-will with which the newly acquired empire of the Spartans was regarded by the other Grecian states had not escaped the notice of the Persians; and when Tithraustes succeeded to the satrapy of Tissaphernes he resolved to avail himself of this feeling by exciting a war against Sparta in the heart of Greece itself. With this view he despatched one Timocrates, a Rhodian, to the leading Grecian cities which appeared hostile to Sparta, carrying with him a sum of 50 talents to be distributed among the chief men in each for the purpose of bringing them over to the views of Persia. Timocrates was successful in Thebes, Corinth, and Argos but he appears not to have visited Athens.

Hostilities were at first confined to Sparta and Thebes. A quarrel having arisen between the Opuntian Locrians and the Phocians respecting a strip of border land, the former people appealed to the Thebans, who invaded Phocis. The Phocians on their side invoked the aid of the Lacedaemonians, who, elated with the prosperous state of their affairs in Asia, and moreover desirous of avenging the affronts they had received from the Thebans, readily listened to the appeal. Lysander, who took an active part in promoting the war, was directed to attack the town of Haliartus; and it was arranged that King Pausanias should join him on a fixed day under the walls of that town, with the main body of the Lacedaemonians and their Peloponnesian allies.

Nothing could more strikingly denote the altered state of feeling in Greece than the request for assistance which the Thebans, thus menaced, made to their ancient enemies and rivals the Athenians. Nor were the Athenians backward in responding to the appeal. Lysander arrived at Haliartus before Pausanias. Here, in a sally made by the citizens, opportunely supported by the unexpected arrival of a body of Thebans, the army of Lysander was routed, and himself slain. His troops disbanded and dispersed themselves in the night time. Thus, when Pausanias at last came up, he found no army to unite with; and as an imposing Athenian force had arrived, he now, with the advice of his council took the humiliating step--always deemed a confession of inferiority--of requesting a truce in order to bury the dead who had fallen in the preceding battle. Even this, however, the Thebans would not grant except on the condition that the Lacedaemonians should immediately quit their territory. With these terms Pausanias was forced to comply; and after duly interring the bodies of Lysander and his fallen comrades, the Lacedaemonians dejectedly pursued their homeward march. Pausanias, afraid to face the public indignation of the Spartans took refuge in the temple of Athena Alea at Tegea; and being condemned to death in his absence, only escaped that fate by remaining in the sanctuary. He was succeeded by his son Agesipolis.

The enemies of Sparta took fresh courage from this disaster to her arms. Athens, Corinth, and Argos now formed with Thebes a solemn alliance against her. The league was soon joined by the Euboeans, the Acarnanians, and other Grecian states. In the spring of 394 B.C. the allies assembled at Corinth, and the war, which had been hitherto regarded as merely Boeotian, was now called the CORINTHIAN, by which name it is known in history. This threatening aspect of affairs determined the Ephors to recall Agesilaus, as already related.

The allies were soon in a condition to take the field with a force of 24,000 hoplites, of whom one-fourth were Athenians, together with a considerable body of light troops and cavalry. The Lacedaemonians had also made the most active preparations. In the neighbourhood of Corinth a battle was fought, in which the Lacedaemonians gained the victory, though their allied troops were put to the rout. This battle, called the battle of Corinth, was fought in July 394 B.C.

Agesilaus, who had relinquished with a heavy heart his projected expedition into Asia, was now on his homeward march. By the promise of rewards he had persuaded the bravest and most efficient soldiers in his army to accompany him, amongst whom were many of the Ten Thousand, with Xenophon at their head. The route of Agesilaus was much the same as the one formerly traversed by Xerxes, and the camels which accompanied the army gave it somewhat of an oriental aspect. At Amphipolis he received the news of the victory at Corinth; but his heart was so full of schemes against Persia, that the feeling which it awakened in his bosom was rather one of regret that so many Greeks had fallen, whose united efforts might have emancipated Asia Minor, than of joy at the success of his countrymen. Having forced his way through a desultory opposition offered by the Thessalian cavalry, he crossed Mount Othrys, and marched unopposed the rest of the way through the straits of Thermopylae to the frontiers of Phocis and Boeotia. Here the evil tidings reached him of the defeat and death of his brother-in-law, Pisander, in a great sea-fight off Cnidus in Caria (August 394 B.C.) Conon, with the assistance of Pharnabazus, had succeeded in raising a powerful fleet, partly Phoenician and partly Grecian, with which he either destroyed or captured more than half of the Lacedaemonian fleet. Agesilaus, fearing the impression which such sad news might produce upon his men, gave out that the Lacedaemonian fleet had gained a victory; and, having offered sacrifice as if for a victory, he ordered an advance.

Agesilaus soon came up with the confederate army, which had prepared to oppose him in the plain of Coronea. The Thebans succeeded in driving in the Orchomenians, who formed the left wing of the army of Agesilaus, and penetrated as far as the baggage in the rear. But on the remainder of the line Agesilaus was victorious, and the Thebans now saw themselves cut off from their companions, who had retreated and taken up a position on Mount Helicon. Facing about and forming in deep and compact order, the Thebans sought to rejoin the main body, but they were opposed by Agesilaus and his troops. The shock of the conflicting masses which ensued was one of the most terrible recorded in the annals of Grecian warfare. The shields of the foremost ranks were shattered, and their spears broken, so that daggers became the only available arm. Agesilaus, who was in the front ranks, unequal by his size and strength to sustain so furious an onset, was flung down, trodden on, and covered with wounds; but the devoted courage of the 50 Spartans forming his body-guard rescued him from death. The Thebans finally forced their may through, but not without severe loss. The victory of Agesilaus was not very decisive; but the Thebans tacitly acknowledged their defeat by soliciting the customary truce for the burial of their dead.

Agesilaus, on his arrival at Sparta, was received with the most lively demonstrations of gratitude and esteem, and became hence-forward the sole director of Spartan policy.

Thus in less than two months the Lacedaemonians had fought two battles on land, and one at sea; namely, those of Corinth, Coronea, and Cnidus. But, though they had been victorious in the land engagements, they were so little decisive as to lead to no important result; whilst their defeat at Cnidus produced the most disastrous consequences. It was followed by the loss of nearly all their maritime empire, even faster than they had acquired it after the battle of Ægospotami. For as Conon and Pharnabazus sailed with their victorious fleet from island to island, and from port to port, their approach was everywhere the signal for the flight or expulsion of the Spartan harmosts.

In the spring of the following year (B.C. 393) Conon and Pharnabazus sailed to the isthmus of Corinth, then occupied as a central post by the allies. The appearance of a Persian fleet in the Saronic gulf was a strange sight to Grecian eyes, and one which might have served as a severe comment on the effect of their suicidal wars. Conon dexterously availed himself of the hatred of Pharnabazus towards Sparta to procure a boon for his native city. As the satrap was on the point of proceeding homewards, Conon obtained leave to employ the seamen in rebuilding the fortifications of Piraeus and the long walls of Athens. Pharnabazus also granted a large sum for the same purpose; and Conon had thus the glory of appearing, like a second Themistocles, the deliverer and restorer of his country. Before the end of autumn the walls were rebuilt. Having thus, as it were, founded Athens a second time, Conon sailed to the islands to lay again the foundations of an Athenian maritime empire.

During the remainder of this and the whole of the following year (B.C. 392) the war was carried on in the Corinthian territory.

One of the most important events at this time was the destruction of a whole Lacedaemonian MORA, or battalion, by the light-armed mercenaries of the Athenian Iphicrates. For the preceding two years Iphicrates had commanded a body of mercenaries, consisting of peltasts, [So called from the pelta, or kind of shield which they carried.] who had been first organised by Conon after rebuilding the walls of Athens. For this force Iphicrates introduced those improved arms and tactics which form an epoch in the Grecian art of war. His object was to combine as far as possible the peculiar advantages of the hoplites and light-armed troops. He substituted a linen corslet for the coat of mail worn by the hoplites, and lessened the shield, while he rendered the light javelin and short sword of the peltasts more effective by lengthening them both one-half These troops soon proved very effective. After gaining several victories he ventured to make a sally from Corinth, and attacked a Lacedaemonian mora in flank and rear. So many fell under the darts and arrows of the peltasts that the Lacedaemonian captain called a halt, and ordered the youngest and most active of his hoplites to rush forward and drive off the assailants. But their heavy arms rendered them quite unequal to such a mode of fighting; nor did the Lacedaemonian cavalry, which now came up, but which acted with very little vigour and courage, produce any better effect. At length the Lacedaemonians succeeded in reaching an eminence, where they endeavoured to make a stand; but at this moment Callias arrived with some Athenian hoplites from Corinth, whereupon the already disheartened Lacedaemonians broke and fled in confusion, pursued by the peltasts, who committed such havoc, chasing and killing some of them even in the sea, that but very few of the whole body succeeded in effecting their escape.

The maritime war was prosecuted with vigour. Thrasybulus, and after his death Iphicrates, were successful upon the coast of Asia Minor, and made the Athenians again masters of the Hellespont. Under these circumstances the Lacedaemonians resolved to spare no efforts to regain the good will of the Persians. Antalcidas, the Lacedaemonian commander on the Asiatic coast, entered into negotiations with Tiribazus, who had succeeded Tithraustes in the satrapy of Ionia, in order to bring about a general peace under the mediation of Persia. Conducted by Tiribazus, Antalcidas repaired to the Persian court, and prevailed an the Persian monarch both to adopt the peace, and to declare war against those who should reject it. Antalcidas and Tiribazus returned to the coasts of Asia Minor, not only armed with these powers, but provided with an ample force to carry them into execution. In addition to the entire fleet of Persia, Dionysius of Syracuse had placed 20 triremes at the service of the Lacedaemonians; and Antalcidas now sailed with a large fleet to the Hellespont, where Iphicrates and the Athenians were still predominant. The overwhelming force of Antalcidas, the largest that had been seen in the Hellespont since the battle of AEgospotami, rendered all resistance hopeless. The supplies of corn from the Euxine no longer found their way to Athens: and the Athenians, depressed at once both by what they felt and by what they anticipated, began to long for peace. As without the assistance of Athens it seemed hopeless for the other allies to struggle against Sparta, all Greece was inclined to listen to an accommodation.

Under these circumstances deputies from the Grecian states were summoned to meet Tiribazus; who, after exhibiting to them the royal seal of Persia, read to them the following terms of a peace: "King Artaxerxes thinks it just that the cities in Asia and the islands of Clazomenae and Cyprus should belong to him. He also thinks it just to leave all the other Grecian cities, both small and great, independent--except Lemnos, Imbros, and Scyros, which are to belong to Athens, as of old. Should any parties refuse to accept this peace, I will make war upon them, along with those who are of the same mind, both by land and sea, with ships and with money." All the Grecian states accepted these terms.

This disgraceful peace, called the PEACE OF ANTALCIDAS, was concluded in the year B.C. 387. By it Greece seemed prostrated at the feet of the barbarians; for its very terms, engraven on stone and set up in the sanctuaries of Greece, recognised the Persian king as the arbiter of her destinies. Although Athens cannot be entirely exonerated from the blame of this transaction, the chief guilt rests upon Sparta, whose designs were far deeper and more hypocritical than they appeared. Under the specious pretext of securing the independence of the Grecian cities, her only object was to break up the confederacies under Athens and Thebes, and, with the assistance of Persia, to pave the way for her own absolute dominion in Greece.

No sooner was the peace of Antalcidas concluded than Sparta, directed by Agesilaus, the ever-active enemy of Thebes, exerted all her power to weaken that city. She began by proclaiming the independence of the various Boeotian cities, and by organizing in each a local oligarchy, adverse to Thebes and favourable to herself.

Lacedaemonian garrisons were placed in Orchomenus and Thespiae, and Plataea was restored in order to annoy and weaken Thebes. Shortly afterwards the Lacedaemonians obtained possession of Thebes itself by an act of shameful treachery. They had declared war against Olynthus, a town situated at the head of the Toronaic gulf, in the peninsula of the Macedonian Chalcidice, the head of a powerful confederation which included several of the adjacent Grecian cities. The Thebans had entered into an alliance with Olynthus, and had forbidden any of their citizens to join the Lacedaemonian army destined to act against it; but they were not strong enough to prevent its marching through their territory. Phoebidas, who was conducting a Lacedaemonian force against Olynthus, halted on his way through Boeotia not far from Thebes; where he was visited by Leontiades, one of the polemarchs of the city, and two or three other leaders of the Lacedaemonian party in Thebes. It happened that the festival of the Thesmophoria was on the point of being celebrated, during which the Cadmea, or Theban Acropolis, was given up for the exclusive use of the women. The opportunity seemed favourable for a surprise; and Leontiades and Phoebidas concerted a plot to seize it. Whilst the festival was celebrating, Phoebidas pretended to resume his march, but only made a circuit round the city walls; whilst Leontiades, stealing out of the senate, mounted his horse, and, joining the Lacedaemonian troops, conducted them towards the Cadmea. It was a sultry summer's afternoon, so that the very streets were deserted; and Phoebidas, without encountering any opposition, seized the citadel and all the women in it, to serve as hostages for the quiet submission of the Thebans (B.C. 382). This treacherous act during a period of profound peace awakened the liveliest indignation throughout Greece. Sparta herself could not venture to justify it openly, and Phoebidas was made the scape-goat of her affected displeasure. As a sort of atonement to the violated feeling of Greece, he was censured, fined, and dismissed. But that this was a mere farce is evident from the fact, of his subsequent restoration to command; and, however indignant the Lacedaemonians affected to appear at the act of Phoebidas, they took care to reap the fruits of it by retaining their garrison in the Cadmea.

The once haughty Thebes was now enrolled a member of the Lacedaemonian alliance, and furnished her contingent--the grateful offering of the new Theban government--for the war which Sparta was prosecuting with redoubled vigour against Olynthus. This city was taken by the Lacedaemonians in B.C. 379; the Olynthian confederacy was dissolved; the Grecian cities belonging to it were compelled to join the Lacedaemonian alliance; whilst the maritime towns of Macedonia were reduced under the dominion of Amyntas, the king of Macedon.

The power of Sparta on land had now attained its greatest height. Her unpopularity in Greece was commensurate with the extent of her harshly administered dominion. She was leagued on all slides with the enemies of Grecian freedom-- with the Persians, with Amyntas of Macedon, and with Dionysius of Syracuse. But she had now reached the turning-point of her fortunes, and her successes, which had been earned without scruple, were soon to be followed by misfortunes and disgrace. The first blow came from Thebes, where she had perpetrated her most signal injustice.

That city had been for three years in the hands of Leontiades and the Spartan party. During this time great discontent had grown up among the resident citizens; and there was also the party of exasperated exiles, who had taken refuge at Athens. Among these exiles was Pelopidas, a young man of birth and fortune, who had already distinguished himself by his disinterested patriotism and ardent character. He now took the lead in the plans formed the the liberation of his country, and was the heart and soul of the enterprise. His warm and generous heart was irresistibly attracted by everything great and noble; and hence he was led to form a close and intimate friendship with Epaminondas, who was several years older than himself and of a still loftier character. Their friendship is said to have originated in a campaign in which they served together, when, Pelopidas having fallen in battle apparently dead, Epaminondas protected his body at the imminent risk of his own life. Pelopidas afterwards endeavoured to persuade Epaminondas to share his riches with him; and when he did not succeed, he resolved to live on the same frugal fare as his great friend. A secret correspondence was opened with his friends at Thebes, the chief of whom were Phyllidas, secretary to the polemarchs, and Charon. The dominant faction, besides the advantage of the actual possession of power, was supported by a garrison of 1500 Lacedaemonians. The enterprise, therefore, was one of considerable difficulty and danger. In the execution of it Phyllidas took a leading part. It was arranged that he should give a supper to Archias and Philippus, the two polemarchs, and after they had partaken freely of wine the conspirators were to be introduced, disguised as women, and to complete their work by the assassination of the polemarchs. On the day before the banquet, Pelopidas, with six other exiles, arrived at Thebes from Athens, and, straggling through the gates towards dusk in the disguise of rustics and huntsmen, arrived safely at the house of Charon, where they remained concealed till the appointed hour. While the polemarchs were at table a messenger arrived from Athens with a letter for Archias, in which the whole plot was accurately detailed. The messenger, in accordance with his instructions, informed Archias that the letter related to matters of serious importance. But the polemarch, completely engrossed by the pleasures of the table, thrust the letter under the pillow of his couch, exclaiming, "Serious matters to-morrow."

The hour of their fate was now ripe. The conspirators, disguised with veils, and in the ample folds of female attire, were ushered into the room. For men in the state of the revelers the deception was complete; but when they attempted to lift the veils from the women, their passion was rewarded by the mortal thrust of a dagger. After thus slaying the two polemarchs, the conspirators went to the house of Leontiades whom they also despatched.

The news of the revolution soon spread abroad. Proclamations were issued announcing that Thebes was free, and calling upon all citizens who valued their liberty to muster in the market-place. As soon as day dawned, and the citizens became aware that they were summoned to vindicate their liberty, their joy and enthusiasm were unbounded. For the first time since the seizure of their citadel they met in public assembly; the conspirators, being introduced, were crowned by the priests with wreaths, and thanked in the name of their country's gods; whilst the assembly, with grateful acclamation, unanimously nominated Pelopidas, Charon, and Mellon as the first restored Boeotarchs.

Meanwhile the remainder of the Theban exiles, accompanied by a body of Athenian volunteers, assembled on the frontiers of Boeotia; and, at the first news of the success of the conspiracy, hastened to Thebes to complete the revolution. The Thebans, under their new Boeotarchs, were already mounting to the assault of the Cadmea, when the Lacedaemonians capitulated, and were allowed to march out with the honours of war. The Athenians formed an alliance with the Thebans, and declared war against Sparta.

From this time must be dated the era of a new political combination in Greece. Athens strained every nerve to organize a fresh confederacy. Thebes did not scruple to enrol herself as one of its earliest members. The basis on which the confederacy was formed closely resembled that of Delos. The cities composing it were to be independent, and to send deputies to a congress at Athens, for the purpose of raising a common fund for the support of a naval force. Care was taken to banish all recollections connected with the former unpopularity of the Athenian empire. The name of the tribute was no longer PHOROS, but SYNTAXIS, or "contribution." The confederacy, which ultimately numbered 70 cities, was chiefly organised through the exertions of Chabrias, and of Timotheus the son of Conon. Nor were the Thebans less zealous, amongst whom the Spartan government had left a lively feeling of antipathy. The military force was put in the best training, and the famous "Sacred Band" was now for the first time instituted. This band was a regiment of 300 hoplites. It was supported at the public expense and kept constantly under arms. It was composed of young and chosen citizens of the best families, and organized in such a manner that each man had at his side a dear and intimate friend. Its special duty was the defence of the Cadmea.

The Thebans had always been excellent soldiers; but their good fortune now gave them the greatest general that Greece had hitherto seen. Epaminondas, who now appears conspicuously in public life, deserves the reputation not merely of a Theban but of a Grecian hero. Sprung from a poor but ancient family, Epaminondas possessed all the best qualities of his nation without that heaviness, either of body or of mind, which characterized and deteriorated the Theban people. By the study of philosophy and by other intellectual pursuits his mind was enlarged beyond the sphere of vulgar superstition, and emancipated from that timorous interpretation of nature which caused even some of the leading men of those days to behold a portent in the most ordinary phenomenon. A still rarer accomplishment for a Theban was that of eloquence, which he possessed in no ordinary degree. These intellectual qualities were matched with moral virtues worthy to consort with them. Though eloquent, he was discreet; though poor, he was neither avaricious nor corrupt; though naturally firm and courageous, he was averse to cruelty, violence, and bloodshed; though a patriot, he was a stranger to personal ambition, and scorned the little arts by which popularity is too often courted. Pelopidas, as we have already said, was his bosom friend. It was natural therefore, that, when Pelopidas was named Boeotarch, Epaminondas should be prominently employed in organizing the means of war; but it was not till some years later that his military genius shone forth in its full lustre.

The Spartans were resolved to avenge the repulse they had received; and in the summer of B.C. 378 Agesilaus marched with a large army into Boeotia. He was unable, however, to effect any thing decisive, and subsequent invasions were attended with the like result. The Athenians created a diversion in their favour by a maritime war, and thus for two years Boeotia was free from Spartan invasion, Thebes employed this time in extending her dominion over the neighbouring cities. One of her most important successes during this period was the victory gained by Pelopidas over a Lacedaemonian force near Tegyra, a village dependent upon Orchomenus (B.C. 375). Pelopidas had with him only the Sacred Band and a small body of cavalry when he fell in with the Lacedaemonians, who were nearly twice as numerous. He did not, however, shrink from the conflict on this account; and when one of his men, running up to him, exclaimed, "We are fallen into the midst of the enemy," he replied, "Why so, more than they into the midst of us?" In the battle which ensued the two Spartan commanders fell at the first charge, and their men were put to the rout. So signal a victory inspired the Thebans with new confidence and vigour, as it showed that Sparta was not invincible even in a pitched battle, and with the advantage of numbers on her side. By the year 374 B.C. the Thebans had succeeded in expelling the Lacedaemonians from Boeotia, and revived the Boeotian confederacy. They also destroyed the restored city of Plataea, and obliged its inhabitants once more to seek refuge at Athens.

The successes of the Thebans revived the jealousy and distrust of Athens. Prompted by these feelings, the Athenians opened negotiations for a peace with Sparta; a resolution which was also adopted by the majority of the allies.

A congress was accordingly opened in Sparta in the spring of 371 B.C. The Athenians were represented by Callias and two other envoys; the Thebans by Epaminondas, then one of the polemarchs. The terms of a peace were agreed upon, by which the independence of the various Grecian cities was to be recognised; and the Spartan harmosts and garrisons everywhere dismissed. Sparta ratified the treaty for herself and her allies; but Athens took the oaths only for herself, and was followed separately by her allies. As Epaminondas refused to sign except in the name of the Boeotian confederation, Agesilaus directed the name of the Thebans to be struck out of the treaty, and proclaimed them excluded from it.

The peace concluded between Sparta, Athens, and their respective allies, was called the PEACE OF CALLIAS. The result with regard to Thebes and Sparta will appear in the following chapter.

CHAPTER XVII.
THE SUPREMACY OF THEBES, B.C. 371-361.

In pursuance of the treaty, the Lacedaemonians withdrew their harmosts and garrisons, whilst the Athenians recalled their fleet from the Ionian sea. Only one feeling prevailed at Sparta--a desire to crush Thebes. This city was regarded as doomed to destruction; and it was not for a moment imagined that, single-handed, she would be able to resist the might of Sparta. At the time when the peace was concluded Cleombrotus happened to be in Phocis at the head of a Lacedaemonian army; and he now received orders to invade Boeotia without delay. The Thebans on their side, were equally determined on resistance. The two armies met on the memorable plain of Leuctra, near Thespiae. The forces on each side are not accurately known, but it seems probable that the Thebans were outnumbered by the Lacedaemonians. The military genius of Epaminondas, however, compensated any inferiority of numbers by novelty of tactics. Up to this time Grecian battles had been uniformly conducted by a general attack in line. Epaminondas now first adopted the manoeuvre, used with such success by Napoleon in modern times, of concentrating heavy masses on a given point of the enemy's array. Having formed his left wing into a dense column of 50 deep, so that its depth was greater than its front, he directed it against the Lacedaemonian right, containing the best troops in their army, drawn up 12 deep, and led by Cleombrotus in person. The shock was terrible. Cleombrotus himself was mortally wounded in the onset, and with difficulty carried off by his comrades. Numbers of his officers, as well as of his men, were slain, and the whole wing was broken and driven back to their camp. The loss of the Thebans was small compared with that of the Lacedaemonians. Out of 700 Spartans in the army of the latter, 400 had fallen; and their king also had been slain, an event which had not occurred since the fatal day of Thermopylae.

The victory of Leuctra was gained within three weeks after the exclusion of the Thebans from the peace of Callias. The effect of it throughout Greece was electrical. It was everywhere felt that a new military power had arisen--that the prestige of the old Spartan discipline and tactics had departed. Yet at Sparta itself though the reverse was the greatest that her arms had ever sustained, the news of it was received with an assumption of indifference characteristic of the people. The Ephors forbade the chorus of men, who were celebrating in the theatre the festival of the Gymnopaedia, to be interrupted. They contented themselves with directing the names of the slain to be communicated to their relatives, and with issuing an order forbidding the women to wail and mourn. Those whose friends had fallen appeared abroad on the morrow with joyful countenances, whilst the relatives of the survivors seemed overwhelmed with grief and shame.

Immediately after the battle the Thebans had sent to Jason of Pherae in Thessaly to solicit his aid against the Lacedaemonians. This despot was one of the most remarkable men of the period. He was Tagus, or Generalissimo, of all Thessaly; and Macedonia was partially dependent on him. He was a man of boundless ambition, and meditated nothing less than extending his dominion over the whole of Greece, for which his central situation seemed to offer many facilities. Upon receiving the invitation of the Thebans, Jason immediately resolved to join them. When he arrived the Thebans were anxious that he should unite with them in an attack upon the Lacedaemonian camp; but Jason dissuaded them from the enterprise, advising them not to drive the Lacedaemonians to despair, and offering his mediation. He accordingly succeeded in effecting a truce, by which the Lacedaemonians were allowed to depart from Boeotia unmolested.

According to Spartan custom, the survivors of a defeat were looked upon as degraded men, and subjected to the penalties of civil infamy. No allowance was made for circumstances. But those who had fled at Leuctra were three hundred in number; all attempt to enforce against them the usual penalties might prove not only inconvenient, but even dangerous; and on the proposal of Agesilaus, they were, for this occasion only, suspended. The loss of material power which Sparta sustained by the defeat was great. The ascendency she had hitherto enjoyed in parts north of the Corinthian gulf fell from her at once, and was divided between Jason of Pherae and the Thebans. Jason was shortly afterwards assassinated. His death was felt as a relief by Greece, and especially by Thebes. He was succeeded by his two brothers, Polyphron and Polydorus; but they possessed neither his ability nor his power.

The Athenians stood aloof from the contending parties. They had not received the news of the battle of Leuctra with any pleasure, for they now dreaded Thebes more than Sparta. But instead of helping the latter, they endeavoured to prevent either from obtaining the supremacy in Greece, and for this purpose called upon the other states to form a new alliance upon the terms of the peace of Antalcidas. Most of the Peloponnesian states joined this new league. Thus even the Peloponnesian cities became independent of Sparta. But this was not all. Never did any state fall with greater rapidity. She not only lost the dominion over states which she had exercised for centuries; but two new political powers sprang up in the peninsula, which threatened her own independence.

In the following year (B.C. 370) Epaminondas marched into Laconia, and threatened Sparta itself. The city, which was wholly unfortified, was filled with confusion and alarm. The women, who had never yet seen the face of an enemy, gave vent to their fears in wailing and lamentation. Agesilaus, however, was undismayed, and saved the state by his vigilance and energy. He repulsed the cavalry of Epaminondas as they advanced towards Sparta; and so vigorous were his measures of defence, that the Theban general abandoned all further attempt upon the city, and proceeded southwards as far as Helos and Gythium on the coast, the latter the port and arsenal of Sparta after laying waste with fire and sword the valley of the Eurotas, he retraced his steps to the frontiers of Arcadia.

Epaminondas now proceeded to carry out the two objects for which his march had been undertaken; namely, the consolidation of the Arcadian confederation, and the establishment of the Messenians as an independent community. In the prosecution of the former of these designs the mutual jealousy of the various Arcadian cities rendered it necessary that a new one should be founded, which should be regarded as the capital of the confederation. Consequently, a new city was built on the banks of the Helisson, called Megalopolis, and peopled by the inhabitants of forty distinct Arcadian townships. Here a synod of deputies from the towns composing the confederation, called "The Ten Thousand" was to meet periodically for the despatch of business. Epaminondas next proceeded to re-establish the Messenian state. The Messenians had formerly lived under a dynasty of their own kings; but for the last three centuries their land had been in the possession of the Lacedaemonians, and they had been fugitives upon the face of the earth. The restoration of these exiles, dispersed in various Hellenic colonies, to their former rights, would plant a bitterly hostile neighbour on the very borders of Laconia. Epaminondas accordingly opened communications with them, and numbers of them flocked to his standard during his march into Peloponnesus. He now founded the town of Messene. Its citadel was placed on the summit of Mount Ithome, which had three centuries before been so bravely defended by the Messenians against the Spartans. The strength of its fortifications was long afterwards a subject of admiration. The territory attached to the new city extended southwards to the Messenian gulf, and northwards to the borders of Arcadia, comprising some of the most fertile land in Peloponnesus.

So low had Sparta sunk, that she was fain to send envoys to beg the assistance of the Athenians. This request was acceded to; and shortly afterwards an alliance was formed between the two states, in which Sparta waived all her claims to superiority and headship. During the next two years the Thebans continued steadily to increase their power and influence in Greece, though no great battle was fought. In B.C. 368 Pelopidas conducted a Theban force into Thessaly and Macedonia. In Thessaly he compelled Alexander, who, by the murder of his two brothers, had become despot of Pherae and Tagus of Thessaly, to relinquish his designs against the independence of Larissa and other Thessalian cities, and to solicit peace. In Macedonia he formed an alliance with the regent Ptolemy: and amongst the hostages given for the observance of this treaty was the youthful Philip, son of Amyntas, afterwards the celebrated king of Macedon, who remained for some years at Thebes.

In the following year Pelopidas and Ismenias proceeded on an embassy to Persia. Ever since the peace of Antalcidas the Great King had become the recognised mediator between the states of Greece; and his fiat seemed indispensable to stamp the claims of that city which pretended to the headship. The recent achievements of Thebes might entitle her to aspire to that position: and at all events the alterations which she had produced in the internal state, of Greece, by the establishment of Megalopolis and Messene, seemed to require for their stability the sanction of a Persian rescript. This was obtained without difficulty, as Thebes was now the strongest state in Greece; and it was evidently easier to exercise Persian ascendency there by her means, than through a weaker power. The Persian rescript pronounced the independence of Messene and Amphipolis; the Athenians were directed to lay up their ships of war in ordinary; and Thebes was declared the head of Greece.

It was, in all probability, during a mission undertaken by Pelopidas and Ismonias, for the purpose of procuring the acknowledgment of the rescript in Thessaly and the northern parts of Greece, that they were seized and imprisoned by Alexander of Pherae. The Thebans immediately despatched an army of 8000 hoplites and 600 cavalry to recover or avenge their favourite citizen. Unfortunately, however, they were no longer commanded by Epaminondas. Their present commanders were utterly incompetent. They were beaten and forced to retreat, and the army was in such danger from the active pursuit of the Thessalians and Athenians, that its destruction seemed inevitable. Luckily, however, Epaminondas was serving as a hoplite in the ranks. By the unanimous voice of the troops he was now called to the command, and succeeded in conducting the army safely back to Thebes. Here the unsuccessful Boeotarchs were disgraced; Epaminondas was restored to the command, and placed at the head of a second Theban army destined to attempt the release of Pelopidas. Directed by his superior skill the enterprise proved successful, and Pelopidas (B.C. 367) returned in safety to Thebes.

In B.C. 364 Pelopidas again marched into Thessaly against Alexander of Pherae. Strong complaints of the tyranny of that despot arrived at Thebes, and Pelopidas, who probably also burned to avenge his private wrongs, prevailed upon the Thebans to send him into Thessaly to punish the tyrant. The battle was fought on the hills of Cynoscephalae; the troops of Alexander were routed: and Pelopidas, observing his hated enemy endeavouring to rally them, was seized with such a transport of rage that, regardless of his duties as a general, he rushed impetuously forwards and challenged him to single combat. Alexander shrunk back within the ranks of his guards, followed impetuously by Pelopidas, who was soon slain, fighting with desperate bravery. Although the army of Alexander was defeated with severe loss, the news of the death of Pelopidas deprived the Thebans and their Thessalian allies of all the joy which they would otherwise have felt at their victory.

Meantime a war had been carried on between Elis and Arcadia which had led to disunion among the Arcadians themselves. The Mantineans supported the Eleans, who were also assisted by the Spartans; whilst the rest of the Arcadians, and especially the Tegeans, favoured Thebes. In B.C. 362 Epaminondas marched into

Peloponnesus to support the Theban party in Arcadia, The Spartans sent a powerful force to the assistance of the Mantineans in whose territory the hostile armies met. In the battle which ensued Epaminondas formed his Boeotian troops into a column of extraordinary depth, with which he bore down all before them. The Mantineans and Lacedaemonians turned and fled, and the rest followed their example. The day was won; but Epaminondas, who fought in the foremost ranks, fell pierced with a mortal wound. His fall occasioned such consternation among his troops, that, although the enemy were in full flight, they did not know how to use their advantage, and remained rooted to the spot. Epaminondas was carried off the field with the spear-head still fixed in his breast. Having satisfied himself that his shield was safe, and that the victory was gained, he inquired for Iolaidas and Daiphantus, whom he intended to succeed him in the command. Being informed that both were slain: "Then" he observed "you must make peace." After this he ordered the spear-head to be withdrawn; when the gush of blood which followed soon terminated his life. Thus died this truly great man; and never was there one whose title to that epithet has been less disputed. Antiquity is unanimous in his praise, and some of the first men of Greece subsequently took him for their model. With him the commanding influence of Thebes began and ended. His last advice was adopted, and peace was concluded probably before the Theban army quitted Peloponnesus. Its basis was a recognition of the STATUS QUO--to leave everything as it was, to acknowledge the Arcadian constitution and the independence of Messene. Sparta alone refused to join it on account of the last article, but she was not supported by her allies.

Agesilaus had lived to see the empire of Sparta extinguished by her hated rival. Thus curiously had the prophecy been fulfilled which warned Sparta of the evils awaiting her under a "lame sovereignty." But Agesilaus had not yet abandoned all hope; and he now directed his views towards the east as the quarter from which Spartan power might still be resuscitated. At the age of 80 the indomitable old man proceeded with a force of 1000 hoplites to assist Tachos, king of Egypt, in his revolt against Persia. He died at Cyrene on his return to Greece. His body was embalmed in wax and splendidly buried in Sparta.

CHAPTER XVIII.
HISTORY OF THE SICILIAN GREEKS FROM THE DESTRUCTION OF THE ATHENIAN ARMAMENT TO THE DEATH OF TIMOLEON.

The affairs of the Sicilian Greeks, an important branch of the Hellenic race, deserve a passing notice. A few years after the destruction of the Athenian armament, Dionysius made himself master of Syracuse, and openly seized upon the supreme power (B.C. 405). His reign as tyrant or despot was long and prosperous. After conquering the Carthaginians, who more than once invaded Sicily, he extended his dominion over a great part of the island, and over a considerable portion of Magna Graecia. He raised Syracuse to be one of the chief Grecian states, second in influence, if indeed second, to Sparta alone. Under his sway Syracuse was strengthened and embellished with new fortifications, docks, arsenals, and other public buildings, and became superior even to Athens in extent and population.

Dionysius was a warm patron of literature, and was anxious to gain distinction by his literary compositions. In the midst of his political and military cares he devoted himself assiduously to poetry, and not only caused his poems to be publicly recited at the Olympic games, but repeatedly contended for the prize of tragedy at Athens. In accordance with the same spirit we find him seeking the society of men distinguished in literature and philosophy. Plato, who visited Sicily about the year 389 from a curiosity to see Mount AEtna, was introduced to Dionysius by Dion. The high moral tone of Plato's conversation did not however prove so attractive to Dionysius as it had done to Dion; and the philosopher was not only dismissed with aversion and dislike, but even, it seems through the machinations of Dionysius, seized, bound, and sold for a slave in the island of AEgina. He was, however, repurchased by Anniceris of Cyrene, and sent back to Athens.

Dionysius died in B.C. 367, and was succeeded by his eldest son, commonly called the younger Dionysius, who was about 25 years of age at the time of his father's death. At first he listened to the counsels of Dion, who had always enjoyed the respect and confidence of his father. At the advice of Dion he invited Plato to Syracuse, where the philosopher was received with the greatest honour. His illustrious pupil immediately began to take lessons in geometry; superfluous dishes disappeared from the royal table; and Dionysius even betrayed some symptoms of a wish to mitigate the former rigours of the despotism. But now the old courtiers took the alarm. It was whispered to Dionysius that the whole was a deep-laid scheme on the part of Dion for the purpose of effecting a revolution and placing his own nephews on the throne. [The elder Dionysius had married two wives at the same time: one of these was a Locrian woman named Doris; the other, Aristomache, was a Syracusan, and the sister of Dion. The younger Dionysius was his elder son by Doris; but he also had children by Aristomache.] These accusations had the desired effect on the mind of Dionysius, who shortly afterwards expelled Dion from Sicily. Plato with difficulty obtained permission to return to Greece (B.C. 366). Dionysius now gave way to his vices without restraint, and became an object of contempt to the Syracusans. Dion saw that the time had come for avenging his own wrongs as well as those of his country. Collecting a small force, he sailed to Sicily, and suddenly appeared before the gates of Syracuse during the absence of Dionysius on an expedition to the coasts of Italy. The inhabitants, filled with joy, welcomed Dion as their deliverer: and Dionysius on his return from Italy found himself compelled to quit Syracuse (B.C. 356), leaving Dion undisputed master of the city. The latter was now in a condition to carry out all those exalted notions of political life which he had sought to instil into the mind of Dionysius. He seems to have contemplated some political changes; but his immediate and practical acts were tyrannical, and were rendered still more unpopular by his overbearing manners. His unpopularity continued to increase, till at length one of his bosom friends--the Athenian Callippus--seized the opportunity to mount to power by his murder, and caused him to be assassinated in his own house. This event took place in 353, about three years after the expulsion of the Dionysian dynasty. Callippus contrived to retain the sovereign power only a twelvemonth. A period of anarchy followed, during which Dionysius made himself master of the city by treachery, about B.C. 346. Dionysius, however, was not able to re-establish himself firmly in his former power. Most of the other cities of Sicily had shaken off the yoke of Syracuse, and were governed by petty despots. Meantime the Carthaginians prepared to take advantage of the distracted condition of Sicily. In the extremity of their sufferings, several of the Syracusan exiles appealed for aid to Corinth, their mother-city. The application was granted, and Timoleon was appointed to command an expedition destined for the relief of Syracuse.

Timoleon was distinguished for gentleness as well as for courage, but towards traitors and despots his hatred was intense. He had once saved the life of his elder brother Timophanes in battle at the imminent peril of his own; but when Timophanes, availing himself of his situation as commander of the garrison in the Acrocorinthus, endeavoured to enslave his country, Timoleon did not hesitate to consent to his death. Twice before had Timoleon pleaded with his brother, beseeching him not to destroy the liberties of his country; but when Timophanes turned a deaf ear to those appeals, Timoleon connived at the action of his friends, who put him to death, whilst he himself, bathed in a flood of tears, stood a little way aloof. The great body of the citizens regarded the conduct of Timoleon with love and admiration. In the mind of Timoleon, however, their approving verdict was far more than outweighed by the reproaches and execrations of his mother. For many years nothing could prevail upon him to return to public life. He buried, himself in the country far from the haunts of men, till a chance voice in the Corinthian assembly nominated him as the leader of the expedition against Dionysius.

Roused by the nature of the cause, and the exhortations of his friends, Timoleon accepted the post thus offered to him. His success exceeded his hopes. As soon as he appeared before Syracuse, Dionysius, who appears to have abandoned all hope of ultimate success, surrendered the citadel into his hands, on condition of being allowed to depart in safety to Corinth (B.C. 343). Dionysius passed the remainder of his life at Corinth, where he is said to have displayed some remnants of his former luxury by the fastidious taste which he showed in the choice of his viands, unguents, dress, and furniture; whilst his literary inclinations manifested themselves in teaching the public singers and actors, and in opening a school for boys.

Timoleon also expelled the other tyrants from the Sicilian cities, and gained a great victory over the Carthaginians at the river Crimesus (or Crimissus). He restored a republican constitution to Syracuse; and his first public act was to destroy the impregnable fortifications of the citadel of Ortygia, the stronghold of the elder and the younger Dionysius. All the rewards which Timoleon received for his great services were a house in Syracuse, and some landed property in the neighbourhood of the city. He now sent for his family from Corinth, and became a Syracusan citizen. He continued, however, to retain, though in a private station, the greatest influence in the state. During the latter part of his life, though he was totally deprived of sight, yet, when important affairs were discussed in the assembly, it was customary to send for Timoleon, who was drawn in a car into the middle of the theatre amid the shouts and affectionate greetings of the assembled citizens. When the tumult of his reception had subsided he listened patiently to the debate. The opinion which he pronounced was usually ratified by the vote of the assembly; and he then left the theatre amidst the same cheers which had greeted his arrival. In this happy and honoured condition he breathed his last in B.C. 336, a few years after the battle of Crimesus. He was splendidly interred at the public cost, whilst the tears of the whole Syracusan population followed him to the grave.

CHAPTER XIX.
PHILIP OF MACEDON, B.C. 359-336.

The internal dissensions of Greece produced their natural fruits; and we shall have now to relate the downfall of her independence and her subjugation by a foreign power. This power was Macedonia, an obscure state to the north of Thessaly, hitherto overlooked and despised, and considered as altogether barbarous, and without the pale of Grecian civilization. But though the Macedonians were not Greeks, their sovereigns claimed to be descended from an Hellenic race, namely, that of Temenus of Argos; and it is said that Alexander I. proved his Argive descent previously to contending at the Olympic games. Perdiccas is commonly regarded as the founder of the monarchy; of the history of which, however, little is known till the reign of Amyntas I., his fifth successor, who was contemporary with the Pisistratidae at Athens. Under Amyntas, who submitted to the satrap Megabyzus, Macedonia became subject to Persia, and remained so till after the battle of Plataea. The reigns of the succeeding sovereigns present little that is remarkable, with the exception of that of Archelaus (B.C. 413). This monarch transferred his residence from AEgae to Pella, which thus became the capital. He entertained many literary men at his court, such as Euripides, who ended his days at Pella. Archelaus was assassinated in B.C. 399, and the crown devolved upon Amyntas II., a representative of the ancient line. Amyntas left three sons, the youngest being the celebrated Philip, of whom we have now to speak.

It has been already mentioned that the youthful Philip was one of the hostages delivered to the Thebans as security for the peace effected by Pelopidas. His residence at Thebes gave him some tincture of Grecian philosophy and literature; but the most important lesson which he learned at that city was the art of war, with all the improved tactics introduced by Epaminondas. Philip succeeded to the throne at the age of 23 (B.C. 359), and displayed at the beginning of his reign his extraordinary energy and abilities. After defeating the Illyrians he established a standing army, in which discipline was preserved by the severest punishments. He introduced the far-famed Macedonian phalanx, which was 16 men deep, armed with long projecting spears.

Philip's views were first turned towards the eastern frontiers of his dominions, where his interests clashed with those of the Athenians. A few years before the Athenians had made various unavailing attempts to obtain possession of Amphipolis, once the jewel of their empire, but which they had never recovered since its capture by Brasidas in the eighth year of the Peloponnesian war. Its situation at the mouth of the Strymon rendered it also valuable to Macedonia, not only as a commercial port, but as opening a passage into Thrace. The Olynthians were likewise anxious to enrol Amphipolis as a member of their confederacy, and accordingly proposed to the Athenians to form an alliance for the purpose of defending Amphipolis against their mutual enemy. An alliance between these two powerful states would have proved an insurmountable obstacle to Philip's views: and it was therefore absolutely necessary to prevent this coalition. Here we have the first instance of Philip's skill and duplicity in negotiation. By secretly promising the Athenians that he would put Amphipolis into their hands if they would give him possession of Pydna, he induced them to reject the overtures of the Olynthians; and by ceding to the latter the town of Anthemus, he bought off their opposition. He now laid siege to Amphipolis, which, being thus left unaided, fell into his hands (B.C. 358). He then forthwith marched against Pydna, which surrendered to him; but on the ground that it was not the Athenians who had put him in possession of this town, he refused to give up Amphipolis to them.

Philip had now just reason to dread the enmity of the Athenians, and accordingly it was his policy to court the favour of the Olynthians, and to prevent them from renewing their negotiations with the Athenians. In order to separate them more effectually, he assisted the Olynthians in recovering Potidaea, which had formerly belonged to their confederacy, but was now in the hands of the Athenians. On the capture of the town he handed it over to the Olynthians. Plutarch relates that the capture of Potidaea was accompanied with three other fortunate events in the life of Philip, namely, the prize gained by his chariot at the Olympic games, a victory of his general Parmenio over the Illyrians, and the birth of his son Alexander. These events happened in B.C. 356.

Philip now crossed the Strymon, on the left bank of which lay Pangaeus, a range of mountains abounding in gold-mines. He conquered the district, and founded there a new town called Philippi, on the site of the ancient Thracian town of Crenides. By improved methods of working the mines he made them yield an annual revenue of 1000 talents, nearly 250,000l.

Meanwhile Athens was engaged in a war with her allies, which has been called the SOCIAL WAR; and which was, perhaps, the reason why she was obliged to look quietly on whilst Philip was thus aggrandizing himself at her expense. This war broke out in B.C. 357. The chief causes of it seem to have been the contributions levied upon the allies by the Athenian generals. The war lasted three years; and as Artaxerxes, the Persian king, threatened to support the allies with a fleet of 300 ships, the Athenians were obliged to consent to a disadvantageous peace, which secured the independence of the more important allies (B.C. 355).

Another war, which had been raging during the same time, tended still further to exhaust the Grecian states, and thus pave the way for Philip's progress to the supremacy. This was the SACRED WAR, which broke out between Thebes and Phocis in the same year as the Social War (B.C. 357). An ill-feeling had long subsisted between those two countries. The Thebans now availed themselves of the influence which they possessed in the Amphictyonic council to take vengeance upon the Phocians and accordingly induced this body to impose a heavy fine upon the latter people, because they had cultivated a portion of the Cirrhaean plain, which had been consecrated to the Delphian god, and was to lie waste for ever. The Phocians pleaded that the payment of the fine would ruin them; but instead of listening to their remonstrances, the Amphictyons doubled the amount, and threatened, in case of their continued refusal to reduce them to the condition of serfs. Thus driven to desperation, the Phocians resolved to complete the sacrilege with which they had been branded, by seizing the very temple of Delphi itself. The leader and counsellor of this enterprise was Philomelus, who, with a force of no more than 2000 men, surprised and took Delphi. At first, however, he carefully abstained from touching the sacred treasure; but being hard pressed by the Thebans and their allies, he threw off the scruples which he had hitherto assumed, and announced that the sacred treasures should be converted into a fund for the payment of mercenaries. On the death of Philomelus, who fell in battle, the command was assumed by his brother Onomarchus, who carried on the war with vigour and success. But he was checked in his career by Philip, who had previously been extending his dominion over Thessaly, and who now assumed the character of a champion of the Delphic god, and made his soldiers wear wreaths of laurel plucked in the groves of Tempe. He penetrated into Thessaly, and encountered the Phocians near the gulf of Pagassae. In the battle which ensued, Onomarchus was slain, and his army totally defeated (B.C. 352). This victory made Philip master of Thessaly. He now directed his march southwards with the view of subduing the Phocians; but upon reaching Thermopylae he found the pass guarded by a strong Athenian force, and was compelled, or considered it more prudent, to retreat.

After his return from Thessaly Philip's views were directed towards Thrace and the Chersonese. It was at this juncture that Demosthenes stepped forwards as the proclaimed opponent of Philip, and delivered the first of those celebrated orations which from their subject have been called "the Philippics." This most famous of all the Grecian orators was born in B.C. 382-381. Having lost his father at the early age of seven, his guardians abused their trust, and defrauded him of the greater part of his paternal inheritance. This misfortune, however, proved one of the causes which tended to make him an orator. Demosthenes, as he advanced towards manhood, perceived with indignation the conduct of his guardians, for which he resolved to make them answerable when the proper opportunity should arrive, by accusing them himself. His first attempt to speak in public proved a failure, and he retired from the bema amidst the hootings and laughter of the citizens. The more judicious and candid among his auditors perceived, however, marks of genius in his speech, and rightly attributed his failure to timidity and want of due preparation. Eunomus, an aged citizen, who met him wandering about the Piraeus in a state of dejection at his ill success, bade him take courage and persevere. Demosthenes now withdrew awhile from public life, and devoted himself perseveringly to remedy his defects. They were such as might be lessened, if not removed, by practice, and consisted chiefly of a weak voice, imperfect articulation, and ungraceful and inappropriate action. He derived much assistance from Satyrus the actor, who exercised him in reciting passages from Sophocles and Euripides. He studied the best rhetorical treatises and orations, and is said to have copied the work of Thucydides with his own hand no fewer than eight times. He shut himself up for two or three months together in a subterranean chamber in order to practise composition and declamation. His perseverance was crowned with success; and he who on the first attempt had descended from the bema amid the ridicule of the crowd, became at last the most perfect orator the world has ever seen.

Demosthenes had established himself as a public speaker before the period which we have now reached; but it is chiefly in connexion with Philip that we are to view him as a statesman as well as an orator. Philip had shown his ambition by the conquest of Thessaly, and by the part he had taken in the Sacred War; and Demosthenes now began to regard him as the enemy of the liberties of Athens and of Greece. In his first "Philippic" Demosthenes tried to rouse his countrymen to energetic measures against this formidable enemy; but his warnings and exhortations produced little effect, for the Athenians were no longer distinguished by the same spirit of enterprise which had characterized them in the days of their supremacy. No important step was taken to curb the growing power of Philip; and it was the danger of Olynthus which first induced the Athenians to prosecute the war with a little more energy. In 350 B.C., Philip having captured a town in Chalcidice, Olynthus began to tremble for her own safety, and sent envoys to Athens to crave assistance. Olynthus was still at the head of thirty-two Greek towns, and the confederacy was a sort of counterpoise to the power of Philip. It was on this occasion that Demosthenes delivered his three Olynthaic orations, in which he warmly advocated an alliance with Olynthus.

Demosthenes was opposed by a strong party, with which Phocion commonly acted. Phocion is one of the most singular and original characters in Grecian history. He viewed the multitude and their affairs with a scorn which he was at no pains to disguise; receiving their anger with indifference, and their praises with contempt. His known probity also gave him weight with the assembly. He was the only statesman of whom Demosthenes stood in awe; who was accustomed to say, when Phocion rose, "Here comes the pruner of my periods." But Phocion's desponding views, and his mistrust of the Athenian people, made him an ill statesman at a period which demanded the most active patriotism. He doubtless injured his country by contributing to check the more enlarged and patriotic views of Demosthenes; and though his own conduct was pure and disinterested, he unintentionally threw his weight on the side of those who, like Demades and others, were actuated by the basest motives. This division of opinion rendered the operations of the Athenians for the aid of the Olynthians languid and desultory. Town after town of the confederacy fell before Philip; and in 347 Olynthus itself was taken. The whole of the Chalcidian peninsula thus became a Macedonian province.

The prospects of Athens now became alarming, her possessions in the Chersonese were threatened, as well as the freedom of the Greek towns upon the Hellespont. The Athenians had supported the Phocians in the Sacred War, and were thus at war with Thebes. In order to resist Philip the attention of the Athenians was now directed towards a reconciliation with Thebes, especially since the treasures of Delphi were nearly exhausted, and on the other hand the war was becoming every year more and more burthensome to the Thebans. Nor did it seem improbable that a peace might be concluded not only between those two cities, but among the Grecian states generally. It seems to have been this aspect of affairs that induced Philip to make several indirect overtures to the Athenians in the summer of B.C. 347. In spite of subsidies from Delphi the war had been very onerous to them, and they received these advances with joy, and eventually agreed to the terms of a peace. Having thus gained over the Athenians, Philip marched through Thermopylae, and entered Phocis, which surrendered unconditionally at his approach. He then occupied Delphi, where he assembled the Amphictyons to pronounce sentence upon those who bad been concerned in the sacrilege committed there. The council decreed that all the cities of Phocia, except Abae, should be destroyed, and their inhabitants scattered into villages containing not more than fifty houses each. Sparta was deprived of her share in the Amphictyonic privileges; the two votes in the council possessed by the Phocians were transferred to the kings of Macedonia; and Philip was to share with the Thebans and Thessalians the honour of presiding at the Pythian games (B.C. 346).

The result of the Sacred War rendered Macedon the leading state in Greece. Philip at once acquired by it military glory, a reputation for piety, and an accession of power. His ambitious designs were now too plain to be mistaken. The eyes of the blindest among the Athenians were at last opened; the promoters of the peace which had been concluded with Philip incurred the hatred and suspicion of the people; whilst on the other hand Demosthenes rose higher than ever in public favour.

Philip was now busy with preparations for the vast projects which he contemplated, and which embraced an attack upon the Athenian colonies, as well as upon the Persian empire. For this purpose he had organized a considerable naval force as well as an army; and in the spring of 342 B.C. he set out on an expedition against Thrace. His progress soon appeared to menace the Chersonese and the Athenian possessions in that quarter; and at length the Athenian troops under Diopithes came into actual collision with the Macedonians. In the following year Philip began to attack the Greek cities north of the Hellespont. He first besieged and captured Selymbria on the Propontis, and then turned his arms against Perinthus and Byzantium. This roused the Athenians to more vigorous action. War was formally declared against Philip, and a fleet equipped for the immediate relief of Byzantium. Philip was forced to raise the siege not only of that town but of Perinthus also, and finally to evacuate the Chersonesus altogether. For these acceptable services the grateful Byzantians erected a colossal statue in honour of Athens.

After this check Philip undertook an expedition against the Thracians; but meantime his partisans procured for him an opportunity of marching again into the very heart of Greece.

Amphissa, a Locrian town, having been declared by the Amphictyonic council guilty of sacrilege, Philip was appointed by the council as their general to inflict punishment on the inhabitants of the guilty town. Accordingly he marched southwards early in B.C. 338; but instead of proceeding in the direction of Amphissa, he suddenly seized Elatea, the chief town in the eastern part of Phocis, thus showing clearly enough that his real design was against Boeotia and Attica. Intelligence of this event reached Athens at night, and caused extraordinary alarm, In the following morning Demosthenes pressed upon the assembly the necessity for making the most vigorous preparations for defence, and especially recommended them to send an embassy to Thebes, in order to persuade the Thebans to unite with them against the common enemy.

The details of the war that followed are exceedingly obscure. Philip appears to have again opened negotiations with the Thebans, which failed; and we then find the combined Theban and Athenian armies marching out to meet the Macedonians.

The decisive battle was fought on the 7th of August, in the plain of Chaeronea in Boeotia, near the frontier of Phocis (B.C. 338). In the Macedonian army was Philip's son, the youthful Alexander, who was intrusted with the command of one of the wings; and it was a charge made by him on the Theban sacred band that decided the fortune of the day. The sacred band was cut to pieces, without flinching from the ground which it occupied, and the remainder of the combined army was completely routed. Demosthenes, who was serving as a foot-soldier in the Athenian ranks, has been absurdly reproached with cowardice because he participated in the general flight.

The battle of Chaeronea crushed the liberties of Greece, and made it in reality a province of the Macedonian monarchy. To Athens herself the blow was almost as fatal as that of AEgospotami. But the manner in which Philip used his victory excited universal surprise. He dismissed the Athenian prisoners without ransom, and voluntarily offered a peace on terms more advantageous than the Athenians themselves would have ventured to propose. Philip, indeed, seems to have regarded Athens with a sort of love and respect, as the centre of art and refinement, for his treatment of the Thebans was very different, and marked by great harshness and severity. They were compelled to recall their exiles, in whose hands the government was placed, whilst a Macedonian garrison was established in the Cadmea.

A congress of the Grecian states was now summoned at Corinth, in which war was declared against Persia, and Philip was appointed generalissimo of the expedition.

In the spring of B.C. 336 Philip sent some forces into Asia, under the command of Attalus, Parmenio, and Amyntas, which were designed to engage the Greek cities of Asia in the expedition. But before quitting Macedonia, Philip determined to provide for the safety of his dominions by celebrating the marriage of his daughter with Alexander of Epirus. It was solemnized at AEgae, the ancient capital of Macedonia, with much pomp, including banquets, and musical and theatrical entertainments. The day after the nuptials was dedicated to theatrical entertainments. The festival was opened with a procession of the images of the twelve Olympian deities, with which was associated that of Philip himself. The monarch took part in the procession, dressed in white robes, and crowned with a chaplet. Whilst thus proceeding through the city, a youth suddenly rushed out of the crowd, and, drawing a long sword which he had concealed under his clothes, plunged it into Philip's side, who fell dead upon the spot. The assassin was pursued by some of the royal guards, and, having stumbled in his flight, was despatched before he could reach the place where horses had been provided for his escape. His name was Pausanias. He was a youth of noble birth, and we are told that his motive for taking Philip's life was that the king had refused to punish an outrage which Attalus had committed against him.

Thus fell Philip of Macedon in the twenty-fourth year of his reign and forty-seventh of his age (B.C. 336). When we reflect upon his achievements, and how, partly by policy and partly by arms, he converted his originally poor and distracted kingdom into the mistress of Greece, we must acknowledge him to have been an extraordinary, if not a great man, in the better sense of that term. His views and his ambition were certainly as large as those of his son Alexander, but he was prevented by a premature death from carrying them out; nor would Alexander himself have been able to perform his great achievements had not Philip handed down to him all the means and instruments which they required.

CHAPTER XX.
ALEXANDER THE GREAT, B.C. 336-323.

Alexander, at the time of his father's death, was in his twentieth year, having been born in B.C. 356. His early education was entrusted to Leonidas, a kinsman of his mother, a man of severe and parsimonious character, who trained him with Spartan simplicity and hardihood; whilst Lysimachus, a sort of under-governor, early inspired the young prince with ambitious notions, by teaching him to love and emulate the heroes of the Iliad. According to the traditions of his family, the blood of Achilles actually ran in the veins of Alexander; [His mother Olympias was the daughter of Neoptolemus, king of Epirus who claimed descent from Pyrrhus, the son of Achilles.] and Lysimachus nourished the feeling which that circumstance was calculated to awaken by giving him the name of that hero, whilst he called Philip Peleus, and himself Phoenix. But the most striking feature in Alexander's education was, that he had Aristotle for his teacher, and that thus the greatest conqueror of the material world received the instructions of him who has exercised the most extensive empire over the human intellect. It was probably at about the age of thirteen that he first received the lessons of Aristotle, and they can hardly have continued more than three years, for Alexander soon left the schools for the employments of active life. At the age of sixteen we find him regent of Macedonia during Philip's absence; and at eighteen we have seen him filling a prominent military post at the battle of Chaeronea.

On succeeding to the throne Alexander announced his intention of prosecuting his father's expedition into Asia; but it was first necessary for him to settle the affairs of Greece, where the news of Philip's assassination, and the accession of so young a prince, had excited in several states a hope of shaking off the Macedonian yoke. Athens was the centre of these movements. Demosthenes, although in mourning for the recent loss of an only daughter, now came abroad dressed in white, and crowned with a chaplet, in which attire he was seen sacrificing at one of the public altars. He also moved a decree that Philip's death should be celebrated by a public thanksgiving, and that religious honours should be paid to the memory of Pausanias. At the same time he made vigorous preparations for action. He despatched envoys to the principal Grecian states for the purpose of inciting them against Macedon. Sparta, and the whole Peloponnesus, with the exception of Megalopolis and Messenia, seemed inclined to shake off their compulsory alliance. Even the Thebans rose against the dominant oligarchy, although the Cadmea was in the hands of the Macedonians.

The activity of Alexander disconcerted all these movements. Having marched through Thessaly, he assembled the Amphictyonic council at Thermopylae, who conferred upon him the command with which they had invested his father during the Sacred War. He then advanced rapidly upon Thebes, and thus prevented the meditated revolution, The Athenians sent ambassadors to deprecate his wrath, who were graciously accepted. He then convened a general congress at Corinth, where he was appointed generalissimo for the Persian war in place of his father. Most of the philosophers and persons of note near Corinth came to congratulate him on this occasion; but Diognes of Sinope who was then living in one of the suburbs of Corinth, did not make his appearance. Alexander therefore resolved to pay a visit to the eccentric cynic, whom he found basking in the sun. On the approach of Alexander with a numerous retinue, Diogenes raised himself up a little, and the monarch affably inquired how he could serve him? "By standing out of my sunshine," replied the churlish philosopher. Alexander was stung with surprise at a behaviour to which he was so little accustomed; but whilst his courtiers were ridiculing the manners of the cynic, he turned to them and said, "Were I not Alexander, I should like to be Diogenes."

The result of the Congress might be considered a settlement of the affairs of Greece. Alexander then returned to Macedonia in the hope of being able to begin his Persian expedition in the spring of B.C. 335; but reports of disturbances among the Thracians and Triballians diverted his attention to that quarter. He therefore crossed Mount Haemus (the Balkan) and marched into the territory of the Triballians, defeated their forces, and pursued them to the Danube, which he crossed.

After acquiring a large booty he regained the banks of the Danube, and thence marched against the Illyrians and Taulantians, whom he speedily reduced to obedience.

During Alexander's absence on these expeditions no tidings were heard of him for a considerable time, and a report of his death was industriously spread in Southern Greece. The Thebans rose and besieged the Macedonian garrison in the Cadmea, at the same time inviting other states to declare their independence. Demosthenes was active in aiding the movement. He persuaded the Athenians to furnish the Thebans with subsidies and to assure them of their support and alliance. But the rapidity of Alexander again crushed the insurrection in the bud. Before the Thebans discovered that the report of his death was false he had already arrived at Onchestus in Boeotia. Alexander was willing to afford them an opportunity for repentance, and marched slowly to the foot of the Cadmea. But the leaders of the insurrection, believing themselves irretrievably compromised, replied with taunts to Alexander's proposals for peace, and excited the people to the most desperate resistance. An engagement was prematurely brought on by one of the generals of Alexander, in which some of the Macedonian troops were put to the rout; but Alexander, coming up with the phalanx, whilst the Thebans were in the disorder of pursuit, drove them back in turn and entered the gates along with them, when a fearful massacre ensued committed principally by the Thracians in Alexander's service. Six thousand Thebans are said to have been slain, and thirty thousand were made prisoners. The doom of the conquered city was referred to the allies, who decreed her destruction. The grounds of the verdict bear the impress of a tyrannical hypocrisy. They rested on the conduct of the Thebans during the Persian war, on their treatment of Plataea, and on their enmity to Athens. The inhabitants were sold as slaves, and all the houses, except that of Pindar, were levelled with the ground. The Cadmea was preserved to be occupied by a Macedonian garrison. Thebes seems to have been thus harshly treated as an example to the rest of Greece, for towards the other states, which were now eager to make their excuses and submission, Alexander showed much forbearance and lenity. The conduct of the Athenians exhibits them deeply sunk in degradation. When they heard of the chastisement indicted upon Thebes, they immediately voted, on the motion of Demosthenes, that ambassadors should be sent to congratulate Alexander on his safe return from his northern expeditions, and on his recent success. Alexander in reply wrote a letter, demanding that eight or ten of the leading Athenian orators should be delivered up to him. At the head of the list was Demosthenes. In this dilemma, Phocion, who did not wish to speak upon such a question, was loudly called upon by the people for his opinion; when he rose and said that the persons whom Alexander demanded had brought the state into such a miserable plight that they deserved to be surrendered, and that for his own part he should be very happy to die for the commonwealth. At the same time he advised them to try the effect of intercession with Alexander; and it was at last only by his own personal application to that monarch with whom he was a great favourite, that the orators were spared. According to another account, however, the wrath of Alexander was appeased by the orator Demades, who received from the Athenians a reward of five talents for his services. It was at this time that Alexander is said to have sent a present of 100 talents to Phocion. But Phocion asked the persons who brought the money--"Why he should be selected for such a bounty?" "Because," they replied, "Alexander considers you the only just and honest man." "Then," said Phocion, "let him suffer me to be what I seem, and to retain that character." And when the envoys went to his house and beheld the frugality with which he lived, they perceived that the man who refused such a gift was wealthier than he who offered it.

Having thus put the affairs of Greece on a satisfactory footing, Alexander marched for the Hellespont in the spring of B.C. 334, leaving Antipater regent of Macedonia in his absence, with a force of 12,000 foot and 1500 horse. Alexander's own army consisted of only about 50,000 foot and 5000 horse. Of the infantry about 12,000 were Macedonians, and these composed the pith of the celebrated Macedonian phalanx. Such was the force with which he proposed to attack the immense but ill-cemented empire of Persia, which, like the empires of Turkey or Austria in modern times, consisted of various nations and races with different religions and manners, and speaking different languages; the only bond of union being the dominant military power of the ruling nation, which itself formed only a small numerical portion of the empire. The remote provinces, like those of Asia Minor, were administered by satraps and military governors who enjoyed an almost independent authority. Before Alexander departed he distributed most of the crown property among his friends, and when Perdiccas asked him what he had reserved for himself he replied, "My hopes."

A march of sixteen days brought Alexander to Sestos, where a large fleet and a number of transports had been collected for the embarkation of his army. He steered with his own hand the vessel in which he sailed towards the very spot where the Achaeans were said to have landed when proceeding to the Trojan war. He was, as we have said, a great admirer of Homer, a copy of whose works he always carried with him; and on landing on the Asiatic coast he made it his first business to visit the plain of Troy. He then proceeded to Sigeum, where he crowned with a garland the pillar said to mark the tumulus of his mythical ancestor Achilles, and, according to custom, ran round it naked with his friends.

Alexander then marched northwards along the coast of the Propontis. The satraps of Lydia and Ionia, together with other Persian generals, were encamped on the river Granicus, with a force of 20,000 Greek mercenaries, and about an equal number of native cavalry, with which they prepared to dispute the passage of the river. A Rhodian, named Memnon, had the chief command. The veteran general Parmenio advised Alexander to delay the attack till the following morning; to which he replied, that it would be a bad omen at the beginning of his expedition, if, after passing the Hellespont, he should be stopped by a paltry stream. Thereupon he directed his cavalry to cross the river, and followed himself at the head of the phalanx. The passage, however, was by no means easy. The stream was in many parts so deep as to be hardly fordable, and the opposite bank was steep and rugged. The cavalry had great difficulty in maintaining their ground till Alexander came up to their relief. He immediately charged into the thickest of the fray, and exposed himself so much that his life was often in imminent danger, and on one occasion was saved only by the interposition of his friend Clitus. Having routed the Persians, he next attacked the Greek mercenaries, 2000 of whom were made prisoners, and the rest nearly all cut to pieces, In this engagement he killed two Persian officers with his own hand.

Alexander now marched southwards towards Sardis, which surrendered before he came within sight of its walls. Having left a garrison in that city, he arrived after a four days' march before Ephesus, which likewise capitulated on his approach. Magnesia, Tralles, and Miletus next fell into his hands, the last after a short siege. Halicarnassus made more resistance. It was obliged to be regularly approached;

but at length Memnon, finding it no longer tenable, set fire to it in the night, and crossed over to Cos. Alexander caused it to be razed to the ground, and pursued his march along the southern coast of Asia Minor, with the view of seizing those towns which might afford shelter to a Persian fleet. The winter was now approaching, and Alexander sent a considerable part of his army under Parmenio into winter-quarters at Sardis. He also sent back to Macedonia such officers and soldiers as had been recently married, on condition that they should return in the spring with what reinforcements they could raise; and with the same view he despatched an officer to recruit in the Peloponnesus. Meanwhile he himself with a chosen body proceeded along the coasts of Lycia and Pamphylia, having instructed Parmenio to rejoin him in Phrygia in the spring, with the main body. After he had crossed the Xanthus most of the Lycian towns tendered their submission. On the borders of Lycia and Pamphylia, Mount Climax, a branch of the Taurus range, runs abruptly into the sea, leaving only a narrow passage at its foot, which is frequently overflowed. This was the case at the time of Alexander's approach. He therefore sent his main body by a long and difficult road across the mountains to Perge; but he himself who loved danger for its own sake, proceeded with a chosen band along the shore, wading through water that was breast-high for nearly a whole day. Then forcing his way northwards through the barbarous tribes which inhabited the mountains of Pisidia, he encamped in the neighbourhood of Gordium in Phrygia. Here he was rejoined by Parmenio and by the new levies from Greece. Gordium had been the capital of the early Phrygian kings, and in it was preserved with superstitious veneration the chariot or waggon in which the celebrated Midas, the son of Gordius, together with his parents, had entered the town, and in conformity with an oracle had been elevated to the monarchy. An ancient prophecy promised the sovereignty of Asia to him who should untie the knot of bark which fastened the yoke of the waggon to the pole. Alexander repaired to the Acropolis, where the waggon was preserved, to attempt this adventure. Whether he undid the knot by drawing out a peg, or cut it through with his sword, is a matter of doubt; but that he had fulfilled the prediction was placed beyond dispute that very night by a great storm of thunder and lightning.

In the spring of 333 Alexander pursued his march eastwards, and on arriving at Ancyra received the submission of the Paphlagonians. He then advanced through

Cappadocia without resistance; and forcing his way through the passes of Mount Taurus (the PYLAE CILICIAE), he descended into the plains of Cilicia. Hence he pushed on rapidly to Tarsus, which he found abandoned by the enemy. Whilst still heated with the march Alexander plunged into the clear but cold stream of the Cydnus, which runs by the town. The result was a fever, which soon became so violent as to threaten his life. An Acarnanian physician, named Philip, who accompanied him, prescribed a remedy; but at the same time Alexander received a letter informing him that Philip had been bribed by Darius, the Persian king, to poison him. He had however, too much confidence in the trusty Philip to believe the accusation and handed him the letter whilst he drank the draught. Either the medicine, or Alexander's youthful constitution, at length triumphed over the disorder. After remaining some time at Tarsus, he continued his march along the coast to Mallus, where he first received certain tidings of the great Persian army, commanded by Darius in person. It is said to have consisted of 600,000 fighting men, besides all that train of attendants which usually accompanied the march of a Persian monarch. Alexander found Darius encamped near Issus on the right bank of the little river Pinarus. The Persian king could hardly have been caught in a more unfavourable position, since the narrow and rugged plain between Mount Amanus and the sea afforded no scope for the evolutions of large bodies, and thus entirely deprived him of the advantage of his numerical superiority. Alexander occupied the pass between Syria and Cilicia at midnight, and at daybreak began to descend into the plain of the Pinarus, ordering his troops to deploy into line as the ground expanded and thus to arrive in battle-array before the Persians. Darius had thrown 30,000 cavalry and 20,000 infantry across the river, to check the advance of the Macedonians; whilst on the right bank were drawn up his choicest Persian troops to the number of 60,000, together with 30,000 Greek mercenaries, who formed the centre, and on whom he chiefly relied. These, it appears, were all that the breadth of the plain allowed to be drawn up in line. The remainder of the vast host were posted in separate bodies in the farther parts of the plain, and were unable to take any share in the combat. Darius placed himself in the centre of the line in a magnificent state chariot. The banks of the Pinarus were in many parts steep, and where they were level Darius had caused them to be intrenched. As Alexander advanced, the Persian cavalry which had been thrown across the river were recalled; but the 20,000 infantry had been driven into the mountains, where Alexander held them in check with a small body of horse. The left wing of the Macedonians, under the command of Parmenio, was ordered to keep near the sea, to prevent being outflanked. The right wing was led by Alexander in person, who rushed impetuously into the water, and was soon engaged in close combat with the Persians. The latter were immediately routed; but what chiefly decided the fortune of the day was the timidity of Darius himself, who, on beholding the defeat of his left wing, immediately took to flight. His example was followed by his whole army. One hundred thousand Persians are said to have been left upon the field. On reaching the hills Darius threw aside his royal robes his bow and shield, and, mounting a fleet courser, was soon out of reach of pursuit. The Persian camp became the spoil of the Macedonians; but the tent of Darius, together with his chariot, robes, and arms, was reserved for Alexander himself. It was now that the Macedonian king first had ocular proof of the nature of Eastern royalty. One compartment of the tent of Darius had been fitted up as a bath, which steamed with the richest odours; whilst another presented a magnificent pavilion, containing a table richly spread for the banquet of Darius. But from an adjoining tent issued the wail of female voices, where Sisygambis the mother, and Statira the wife of Darius, were lamenting the supposed death of the Persian monarch. Alexander sent to assure them of his safety, and ordered them to be treated with the most delicate and respectful attention.

Such was the memorable battle of Issus, fought in November, B.C. 333. A large treasure which Parmenio was sent forward with a detachment to seize, fell into the hands of the Macedonians at Damascus. Another favourable result of the victory was that it suppressed some attempts at revolt from the Macedonian power, which with the support of Persia, had been manifested in Greece. But, in order to put a complete stop to all such intrigues, which chiefly depended on the assistance of a Persian fleet, Alexander resolved to seize Phoenicia and Egypt, and thus to strike at the root of the Persian maritime power.

Meanwhile, Darius, attended by a body of only 4000 fugitives, had crossed the Euphrates at Thapsacus. Before he had set out from Babylon the whole forces of the empire had been summoned; but he had not thought it worth while to wait for what he deemed a merely useless encumbrance; and the more distant levies, which comprised some of the best troops of the empire, were still hastening towards Babylon. In a short time, therefore, he would be at the head of a still more numerous host than that which had fought at Issus; yet he thought it safer to open negotiations with Alexander than to trust to the chance of arms. With this view he sent a letter to Alexander, who was now at Marathus in Phoenicia, proposing to become his friend and ally; but Alexander rejected all his overtures, and told him that he must in future be addressed not in the language of an equal, but of a subject.

As Alexander advanced southwards, all the towns of Phoenicia hastened to open their gates; the inhabitants of Sidon even hailed him as their deliverer. Tyre, also, sent to tender her submission; but coupled with reservations by no means acceptable to a youthful conqueror in the full tide of success. Alexander affected to receive their offer as an unconditional surrender, and told them that he would visit their city and offer sacrifices to Melcart, a Tyrian deity, who was considered as identical with the Grecian Hercules. This brought the matter to an issue. The Tyrians now informed him that they could not admit any foreigners within their walls, and that, if he wished to sacrifice to Melcart, he would find another and more ancient shrine in Old Tyre, on the mainland. Alexander indignantly dismissed the Tyrian ambassadors, and announced his intention of laying siege to their city. The Tyrians probably deemed it impregnable. It was by nature a place of great strength, and had been rendered still stronger by art. The island on which it stood was half a mile distant from the mainland; and though the channel was shallow near the coast, it deepened to three fathoms near the island. The shores of the island were rocky and precipitous, and the walls rose from the cliffs to the height of 150 feet in solid masonry. As Alexander possessed no ships, the only method by which he could approach the town was by constructing a causeway, the materials for which were collected from the forests of Libanus and the ruins of Old Tyre. After overcoming many difficulties the mole was at length pushed to the foot of the walls; and as soon as Alexander had effected a practicable breach, he ordered a general assault both by land and sea. The breach was stormed under the immediate inspection of Alexander himself; and though the Tyrians made a desperate resistance, they were at length overpowered, when the city became one wide scene of indiscriminate carnage and plunder. The siege had lasted seven months, and the Macedonians were so exasperated by the difficulties and dangers they had undergone that they granted no quarter. Eight thousand of the citizens are said to have been massacred; and the remainder, with the exception of the king and some of the principal men, who had taken refuge in the temple of Melcart, were sold into slavery to the number of 30,000. Tyre was taken in the month of July in 332.

Whilst Alexander was engaged in the siege of Tyre, Darius made him further and more advantageous proposals. He now offered 10,000 talents as the ransom of his family, together with all the Provinces west of the Euphrates, and his daughter Barsine in marriage, as the conditions of a peace. When these offers were submitted to the council Parmenio was not unnaturally struck with their magnificence, and observed, that were he Alexander he would accept them. "And so would I," replied the king, "were I Parmenio." Darius, therefore, prepared himself for a desperate resistance.

After the fall of Tyre, Alexander marched with his army towards Egypt, whilst his fleet proceeded along the coast. Gaza, a strong fortress on the sea-shore, obstinately held out, and delayed his progress three or four months. After the capture of this city Alexander met his fleet at Pelusium, and ordered it to sail up the Nile as far as Memphis, whither he himself marched with his army across the desert. He conciliated the affection of the Egyptians by the respect with which he treated their national superstitions, whilst the Persians by an opposite line of conduct had incurred their deadliest hatred. He then sailed down the western branch of the Nile, and at its mouth traced the plan of the new city of Alexandria, which for many centuries continued to be not only the grand emporium of Europe, Africa, and India, but also the principal centre of intellectual life. Being now on the confines of Libya, Alexander resolved to visit the celebrated oracle of Zeus (Jupiter) Ammon, which lay in the bosom of the Libyan wilderness. The conqueror was received by the priests with all the honours of sacred pomp. He consulted the oracle in secret, and is said never to have disclosed the answer which he received; though that it was an answer that contented him appeared from the magnificence of the offerings which he made to the god. Some say that Ammon saluted him as the son of Zeus.

Alexander returned to Phoenicia in the spring of 331. He then directed his march through Samaria, and arrived at Thapsacus on the Euphrates about the end of August. After crossing the river he struck to the north-east through a fertile and well-supplied country. On his march he was told that Darius was posted with an immense force on the left bank of the Tigris; but on arriving at that river he found nobody to dispute his passage. He then proceeded southwards along its banks, and after four days' march fell in with a few squadrons of the enemy's cavalry. From some of these who were made prisoners Alexander learned that Darius was encamped with his host on one of the extensive plains between the Tigris and the mountains of Kurdistan, near a village called Gaugamela (the Camel's House). The town of Arbela, after which the battle that ensued is commonly named, lay at about twenty miles distance, and there Darius had deposited his baggage and treasure. That monarch had been easily persuaded that his former defeat was owing solely to the nature of the ground; and, therefore, he now selected a wide plain for an engagement, where there was abundant room for his multitudinous infantry, and for the evolutions of his horsemen and charioteers. Alexander, after giving his army a few days' rest, set out to meet the enemy soon after midnight, in order that he might come up with them about daybreak. On ascending some sand-hills the whole array of the Persians suddenly burst upon the view of the Macedonians, at the distance of three or four miles. Darius, as usual, occupied the centre, surrounded by his body-guard and chosen troops. In front of the royal position were ranged the war-chariots and elephants, and on either side the Greek mercenaries, to the number, it is said, of 50,000. Alexander spent the first day in surveying the ground and preparing for the attack; he also addressed his troops, pointing out to them that the prize of victory would not be a mere province, but the dominion of all Asia. Yet so great was the tranquillity with which he contemplated the result, that at daybreak on the following morning, when the officers came to receive his final instructions, they found him in a deep slumber. His army, which consisted only of 40,000 foot and 7000 horse, was drawn up in the order which he usually observed, namely, with the phalanx in the centre in six divisions, and the Macedonian cavalry on the right, where Alexander himself took his station. The Persians, fearful of being surprised, had stood under arms the whole night, so that the morning found them exhausted and dispirited. Some of them, however, fought with considerable bravery; but when Alexander had succeeded in breaking their line by an impetuous charge, Darius mounted a fleet horse and took to flight, as at Issus, though the fortune of the day was yet far from having been decided. At length, however, the rout became general. Whilst daylight lasted Alexander pursued the flying enemy as far as the banks of the Lycus, or Greater Zab, where thousands of the Persians perished in the attempt to pass the river. After resting his men a few hours Alexander continued the pursuit at midnight in the hope of overtaking Darius at Arbela. The Persian monarch, however, had continued his flight without stopping; but the whole of the royal baggage and treasure was captured.

Finding any further pursuit of Darius hopeless, Alexander now directed his march towards Babylon. At a little distance from the city the greater part of the population came out to meet him, headed by their priests and magistrates, tendering their submission and bearing with them magnificent presents. Alexander then made his triumphant entry into Babylon, riding in a chariot at the head of his army. The streets were strewed with flowers, incense smoked on either hand on silver altars, and the priests celebrated his entry with hymns. Nor was this a mere display of a compulsory obedience. Under the Persian sway the Chaldaean religion had been oppressed and persecuted; the temple of Belus had been destroyed and still lay in ruins; and both priests and people consequently rejoiced at the downfall of a dynasty from which they had suffered so much wrong. Alexander observed here the same politic conduct which he had adopted in Egypt. He caused the ruined temples to be restored, and proposed to offer personally, but under the direction of the priests, a sacrifice to Belus. Alexander contemplated making Babylon the capital of his future empire. His army was rewarded with a large donative from the Persian treasury; and after being allowed to indulge for some time in the luxury of Babylon, was again put in motion, towards the middle of November, for Susa. It was there that the Persian treasures were chiefly accumulated, and Alexander had despatched one of his generals to take possession of the city immediately after the battle of Arbela. It was surrendered without a blow by the satrap Abulites. The treasure found there amounted to 40,000 talents in gold and silver bullion, and 9000 in gold Darics. But among all these riches the interest of the Greeks must have been excited in a lively manner by the discovery of the spoils carried off from Greece by Xerxes. Among them were the bronze statues of Harmodius and Aristogiton, which Alexander now sent back to Athens, and which were long afterwards preserved in the Ceramicus.

At Susa Alexander received reinforcements of about 15,000 men from Greece. He then directed his march south-eastwards towards Persepolis. His road lay through the mountainous territory of the Uxians, who refused him a passage unless he paid the usual tribute which they were in the habit of extorting even from the Persian kings. But Alexander routed them with great slaughter. He then advanced rapidly to Persepolis, whose magnificent ruins still attest its ancient splendour. It was the real capital of the Persian kings, though they generally resided at Susa during the winter, and at Ecbatana in summer. The treasure found there exceeded that both of Babylon and Susa, and is said to have amounted to 120,000 talents or nearly 30,000,000l. sterling. It was here that Alexander is related to have committed an act of senseless folly, by firing with his own hand the ancient and magnificent palace of the Persian kings; of which the most charitable version is that he committed the act when heated with wine at the instigation of Thais, an Athenian courtezan. By some writers, however, the story is altogether disbelieved, and the real destruction of Persepolis referred to the Mahommedan epoch. Whilst at Persepolis, Alexander visited the tomb of Cyrus, the founder of the Persian monarchy, which was situated at a little distance, at a city called Pasargadae.

Thus in between three and four years after crossing the Hellespont Alexander had established himself on the Persian throne. But Darius was not yet in his power. After the battle of Arbela that monarch had fled to Ecbatana. It was not till about four months after the battle of Arbela, and consequently early in 330, that Alexander quitted Persepolis to resume the pursuit of Darius. On approaching Ecbatana he learned that the Persian monarch had already fled with the little army which still adhered to him. Alexander, with his main body, then pursued Darius through Media by forced marches and reached Rhagae, a distance of three hundred miles from Ecbatana, in eleven days. Such was the rapidity of the march that many men and horses died of fatigue. At Rhagae he heard that Darius had already passed the defile called the "Caspian Gates," leading into the Bactrian provinces; and, as that pass was fifty miles distant, urgent pursuit was evidently useless. He therefore allowed his troops five days' rest, and then resumed his march. Soon after passing the Gates he learned that Darius had been seized and loaded with chains by his own satrap Bessus, who entertained the design of establishing himself in Bactria as an independent sovereign. This intelligence stimulated Alexander to make still further haste with part of his cavalry and a chosen body of foot. On the fourth day he succeeded in overtaking the fugitives with his cavalry, having been obliged to leave the infantry behind, with directions to follow more at leisure. The enemy, who did not know his real strength, were struck with consternation at his appearance, and fled precipitately. Bessus and his adherents now endeavoured to persuade Darius to fly with them, and provided a fleet horse for that purpose. But the Persian monarch, who had already experienced the generosity of Alexander in the treatment of his captive family, preferred to fall into his hands, whereupon the conspirators mortally wounded him in the chariot in which they kept him confined, and then took to flight. Darius expired before Alexander could come up, who threw his own cloak over the body. He then ordered him to be magnificently buried in the tomb of his ancestors, and provided for the fitting education of his children.

The next three years were employed by Alexander in subduing Hyrcania, Drangiana, Bactria, and Sogdiana, and the other northern provinces of the Persian empire. In these distant regions he founded several cities, one of which in Aria, called after him (Alexandria Ariorum), is still, under the name of HERAT, one of the chief cities in central Asia. Alexander's stay in Prophthasia, the capital of Drangiana, was signalized by a supposed conspiracy against his life, formed by Philotas, the son of Parmenio. Alexander had long entertained suspicions of Philotas. But the immediate subject of accusation against him was that he had not revealed a conspiracy which was reported to be forming against Alexander's life, and which he had deemed too contemptible to notice. He was consequently suspected of being implicated in it; and on being put to the torture he not only confessed his own guilt in his agonies, but also implicated his father. Philotas was executed, and an order was sent to Ecbatana, where Parmenio then was, directing that veteran general to be put to death. A letter, purporting to be from his son, was handed to him; and whilst the old man was engaged in reading it, Polydamus, his intimate friend, together with some others of Alexander's principal officers, fell upon and slew him. His head was carried to Alexander.

Meantime Bessus had assumed the royal dignity in Bactria; but upon Alexander's approach he fled across the Oxus into Sogdiana. Early in the summer of 329 Alexander followed him across the Oxus; and shortly afterwards Bessus was betrayed by two of his own officers into the hands of Alexander. Bessus was carried to Zariaspa, the capital of Bactria, where he was brought before a Persian court, and put to death in a cruel and barbarous manner.

Alexander even crossed the river Jaxartes (SIR), and defeated the Scythians.

Sogdiana alone of the northern provinces offered any serious resistance to his arms. Accordingly in 328 he again crossed the Oxus. He divided his army into five bodies, ordering them to scour the country in different directions. With the troops under his own command he marched against the fortress called the Sogdian Rock, seated on an isolated hill, so precipitous as to be deemed inaccessible, and so well supplied with provisions as to defy a blockade. The summons to surrender was treated with derision by the commander, who inquired whether the Macedonians had wings? But a small body of Macedonians having succeeded in scaling some heights which overhung the fortress, the garrison became so alarmed that they immediately surrendered. To this place a Bactrian named Oxyartes, an adherent of Bessus, had sent his daughters for safety. One of them, named Roxana, was of surpassing beauty, and Alexander made her the partner of his throne (B.C. 328).

At Maracanda (now SAMARCAND) he appointed his friend Clitus satrap of Bactria. On the eve of the parting of the two friends Alexander celebrated a festival in honour of the Dioscuri (Castor and Pollux), though the day was sacred to Dionysus (Bacchus). The banquet was attended by several parasites and literary flatterers, who magnified the praises of Alexander with extravagant and nauseous flattery. Clitus, whom wine had released from all prudent reserve, sternly rebuked their fulsome adulation; and, as the conversation turned on the comparative merits of the exploits of Alexander and his father Philip, he did not hesitate to prefer the exploits of the latter. He reminded Alexander of his former services, and, stretching forth his hand, exclaimed, "It was this hand Alexander, which saved your life at the battle of the Granicus!" The king, who was also flushed with wine, was so enraged by these remarks, that he rushed at Clitus with the intention of killing him on the spot, but he was held back by his friends, whilst Clitus was at the same time hurried out of the room. Alexander, however, was no sooner released than, snatching a spear, he sprang to the door, and meeting Clitus, who was returning in equal fury to brave his anger, ran him through the body. But when the deed was done he was seized with repentance and remorse. He flung himself on his couch and remained for three whole days in an agony of grief, refusing all sustenance, and calling on the names of Clitus and of his sister Lanice who had been his nurse. It was not till his bodily strength began to fail through protracted abstinence that he at last became more composed, and consented to listen to the consolations of his friends, and the words of the soothsayers, who ascribed the murder of Clitus to a temporary frenzy with which Dionysus had visited him as a punishment for neglecting the celebration of his festival.

After reducing Sogdiana, Alexander returned into Bactria in 327, and began to prepare far his projected expedition into India. While he was thus employed a plot was formed against his life by the royal pages, incited by Hermolaus, one of their number, who had been punished with stripes for anticipating the king during a hunting party in slaying a wild boar. Hermolaus and his associates, among whom was Callisthenes, a pupil of Aristotle, were first tortured, and then put to death. It seems certain that a conspiracy existed; but no less certain that the growing pride and haughtiness of Alexander were gradually alienating from him the hearts of his followers.

Alexander did not leave Bactria till late in the spring. He crossed the Indus by a bridge of boats near Taxila, the present ATTOCK, where the river is about 1000 feet broad, and very deep. He now found himself in the district at present called the PENJ-AB (or the FIVE RIVERS). Taxiles, the sovereign of the district, at once surrendered Taxila, his capital and joined the Macedonian force with 5000 men. Hence Alexander proceeded with little resistance to the river Haydaspes (BEHUT or JELUM). On the opposite bank, Porus, a powerful Indian king, prepared to dispute his progress with a numerous and well-appointed force. Alexander, however, by a skilful stratagem conveyed his army safely across the river. An obstinate battle then ensued. In the army of Porus were many elephants, the sight and smell of which frightened the horses of Alexander's cavalry. But these unwieldy animals ultimately proved as dangerous to the Indians as to the Greeks; for when driven into a narrow space they became unmanageable, and created great confusion in the ranks of Porus. By a few vigorous charges the Indians were completely routed, with the loss of 12,000 slain and 9000 prisoners. Among the latter was Porus himself, who was conducted into the presence of Alexander. The courage which he had displayed in the battle had excited the admiration of the Macedonian king. Mounted on an enormous elephant, he retreated leisurely when the day was lost, and long rejected every summons to surrender; till at length, overcome by thirst and fatigue, he permitted himself to be taken. Even in this situation Porus still retained his majestic bearing, the effect of which was increased by the extraordinary height of his stature. On Alexander's inquiring how he wished to be treated, he replied, "Like a king." "And have you no other request?" asked Alexander. "No," answered Porus; "everything is comprehended in the word king." Struck by his magnanimity, Alexander not only restored him to his dominions, but also considerably enlarged them; seeking by these means to retain him as an obedient and faithful vassal.

Alexander rested a month on the banks of the Hydaspes, where he celebrated his victory by games and sacrifices, and founded two towns one of which he named Nicaea, and the other Bucephala, in honour of his gallant charger Bucephalus, which is said to have died there. He then overran the whole of the PENJ-AB, as far as the Hyphasis (GHARRA), its southern boundary. Upon reaching this river, the army, worn out by fatigues and dangers, positively refused to proceed any farther; although Alexander passionately desired to attack a monarch still more powerful than Porus, whose dominions lay beyond the Hyphasis. All his attempts to induce his soldiers to proceed proving ineffectual, he returned to the Hydaspes, when he ordered part of his army to descend the river on its opposite banks; whilst he himself at the head of 8000 men, embarked on board a fleet of about 2000 vessels, which he had ordered to be prepared with the view of sailing down the Indus to its mouth.

The army began to move in November 327. The navigation lasted several months, but was accomplished without any serious opposition, except from the tribe of the Malli, who are conjectured to have occupied the site of the present MOOLTAN. At the storming of their town the life of Alexander was exposed to imminent danger. He was the first to scale the walls of the citadel, and was followed by four officers; but before a fifth man could mount, the ladder broke, and Alexander was left exposed on the wall to the missiles of the enemy. Leaping down into the citadel among the enemy, he placed his back to the wall, where he succeeded in keeping the enemy at bay, and slew two of their chiefs who had ventured within reach of his sword. But an arrow which pierced his corslet brought him to the ground, fainting with loss of blood. Two of his followers, who had jumped down after him, now stood over and defended him; till at length, more soldiers having scaled the walls and opened one of the gates, sufficient numbers poured in not only to rescue their monarch, but to capture the citadel; when every living being within the place was put to the sword. Upon arriving at the mouth of the Indus, Nearchus with the fleet was directed to explore the Indian Ocean, the Persian Gulf, and the mouths of the Tigris and Euphrates, with the view of establishing a maritime communication between India and Persia. Alexander himself proceeded with his army, in the autumn of 326, through the burning deserts of Gedrosia towards Persepolis; marching himself on foot, and sharing the privations and fatigues of the meanest soldier. In these regions the very atmosphere seems to be composed of a fine dust which, on the slightest wind, penetrates into the mouth and nose, whilst the soil affords no firm footing to the traveller. The march through this inhospitable region lasted 60 days, during which numbers of the soldiers perished from fatigue or disease. At length they emerged into the fertile province of Carmania. Whilst in this country Alexander was rejoined by Nearchus, who had arrived with his fleet at Harmozia (ORMUZ); but who subsequently prosecuted his voyage to the head of the Persian Gulf.

Upon reaching Susa (B.C. 325) Alexander allowed his soldiers to repose from their fatigues, and amused them with a series of brilliant festivities. It was here that he adopted various measures with the view of consolidating his empire. One of the most important was to form the Greeks and Persians into one people by means of intermarriages. He himself celebrated his nuptials with Statira the eldest daughter of Darius, and bestowed the hand of her sister, Drypetis, on Hephaestion. Other marriages were made between Alexander's officers and Asiatic women, to the number, it is said, of about a hundred; whilst no fewer than 10,000 of the common soldiers followed their example and took native wives. As another means of amalgamating the Europeans and Asiatics, he caused numbers of the latter to be admitted into the army, and to be armed and trained in the Macedonian fashion. But these innovations were regarded with a jealous eye by most of the Macedonian veterans; and this feeling was increased by the conduct of Alexander himself, who assumed every day more and more of the state and manners of an eastern despot. Their long-stifled dissatisfaction broke out into open mutiny and rebellion at a review which took place at Opis on the Tigris. But the mutiny was quelled by the decisive conduct of Alexander. He immediately ordered thirteen of the ringleaders to be seized and executed, and then, addressing the remainder, pointed out to them how, by his own and his father's exertions, they had been raised from the condition of scattered herdsmen to be the masters of Greece and the lords of Asia; and that, whilst he had abandoned to them the richest and most valuable fruits of his conquest, he had reserved nothing but the diadem for himself, as the mark of his superior labours and more imminent perils. He then secluded himself for two whole days, during which his Macedonian guard was exchanged for a Persian one, whilst nobles of the same nation were appointed to the most confidential posts about his person. Overcome by these marks of alienation on the part of their sovereign, the Macedonians now supplicated with tears to be restored to favour. A solemn reconciliation was effected, and 10,000 veterans were dismissed to their homes under the conduct of Craterus. That general was also appointed to the government of Macedonia in place of Antipater, who was ordered to repair to Asia with fresh reinforcements.

Soon after these occurrences Alexander proceeded to Ecbatana, where during the autumn he solemnised the festival of Dionysus with extraordinary splendour. But his enjoyment was suddenly converted into bitterness by the death of his friend Hephaestion, who was carried off by a fever. This event threw Alexander into a deep melancholy, from which he never entirely recovered. The memory of Hephaestion was honoured by extravagant marks of public mourning, and his body was conveyed to Babylon, to be there interred with the utmost magnificence.

Alexander entered Babylon in the spring of 324, notwithstanding the warnings of the priests of Belus, who predicted some serious evil to him if he entered the city at that time. Babylon was now to witness the consummation of his triumphs and of his life. Ambassadors from all parts of Greece, from Libya, Italy, and probably from still more distant regions, were waiting to salute him, and to do homage to him as the conqueror of Asia; the fleet under Nearchus had arrived after its long and enterprising voyage; whilst for the reception of this navy, which seemed to turn the inland capital of his empire into a port, a magnificent harbour was in process of construction. The mind of Alexander was still occupied with plans of conquest and ambition; his next design was the subjugation of Arabia; which, however, was to be only the stepping-stone to the conquest of the whole known world. He despatched three expeditions to survey the coast of Arabia; ordered a fleet to be built to explore the Caspian sea; and engaged himself in surveying the course of the Euphrates, and in devising improvements of its navigation. The period for commencing the Arabian campaign had already arrived; solemn sacrifices were offered up for its success, and grand banquets were given previous to departure. At these carousals Alexander drank deep; and at the termination of the one given by his favourite, Medius, he was seized with unequivocal symptoms of fever. For some days, however, he neglected the disorder, and continued to occupy himself with the necessary preparations for the march. But in eleven days the malady had gained a fatal strength, and terminated his life on the 28th of June, B.C. 323, at the early age of 32. Whilst he lay speechless on his deathbed his favourite troops were admitted to see him; but he could offer them no other token of recognition than by stretching out his hand.

Few of the great characters of history have been so differently judged as Alexander. Of the magnitude of his exploits, indeed, and of the justice with which, according to the usual sentiments of mankind, they confer upon him the title of "Great," there can be but one opinion. His military renown, however, consists more in the seemingly extravagant boldness of his enterprises than in the real power of the foes whom he overcame. The resistance he met with was not greater than that which a European army experiences in the present day from one composed of Asiatics; and the empire of the East was decided by the two battles of Issus and Arbela. His chief difficulties were the geographical difficulties of distance, climate, and the nature of the ground traversed. But this is no proof that he was incompetent to meet a foe more worthy of his military skill; and his proceedings in Greece before his departure show the reverse. His motive, it must be allowed, seem rather to have sprung from the love of personal glory and the excitement of conquest, than from any wish to benefit his subjects. Yet on the whole his achievements, though they undoubtedly occasioned great partial misery, must be regarded as beneficial to the human race. By his conquests the two continents were put into closer communication with one another; and both, but particularly Asia, were the gainers. The language, the arts, and the literature of Greece were introduced into the East; and after the death of Alexander, Greek kingdoms were formed in the western parts of Asia, which continued to exist for many generations.

CHAPTER XXI.
FROM THE DEATH OF ALEXANDER THE GREAT TO THE CONQUEST OF GREECE BY THE ROMANS, B.C. 323-146.

The vast empire of Alexander the Great was divided, at his death, among his generals; but, before relating their history, it is necessary to take a brief retrospective glance at the affairs of Greece. Three years after Alexander had quitted Europe the Spartans made a vigorous effort to throw off the Macedonian yoke. They were joined by most of the Peloponnesian states, but though they met with some success at first, they were finally defeated with great slaughter by Antipater near Megalopolis. Agis fell in the battle, and the chains of Greece were riveted more firmly than ever. This victory, and the successes of Alexander in the East, encouraged the Macedonian party in Athens to take active measures against Demosthenes; and AEschines revived an old charge against him which had lain dormant for several years. Soon after the battle of Chaeronea, Ctesiphon had proposed that Demosthenes should be presented with a golden crown in the theatre during the great Dionysiac festival, on account of the services he had conferred upon his country. For proposing this decree AEschines indicted Ctesiphon; but though the latter was the nominal defendant, it was Demosthenes who was really put upon his trial. The case was decided in 330 B.C., and has been immortalised by the memorable and still extant speeches of AEschines 'Against Ctesiphon' and of Demosthenes 'On the Crown.' AEschines, who did not obtain a fifth part of the votes, and consequently became himself liable to a penalty, was so chagrined at his defeat that he retired to Rhodes.

In B.C. 325 Harpalus arrived in Athens. He had been left by Alexander at Ecbatana in charge of the royal treasures, and appears also to have held the important satrapy of Babylon. During the absence of Alexander in India he gave himself up to the most extravagant luxury and profusion, squandering the treasures intrusted to him, at the same time that he alienated the people subject to his rule by his lustful excesses and extortions. He had probably thought that Alexander would never return from the remote regions of the East into which he had penetrated; but when he at length learnt that the king was on his march back to Susa, and had visited with unsparing rigour those of his officers who had been guilty of any excesses during his absence, he at once saw that his only resource was in flight. Collecting together all the treasures which he could, and assembling a body of 6000 mercenaries, he hastened to the coast of Asia, and from thence crossed over to Attica, At first the Athenians refused to receive him; but bribes administered to some of the principal orators induced them to alter their determination. Such a step was tantamount to an act of hostility against Macedonia itself; and accordingly Antipater called upon the Athenians to deliver up Harpalus, and to bring to trial those who had accepted his bribes. The Athenians did not venture to disobey these demands. Harpalus was put into confinement, but succeeded in making his escape from prison. Demosthenes was among the orators who were brought to trial for corruption. He was declared to be guilty, and was condemned to pay a fine of 50 talents. Not being able to raise that sum, he was thrown into prison; but he contrived to make his escape, and went into exile. There are, however, good grounds for doubting his guilt; and it is more probable that he fell a victim to the implacable hatred of the Macedonian party. Upon quitting Athens Demosthenes resided chiefly at AEgina or Troezen, in sight of his native land, and whenever he looked towards her shores it was observed that he shed tears.

When the news of Alexander's death reached Athens, the anti-Macedonian party, which, since the exile of Demosthenes, was led by Hyperides, carried all before it. The people in a decree declared their determination to support the liberty of Greece. Envoys were despatched to all the Grecian states to announce the determination of Athens, and to exhort them to struggle with her for their independence. This call was responded to in the Peloponnesus only by the smaller states, whilst Sparta, Arcadia, and Achaia kept aloof. In northern Greece the confederacy was joined by most of the states except the Boaotians; and Leosthenes was appointed commander-in-chief of the allied forces.

The allied army assembled in the neighbourhood of Thermopylae. Antipater now advanced from the north, and offered battle in the vale of the Spercheus; but being deserted by his Thessalian cavalry, who went over to his opponents during the heat of the engagement, he was obliged to retreat and threw himself into Lamia, a strong fortress on the Malian gulf. Leosthenes, desirous to finish the war at a blow, pressed the siege with the utmost vigour; but his assaults were repulsed, and he was compelled to resort to the slower method of a blockade. From this town the contest between Antipater and the allied Greeks has been called the Lamian War.

The novelty of a victory over the Macedonian arms was received with boundless exultation at Athens, and this feeling was raised to a still higher pitch by the arrival of an embassy from Antipater to sue for peace. But the Athenians were so elated with their good fortune, that they would listen to no terms but the unconditional surrender of Antipater. Meantime Demosthenes, though still an exile, exerted himself in various parts of the Peloponnesus in counteracting the envoys of Antipater, and in endeavouring to gain adherents to the cause of Athens and the allies. The Athenians in return invited Demosthenes back to his native country, and a ship was sent to convey him to Piraeus, where he was received with extraordinary honours.

Meanwhile Leonnatus, governor of the Hellespontine Phrygia, had appeared on the theatre of war with an army of 20,000 foot and 2500 horse. Leosthenes had been slain at Lamia in a sally of the besieged; and Antiphilus, on whom the command of the allied army devolved, hastened to offer battle to Leonnatus before he could arrive at Lamia. The hostile armies met in one of the plains of Thessaly, where Leonnatus was killed and his troops defeated. Antipater, as soon as the blockade of Lamia was raised, had pursued Antiphilus, and on the day after the battle he effected a junction with the beaten army of Leonnatus.

Shortly afterwards Antipater was still further reinforced by the arrival of Craterus with a considerable force from Asia; and being now at the head of an army which outnumbered the forces of the allies, he marched against them and gained a decisive victory over them near Crannon in Thessaly, on the 7th of August, B.C. 322. The allies were now compelled to sue for peace; but Antipater refused to treat with them except as separate states, foreseeing that by this means many would be detached from the confederacy. The result answered his expectations. One by one the various states submitted, till at length all had laid down their arms. Athens, the original instigator of the insurrection, now lay at the mercy of the conqueror. As Antipater advanced, Phocion used all the influence which he possessed with the Macedonians in favour of his countrymen; but he could obtain no other terms than an unconditional surrender. On a second mission Phocion received the final demands of Antipater; which were, that the Athenians should deliver up a certain number of their orators, among whom were Demosthenes and Hyperides; that their political franchise should be limited by a property qualification; that they should receive a Macedonian garrison in Munychia; and that they should defray the expenses of the war. Such was the result of the Lamian war, which riveted the Macedonian fetters more firmly than ever.

After the return of the envoys bringing the ultimatum of Antipater, the sycophant Demades procured a decree for the death of the denounced orators. Demosthenes, and the other persons compromised, made their escape from Athens before the Macedonian garrison arrived. Ægina was their first place of refuge, but they soon parted in different directions. Hyperides fled to the temple of Demeter (Ceres) at Hermione in Peloponnesus, whilst Demosthenes took refuge in that of Poseidon (Neptune) in the isle of Calaurea, near Troezen. But the satellites of Antipater, under the guidance of a Thurian named Archias who had formerly been an actor, tore them from their sanctuaries. Hyperides was carried to Athens, and it is said that Antipater took the brutal and cowardly revenge of ordering his tongue to be cut out, and his remains to be thrown to the dogs. Demosthenes contrived at least to escape the insults of the tyrannical conqueror. Archias at first endeavoured to entice him from his sanctuary by the blandest promises, But Demosthenes, forewarned, it is said, by a dream, fixing his eyes intently on him, exclaimed, "Your acting, Archias, never touched me formerly, nor do your promises now." And when Archias began to employ threats, "Good," said Demosthenes; "now you speak as from the Macedonian tripod; before you were only playing a part. But wait awhile, and let me write my last directions to my family." So taking his writing materials, he put the reed into his mouth, and bit it for some time, as was his custom when composing; after which he covered his head with his garment and reclined against a pillar. The guards who accompanied Archias, imagining this to be a mere trick, laughed and called him coward, whilst Archias began to renew his false persuasions. Demosthenes, feeling the poison work--for such it was that he had concealed in the reed now bade him lead on. "You may now," said he, "enact the part of Creon, and cast me out unburied; but at least, O gracious Poseidon, I have not polluted thy temple by my death which Antipater and his Macedonians would not have scrupled at." But whilst he was endeavouring to walk out, he fell down by the altar and expired.

The history of Alexander's successors is marked from first to last by dissension, crimes, and unscrupulous ambition. It is only necessary for the purpose of the present work to mention very briefly the most important events.

Alexander on his death-bed is said to have given his signet-ring to Perdiccas, but he had left no legitimate heir to his throne, though his wife Roxana was pregnant. On the day after Alexander's death a military council was assembled, in which Perdiccas assumed a leading part; and in which, after much debate, an arrangement was at length effected on the following basis: That Philip Arrhidaeus, a young man of weak intellect, the half-brother of Alexander (being the son of Philip by a Thessalian woman named Philinna), should be declared king, reserving however to the child of Roxana if a son should be born, a share in the sovereignty: that the government of Macedonia and Greece should be divided between Antipater and Craterus: that Ptolemy should preside over Egypt and the adjacent countries: that Antigonus should have Phrygia Proper, Lycia, and Pamphylia: that the Hellespontine Phrygia should be assigned to Leonnatus: that Eumenes should have the satrapy of Paphlagonia and Cappadocia, which countries, however, still remained to be subdued: and that Thrace should be committed to Lysimachus. Perdiccas reserved for himself the command of the horse-guards, the post before held by Hephaestion, in virtue of which he became the guardian of Philip Arrhidaeus, the nominal sovereign. It was not for some time after these arrangements had been completed that the last rites were paid to Alexander's remains. They were conveyed to Alexandria, and deposited in a cemetery which afterwards became the burial-place of the Ptolemies. Nothing could exceed the magnificence of the funeral car, which was adorned with ornaments of massive gold, and was so heavy, that it was more than a year in being conveyed from Babylon to Syria, though drawn by 84 mules. In due time Roxana was delivered of a son, to whom the name of Alexander was given, and who was declared the partner of Arrhidaeus in the empire. Roxana had previously inveigled

Statira and her sister Drypetis to Babylon, where she caused them to be secretly assassinated.

Perdiccas possessed more power than any of Alexander's generals, and he now aspired to the Macedonian throne. His designs, however, were not unknown to Antigonus and Ptolemy; and when he attempted to bring Antigonus to trial for some offence in the government of his satrapy, that general made his escape to Macedonia, where he revealed to Antipater the full extent of the ambitious schemes of Perdiccas, and thus at once induced Antipater and Craterus to unite in a league with him and Ptolemy, and openly declare war against the regent. Thus assailed on all sides, Perdiccas resolved to direct his arms in the first instance against Ptolemy. In the spring of B.C. 321 he accordingly set out on his march against Egypt, at the head of a formidable army, and accompanied by Philip Arrhidaeus, and Roxana and her infant son. He advanced without opposition as far as Pelusium, but he found the banks of the Nile strongly fortified and guarded by Ptolemy, and was repulsed in repeated attempts to force the passage of the river; in the last of which, near Memphis, he lost great numbers of men by the depth and rapidity of the current. Perdiccas had never been popular with the soldiery, and these disasters completely alienated their affections. A conspiracy was formed against him, and some of his chief officers murdered him in his tent.

The death of Perdiccas was followed by a fresh distribution of the provinces of the empire. At a meeting of the generals held at Triparadisus in Syria, towards the end of the year 321 B.C., Antipater was declared regent, retaining the government of Macedonia and Greece; Ptolemy was continued in the government of Egypt; Seleucus received the satrapy of Babylon; whilst Antigonus not only retained his old province, but was rewarded with that of Susiana.

Antipater did not long survive these events. He died in the year 318, at the advanced age of 80, leaving Polysperchon, one of Alexander's oldest generals, regent; much to the surprise and mortification of his son Cassander, who received only the secondary dignity of Chiliarch, or commander of the cavalry. Cassander was now bent on obtaining the regency; but seeing no hope of success in Macedonia, he went over to Asia to solicit the assistance of Antigonus.

Polysperchon, on his side, sought to conciliate the friendship of the Grecian states, by proclaiming them all free and independent, and by abolishing the oligarchies which had been set up by Antipater. In order to enforce these measures, Polysperchon prepared to march into Greece, whilst his son Alexander was despatched beforehand with an army towards Athens to compel the Macedonian garrison under the command of Nicanor to evacuate Munychia. Nicanor, however, refused to move without orders from Cassander, whose general he declared himself to be. Phocion was suspected of intriguing in favour of Nicanor, and being accused of treason, fled to Alexander, now encamped before the walls of Athens. Alexander sent Phocion to his father, who sent him back to Athens in chains, to be tried by the Athenian people. The theatre, where his trial was to take place, was soon full to overflowing. Phocion was assailed on every side by the clamours of his enemies, which prevented his defence; from being heard, and he was condemned to death by a show of hands. To the last Phocion maintained his calm and dignified, but somewhat contemptuous bearing. When some wretched man spat upon him as he passed to the prison, "Will no one," said he, "check this fellow's indecency?" To one who asked him whether he had any message to leave for his son Phocus, he answered, "Only that he bear no grudge against the Athenians." And when the hemlock which had been prepared was found insufficient for all the condemned, and the jailer would not furnish more unless he was paid for it, "Give the man his money," said Phocion to one of his friends, "since at Athens one cannot even die for nothing." He died in B.C. 317, at the age of 85. The Athenians afterwards repented of their conduct towards Phocion. His bones, which had been cast out on the frontiers of Megara, were brought back to Athens, and a bronze statue was erected to his memory.

Whilst Alexander was negotiating with Nicanor about the surrender of Munychia, Cassander arrived in the Piraeus with a considerable army, with which Antigonus had supplied him. Polysperchon was obliged to retire from Athens, and Cassander established an oligarchical government in the city under the presidency of Demetrius of Phalerus.

Although Polysperchon was supported by Olympias, the mother of Alexander the Great, he proved no match for Cassander, who became master of Macedonia after the fall of Pydna in B.C. 316. In this city Olympias had taken refuge together with Roxana and her son; but after a blockade of some months it was obliged to surrender. Olympias had stipulated that her life should be spared, but Cassander soon afterwards caused her to be murdered, and kept Roxana and her son in custody in the citadel of Amphipolis. Shortly afterwards Cassander began the restoration of Thebes (B.C. 315), in the twentieth year after its destruction by Alexander, a measure highly popular with the Greeks.

A new war now broke out in the East. Antigonus had become the most powerful of Alexander's successors. He had conquered Eumenes, who had long defied his arms, and he now began to dispose of the provinces as he thought fit. His increasing power and ambitious projects led to a general coalition against him, consisting of Ptolemy, Seleucus, Cassander, and Lysimachus, the governor of Thrace. The war began in the year 315, and was carried on with great vehemence and alternate success in Syria, Phoenicia, Asia Minor, and Greece. After four years all parties became exhausted with the struggle, and peace was accordingly concluded in 311, on condition that the Greek cities should be free, that Cassander should retain his authority in Europe till Alexander came of age, that Ptolemy and Lysimachus should keep possession of Egypt and Thrace respectively, and that Antigonus should have the government of all Asia. This hollow peace, which had been merely patched up for the convenience of the parties concerned, was not of long duration. It seems to have been the immediate cause of another of those crimes which disgrace the history of Alexander's successors. His son, Alexander, who had now attained the age of sixteen, was still shut up with his mother Roxana in Amphipolis; and his partisans, with injudicious zeal, loudly expressed their wish that he should be released and placed upon the throne. In order to avert this event Cassander contrived the secret murder both of the mother and the son.

This abominable act, however, does not appear to have caused a breach of the peace. Ptolemy was the first to break it (B.C. 310), under the pretext that Antigonus, by keeping his garrisons in the Greek cities of Asia and the islands, had not respected that article of the treaty which guaranteed Grecian freedom. After the war had lasted three years Antigonus resolved to make a vigorous effort to wrest Greece from the hands of Cassander and Ptolemy, who held all the principal towns in it. Accordingly, in the summer of 307 B.C. he despatched his son Demetrius from Ephesus to Athens, with a fleet of 250 sail, and 5000 talents in money. Demetrius, who afterwards obtained the surname of "Poliorcetes," or "Besieger of Cities," was a young man of ardent temperament and great abilities. Upon arriving at the Piraeus he immediately proclaimed the object of his expedition to be the liberation of Athens and the expulsion of the Macedonian garrison. Supported by the Macedonians, Demetrius the Phalerean had now ruled Athens for a period of more than ten years. Of mean birth, Demetrius the Phalerean owed his elevation entirely to his talents and perseverance. His skill as an orator raised him to distinction among his countrymen; and his politics, which led him to embrace the party of Phocion, recommended him to Cassander and the Macedonians. He cultivated many branches of literature, and was at once an historian, a philosopher, and a poet; but none of his works have come down to us. The Athenians heard with pleasure the proclamations of the son of Antigonus his namesake, the Phalerean was obliged to surrender the city to him, and to close his political career by retiring to Thebes. The Macedonian garrison in Munychia offered a slight resistance, which was soon overcome, Demetrius Poliorcetes then formally announced to the Athenian assembly the restoration of their ancient constitution, and promised them a large donative of corn and ship-timber. This munificence was repaid by the Athenians with the basest and most abject flattery. Both Demetrius and his father were deified, and two new tribes, those of Antigonias and Demetrias, were added to the existing ten which derived their names from the ancient heroes of Attica.

Demetrius Poliorcetes did not, however, remain long at Athens. Early in 306 B.C. he was recalled by his father, and, sailing to Cyprus, undertook the siege of Salamis. Ptolemy hastened to its relief with 140 vessels and 10,000 troops. The battle that ensued was one of the most memorable in the annals of ancient naval warfare, more particularly on account of the vast size of the vessels engaged. Ptolemy was completely defeated; and so important was the victory deemed by Antigonus, that on the strength of it he assumed the title of king, which he also conferred upon his son. This example was followed by Ptolemy, Seleucus, and Lysimachus.

Demetrius now undertook an expedition against Rhodes, which had refused its aid in the attack upon Ptolemy. It was from the memorable siege of Rhodes that Demetrius obtained his name of "Poliorcetes." After in vain attempting to take the town from the sea-side, by means of floating batteries, from which stones of enormous weight were hurled from engines with incredible force against the walls, he determined to alter his plan and invest it on the land-side. With the assistance of Epimachus, an Athenian engineer, he constructed a machine which, in anticipation of its effect, was called Helepolis, or "the city-taker." This was a square wooden tower, 150 feet high, and divided into nine stories, filled with armed men, who discharged missiles through apertures in the sides. When armed and prepared for attack, it required the strength of 2300 men to set this enormous machine in motion. But though it was assisted by the operation of two battering-rams, each 150 feet long and propelled by the labour of 1000 men, the Rhodians were so active in repairing the breaches made in their walls, that, after a year spent in the vain attempt to take the town, Demetrius was forced to retire and grant the Rhodians peace.

In 301 B.C., the struggle between Antigonus and his rivals was brought to a close by the battle of Ipsus in Phrygia, in which Antigonus was killed, and his army completely defeated. He had attained the age of 81 at the time of his death. A third partition of the empire of Alexander was now made. Seleucus and Lysimachus shared between them the possessions of Antigonus. Lysimachus seems to have had the greater part of Asia Minor, whilst the whole country from the coast of Syria to the Euphrates, as well as a part of Phrygia and Cappadocia, fell to the share of Seleucus. The latter founded on the Orontes a new capital of his empire, which he named Antioch, after his father Antiochus, and which long continued to be one of the most important Greek cities in Asia. The fall of Antigonus secured Cassander in the possession of Greece.

Demetrius was now a fugitive, but in the following year he was agreeably surprised by receiving an embassy from Seleucus, by which that monarch solicited his daughter Stratonice in marriage. Demetrius gladly granted the request, and found himself so much strengthened by this alliance, that in the spring of the year 296 he was in a condition to attack Athens, which he captured after a long siege, and drove out the bloodthirsty tyrant Lachares, who had been established there by Cassander.

Meanwhile Cassander had died shortly before the siege of Athens, and was succeeded on the throne of Macedon by his eldest son, Philip IV. [Philip Arrhidaeus is called Philip III.] But that young prince died in 295, and the succession was disputed between his two brothers, Antipater and Alexander. Demetrius availed himself of the distracted state of Macedonia to make himself master of that country (B.C. 294). He reigned over Macedonia, and the greater part of Greece, about seven years. He aimed at recovering the whole of his father's dominions in Asia; but before he was ready to take the field, his adversaries, alarmed at his preparations, determined to forestall him. In the spring of B.C. 287 Ptolemy sent a powerful fleet against Greece, while Pyrrhus on the one side and Lysimachus on the other simultaneously invaded Macedonia. Demetrius had completely alienated his own subjects by his proud and haughty bearing, and by his lavish expenditure on his own luxuries; while Pyrrhus by his generosity, affability, and daring courage, had become the hero of the Macedonians, who looked upon him as a second Alexander. The appearance of Pyrrhus was the signal for revolt: the Macedonian troops flocked to his standard and Demetrius was compelled to fly. Pyrrhus now ascended the throne of Macedonia; but his reign was of brief duration; and at the end of seven months he was in turn driven out by Lysimachus. Demetrius made several attempts to regain his power in Greece, and then set sail for Asia, where he successively endeavoured to establish himself in the territories of Lysimachus, and of his son-in-law Seleucus. Falling at length into the hands of the latter, he was kept in a kind of magnificent captivity in a royal residence in Syria; where, in 283, at the early age of 55, his chequered career was brought to a close, partly by chagrin, and partly by the sensual indulgences with which he endeavoured to divert it.

Lysimachus, Seleucus, and Ptolemy now divided the empire of Alexander between them. In Egypt the aged Ptolemy had abdicated in 285 in favour of his son by Berenice afterwards known as Ptolemy Philadelphus, and to the exclusion of his eldest son, Ptolemy Ceraunus, by his wife Eurydice. Ptolemy Ceraunus quitted Egypt in disgust, and fled to the court of Lysimachus; and Arsinoe, the wife of Lysimachus, jealous of her stepson Agathocles, the heir apparent to the throne, and desirous of securing the succession for her own children, conspired with Ptolemy Ceraunus against the life of Agathocles. She even procured the consent of Lysimachus to his murder; and after some vain attempts to make away with him by poison, he was flung into prison, where Ptolemy Ceraunus despatched him with his own hand. Lysandra, the mother of Agathocles, fled with the rest of her family to Seleucus, to demand from him protection and vengeance; and Seleucus, induced by the hopes of success, inspired by the discontent and dissensions which so foul an act had excited among the subjects of Lysimachus, espoused her cause. The hostilities which ensued between him and Lysimachus were brought to a termination by the battle of Corupedion, fought near Sardis in 281, in which Lysimachus was defeated and slain. By this victory, Macedonia, and the whole of Alexander's empire, with the exception of Egypt, southern Syria, Cyprus, and part of Phoenicia, fell under the sceptre of Seleucus.

That monarch, who had not beheld his native land since he first joined the expedition of Alexander, now crossed the Hellespont to take possession of Macedonia. Ptolemy Ceraunus, who after the battle of Corupedion had thrown himself on the mercy of Seleucus, and had been received with forgiveness and favour, accompanied him on this journey. The murder of Agathocles had not been committed by Ptolemy merely to oblige Arsinoe. He had even then designs upon the supreme power, which he now completed by another crime. As Seleucus stopped to sacrifice at a celebrated altar near Lysimachia in Thrace, Ptolemy treacherously assassinated him by stabbing him in the back (280). After this base and cowardly act, Ptolemy Ceraunus, who gave himself out as the avenger of Lysimachus, was, by one of those movements wholly inexplicable to our modern notions, saluted king by the army; but the Asiatic dominions of Seleucus fell to his son Antiochus, surnamed Soter. The crime of Ptolemy, however, was speedily overtaken by a just punishment. In the very same year his kingdom of Macedonia and Thrace was invaded by an immense host of Celts, and Ptolemy fell at the head of the forces which he led against them. A second invasion of the same barbarians compelled the Greeks to raise a force for their defence, which was intrusted to the command of the Athenian Callippus (B.C. 279). On this occasion the Celts attracted by the report of treasures which were now perhaps little more than an empty name, penetrated as far southwards as Delphi, with the view of plundering the temple. The god, it is said, vindicated his sanctuary on this occasion in the same supernatural manner as when it was attacked by the Persians: it is at all events certain that the Celts were repulsed with great loss, including that of their leader Brennus. Nevertheless some of their tribes succeeded in establishing themselves near the Danube; others settled on the sea-coast of Thrace whilst a third portion passed over into Asia, and gave their name to the country called Galatia.

After the death of Ptolemy Ceraunus, Macedonia fell for some time into a state of anarchy and confusion, and the crown was disputed by several pretenders. At length, in 278, Antigonus Gonatas, son of Demetrius Poliorcetes, succeeded in establishing himself on the throne of Macedonia; and, with the exception of two or three years (274-272) during which he was temporarily expelled by Pyrrhus, he continued to retain possession of it till his death in 239. The struggle between Antigonus and Pyrrhus was brought to a close at Argos in 272. Pyrrhus had marched into the Peloponnesus with a large force in order to make war upon Sparta, but with the collateral design of reducing the places which still held out for Antigonus. Pyrrhus having failed in an attempt to take Sparta, marched against Argos, where Antigonus also arrived with his forces. Both armies entered the city by opposite gates; and in a battle which ensued in the streets Pyrrhus was struck from his horse by a tile hurled by a woman from a house-top, and was then despatched by some soldiers of Antigonus. Such was the inglorious end of one of the bravest and most warlike monarchs of antiquity; whose character for moral virtue, though it would not stand the test of modern scrutiny, shone out conspicuously in comparison with that of contemporary sovereigns.

Antigonus Gonatas now made himself master of the greater part of Peloponnesus, which he governed by means of tyrants whom he established in various cities.

While all Greece, with the exception of Sparta, seemed hopelessly prostrate at the feet of Macedonia, a new political power, which sheds a lustre on the declining period of Grecian history, arose in a small province in Peloponnesus, of which the very name has been hitherto rarely mentioned since the heroic age. In Achaia, a narrow slip of country upon the shores of the Corinthian gulf, a league, chiefly for religious purposes, had existed from a very early period among the twelve chief cities of the province. The league, however, had never possessed much political importance, and it had been suppressed by the Macedonians. At the time of which we are speaking Antigonus Gonatas was in possession of all the cities formerly belonging to the league, either by means of his garrisons or of the tyrants who were subservient to him. It was, however, this very oppression that led to a revival of the league. The Achaean towns, now only ten in number, as two had been destroyed by earthquakes, began gradually to coalesce again; but Aratus of Sicyon, one of the most remarkable characters of this period of Grecian history, was the man who, about the year 251 B.C., first called the new league into active political existence. He had long lived in exile at Argos, whilst his native city groaned under the dominion of a succession of tyrants. Having collected a band of exiles, he surprised Sicyon in the night time, and drove out the last and most unpopular of these tyrants.

Instead of seizing the tyranny for himself, as he might easily have done, Aratus consulted only the advantage of his country, and with this view united Sicyon with the Achaean league. The accession of so important a town does not appear to have altered the constitution of the confederacy. The league was governed by a STRATEGUS, or general, whose functions were both military and civil; a GRAMMATEUS, or secretary; and a council of ten DEMIURGI. The sovereignty, however, resided in the general assembly, which met twice a year in a sacred grove near AEgium. It was composed of every Achaean who had attained the age of thirty, and possessed the right of electing the officers of the league, and of deciding all questions of war, peace, foreign alliances, and the like. In the year 245 B.C. Aratus was elected STRATEGUS of the league, and again in 243. In the latter of these years he succeeded in wresting Corinth from the Macedonians by another nocturnal surprise, and uniting it to the league. The confederacy now spread with wonderful rapidity. It was soon joined by Troezen, Epidaurus, Hermione and other cities; and ultimately embraced Athens, Megara, AEgina, Salamis, and the whole Peloponnesus, with the exception of Sparta, Elis, and some of the Arcadian towns.

Sparta, it is true, still continued to retain her independence, but without a shadow of her former greatness and power. The primitive simplicity of Spartan manners had been completely destroyed by the collection of wealth into a few hands, and by the consequent progress of luxury. The number of Spartan citizens had been reduced to 700; but even of these there were not above a hundred who possessed a sufficient quantity of land to maintain themselves in independence. The young king, Agis IV., who succeeded to the crown in 244, attempted to revive the ancient Spartan virtue, by restoring the institutions of Lycurgus, by cancelling all debts, and by making a new distribution of lands; and with this view he relinquished all his own property, as well as that of his family, for the public good. But Agis perished in this attempt, and was put to death as a traitor to his order. A few years afterwards, however, Cleomenes, the son of Leonidas, succeeded in effecting the reforms which had been contemplated by Agis, as well as several others which regarded military discipline. The effect of these new measures soon became visible in the increased success of the Spartan arms. Aratus was so hard pressed that he was compelled to solicit the assistance of the Macedonians. Both Antigonus Gonatas and his son Demetrius II.--who had reigned in Macedonia from 239 to 229 B.C. were now dead, and the government was administered by Antigonus Doson, as guardian of Philip, the youthful son of Demetrius II. Antigonus Doson was the grandson of Demetrius Poliorcetes, and the nephew of Antigonus Gonatas. The Macedonians compelled him to accept the crown; but he remained faithful to his trust as guardian of Philip, whose mother he married; and though he had children of his own by her, yet Philip succeeded him on his death. It was to Antigonus Doson that Aratus applied for assistance; and though Cleomenes maintained his ground for some time, he was finally defeated by Antigonus Doson in the fatal battle of Sellasia in Laconia (B.C. 221). The army of Cleomenes was almost totally annihilated; he himself was obliged to fly to Egypt; and Sparta, which for many centuries bad remained unconquered, fell into the hands of the victor.

The succession of Macedonian kings from Alexander the Great to the extinction of the monarchy will be seen from the following table:--

	B.C.
Philip III. Arrhidaeus	323-316
Cassander	316-296
Philip IV.	296-295
Demetrius I. Poliorcetes	294-287
Pyrrhus	287-286
Lysimachus	286-280
Ptolemy Ceraunus and others	280-277
Antigonus Gonatas	277-239
Demetrius II	239-229
Antigonus Doson	229-220
Philip V	220-178
Perseus	178-167

In the following year Antigonus was succeeded by Philip V., the son of Demetrius II., who was then about sixteen or seventeen years of age. His youth encouraged the AEtolians to make predatory incursions into the Peloponnesus. That people were a species of freebooters, and the terror of their neighbours; yet they were united, like the Achaeans, in a confederacy or league. The Aetolian League was a confederation of tribes instead of cities, like the Achaean. The diet or council of the league, called the Panaetolicum, assembled every autumn, generally at Thermon, to elect the strategus and other officers; but the details of its affairs were conducted by a committee called APOCLETI, who seem to have formed a sort of permanent council, The AEtolians had availed themselves of the disorganised state of Greece consequent upon the death of Alexander to extend their power, and had gradually made themselves masters of Locris, Phocis, Boeotia, together with portions of Acarnania, Thessaly, and Epirus. Thus both the Amphictyonic Council and the oracle of Delphi were in their power. They had early wrested Naupactus from the Achaeans, and had subsequently acquired several Peloponnesian cities.

Such was the condition of the AEtolians at the time of Philip's accession. Soon after that event we find them, under the leadership of Dorimachus, engaged in a series of freebooting expeditions in Messenia, and other parts of Peloponnesus. Aratus marched to the assistance of the Messenians at the head of the Achaean forces, but was totally defeated in a battle near Caphyae. The Achaeans now saw no hope of safety except through the assistance of Philip. That young monarch was ambitious and enterprising possessing considerable military ability and much political sagacity. He readily listened to the application of the Achaeans, and in 220 entered into an alliance with them. The war which ensued between the AEtolians on the one side, and the Achaeans, assisted by Philip, on the other, and which lasted about three years, has been called the Social War. Philip gained several victories over the AEtolians, but he concluded a treaty of peace with them in 217, because he was anxious to turn his arms against another and more formidable power.

The great struggle now going on between Rome and Carthage attracted the attention of the whole civilized world. If was evident that Greece, distracted by intestine quarrels, must be soon swallowed up by whichever of those great states might prove successful; and of the two, the ambition of the Romans, who had already gained a footing on the eastern shores of the Adriatic was by far the more formidable to Greece. After the conclusion of the peace with the AEtolians Philip prepared a large fleet, which he employed to watch the movements of the Romans, and in the following year (216) he concluded a treaty with Hannibal, which, among other clauses, provided that the Romans should not be allowed to retain their conquests on the eastern side of the Adriatic. He even meditated an invasion of Italy, and with that view endeavoured to make himself master of Apollonia and Oricum. But though he succeeded in taking the latter city, the Romans surprised his camp whilst he was besieging Apollonia, and compelled him to burn his ships and retire. Meanwhile Philip had acted in a most arbitrary manner in the affairs of Greece; and when Aratus remonstrated with him respecting his proceedings, he got rid of his former friend and counsellor by means of a slow and secret poison (B.C. 213).

In B.C., 209 the Achaeans, being hard pressed by the AEtolians, were again induced to call in the aid of Philip. The spirit of the Achaeans was at this time revived by Philopoemen, one of the few noble characters of the period, and who has been styled by Plutarch "the last of the Greeks." He was a native of Megalopolis in Arcadia, and in 208 was elected Strategus of the league. In both these posts Philopoemen made great alterations and improvements in the arms and discipline of the Achaean forces, which he assimilated to those of the Macedonian phalanx. These reforms, as well as the public spirit with which he had inspired the Achaeans were attended with the most beneficial results. In 207 Philopoemen gained at Mantinea a signal victory over the Lacedaemonians, who had joined the Roman alliance; 4000 of them were left upon the field, and among them Machanidas who had made himself tyrant of Sparta. This decisive battle, combined with the withdrawal of the Romans, who, being desirous of turning their undivided attention towards Carthage, had made peace with Philip (205), secured for a few years the tranquillity of Greece. It also raised the fame of Philopoemen to its highest point; and in the next Nemean festival, being a second time general of the league, he was hailed by the assembled Greeks as the liberator of their country.

Upon the conclusion of the second Punic war the Romans renewed their enterprises in Greece, and declared war against Philip (B.C. 200). For some time the war lingered on without any decided success on either side; but in 198 the consul T. Quinctius Flamininus succeeded in gaining over the Achaean league to the Roman alliance; and as the AEtolians had previously deserted Philip, both those powers fought for a short time on the same side. In 197 the struggle was brought to a termination by the battle of Cynoscephalae, near Scotussa, in Thessaly, which decided the fate of the Macedonian monarchy. Philip was obliged to sue for peace, and in the following year (196) a treaty was ratified by which the Macedonians were compelled to renounce their supremacy, to withdraw their garrisons from the Grecian towns, to surrender their fleet, and to pay 1000 talents for the expenses of the war. At the ensuing Isthmian games Flamininus solemnly proclaimed the freedom of the Greeks, and was received by them with overwhelming joy and gratitude.

The AEtolians, dissatisfied with these arrangements, persuaded Antiochus III., king of Syria, to enter into a league against the Romans. He passed over into Greece with a wholly inadequate force, and was defeated by the Romans at Thermopylae (B.C. 191). The AEtolians were now compelled to make head against the Romans by themselves. After some ineffectual attempts at resistance they were reduced to sue for peace, which they at length obtained, but on the most humiliating conditions (B.C. 189). They were required to acknowledge the supremacy of Rome, to renounce all the conquests they had recently made, to pay an indemnity of 500 talents and to engage in future to aid the Romans in their wars. The power of the AEtolian league was thus for ever crushed, though it seems to have existed, in name at least, till a much later period.

The Achaean league still subsisted but was destined before long to experience the same fate as its rival. At first, indeed, it enjoyed the protection of the Romans, and even acquired an extension of members through their influence, but this protectorate involved a state of almost absolute dependence. Philopoemen also had succeeded, in the year 192, in adding Sparta to the league, which now embraced the whole of Peloponnesus. But Sparta having displayed symptoms of insubordination, Philopoemen marched against it in 188, and captured the city; when he put to death eighty of the leading men, razed the walls and fortifications, abolished the institutions of Lycurgus, and compelled the citizens to adopt the democratic constitution of the Achaeans. Meanwhile the Romans regarded with satisfaction the internal dissensions of Greece, which they foresaw would only render her an easier prey, and neglected to answer the appeals of the Spartans for protection. In 183 the Messenians, under the leadership of Dinocrates, having revolted from the league, Philopoemen, who had now attained the age of 70, led an expedition against them; but having fallen from his horse in a skirmish of cavalry, he was captured, and conveyed with many circumstances of ignominy to Messene, where, after a sort of mock trial, he was executed. His fate was avenged by Lycortas, the commander of the Achaean cavalry, the father of the historian Polybius.

In B.C. 179 Philip died, and was succeeded by his son Perseus, the last monarch of Macedonia. The latter years of the reign of Philip had been spent in preparations for a renewal of the war, which he foresaw to be inevitable; yet a period of seven years elapsed after the accession of Perseus before the mutual enmity of the two powers broke out into open hostilities. The war was protracted three years without any decisive result; but was brought to a conclusion in 168 by the consul L. AEmilius Paulus, who defeated Perseus with great loss near Pydna. Perseus was carried to Rome to adorn the triumph of Paulus (167), and was permitted to spend the remainder of his life in a sort of honourable captivity at Alba. Such was the end of the Macedonian empire, which was now divided into four districts, each under the jurisdiction of an oligarchical council.

The Roman commissioners deputed to arrange the affairs of Macedonia did not confine their attention to that province, but evinced their design of bringing all Greece under the Roman sway. In these views they were assisted by various despots and traitors in different Grecian cities, and especially by Callicrates, a man of great influence among the Achaeans, and who for many years lent himself as the base tool of the Romans to effect the enslavement of his country. After the fall of Macedonia, Callicrates denounced more than a thousand leading Achaeans who had favoured the cause of Perseus. These, among whom was Polybius the historian, were apprehended and sent to Rome for trial. A still harder fate was experienced by AEtolia, Boeotia, Acarnania, and Epirus. In the last-named country, especially, no fewer than seventy of the principal towns were abandoned by Paulus to his soldiers for pillage, and 150,000 persons are said to have been sold into slavery.

A quarrel between the Achaeans and Sparta afforded the Romans a pretence for crushing the small remains of Grecian independence by the destruction of the Achaean league.

The Spartans, feeling themselves incompetent to resist the Achaeans, appealed to the Romans for assistance; and in 147 two Roman commissioners were sent to Greece to settle the disputes between the two states. These commissioners decided that not only Sparta, but Corinth, and all the other cities, except those of Achaia, should be restored to their independence. This decision occasioned serious riots at Corinth, the most important city of the league. All the Spartans in the town were seized, and even the Roman commissioners narrowly escaped violence. On their return to Rome a fresh embassy was despatched to demand satisfaction for these outrages. But the violent and impolitic conduct of Critolaus, then Strategus of the league, rendered all attempts at accommodation fruitless, and after the return of the ambassadors the Senate declared war against the league. The cowardice and incompetence of Critolaus as a general were only equalled by his previous insolence. On the approach of the Romans under Metellus from Macedonia he did not even venture to make a stand at Thermopylae; and being overtaken by them near Scarphea in Locris, he was totally defeated, and never again heard of. Diaeus, who succeeded him as Strategus, displayed rather more energy and courage. But a fresh Roman force under Mummius having landed on the isthmus, Diaeus was overthrown in a battle near Corinth; and that city was immediately evacuated not only by the troops of the league, but also by the greater part of the inhabitants. On entering it Mummius put the few males who remained to the sword; sold the women and children as slaves and having carried away all its treasures, consigned it to the flames (B.C. 146). Corinth was filled with masterpieces of ancient art; but Mummius was so insensible to their surpassing excellence as to stipulate with those who contracted to convey them to Italy, that, if any were lost in the passage, they should be replaced by others of equal value! Mummius then employed himself in chastising and regulating the whole of Greece; and ten commissioners were sent from Rome to settle its future condition. The whole country, to the borders of Macedonia and Epirus, was formed into a Roman province, under the name of ACHAIA, derived from that confederacy which had made the last struggle for its political existence.

CHAPTER XXII.
SKETCH OF THE HISTORY OF GREEK LITERATURE FROM THE EARLIEST TIMES TO THE REIGN OF ALEXANDER THE GREAT.

The Greeks possessed two large collections of epic poetry. The one comprised poems relating to the great events and enterprises of the Heroic age, and characterised by a certain poetical unity; the other included works tamer in character and more desultory in their mode of treatment, containing the genealogies of men and gods, narratives of the exploits of separate heroes, and descriptions of the ordinary pursuits of life. The poems of the former class passed under the name of Homer; while those of the latter were in the same general way ascribed to Hesiod. The former were the productions of the Ionic and AEolic minstrels in Asia Minor, among whom Homer stood pre-eminent and eclipsed the brightness of the rest: the latter were the compositions of a school of bards in the neighbourhood of Mount Helicon in Boeotia, among whom in like manner Hesiod enjoyed the greatest celebrity. The poems of both schools were composed in the hexameter metre and in a similar dialect; but they differed widely in almost every other feature.

Of the Homeric poems the Iliad and the Odyssey were the most distinguished and have alone come down to us. The subject of the Iliad was the exploits of Achilles and of the other Grecian heroes before Ilium or Troy; that of the Odyssey was the wanderings and adventures of Odysseus or Ulysses after the capture of Troy on his return to his native island. Throughout the flourishing period of Greek literature these unrivalled works were universally regarded as the productions of a single mind; but there was very little agreement respecting the place of the poet's birth the details of his life, or the time in which he lived. Seven cities laid claim to Homer's birth, and most of them had legends to tell respecting his romantic parentage, his alleged blindness, and his life of an itinerant bard acquainted with poverty and sorrow. It cannot be disputed that he was an Asiatic Greek; but this is the only fact in his life which can be regarded as certain. Several of the best writers of antiquity supposed him to have been a native of the island of Chios; but most modern scholars believe Smyrna to have been his birthplace. His most probable date is about B.C. 850.

The mode in which these poems were preserved has occasioned great controversy in modern times. Even if they were committed to writing by the poet himself, and were handed down to posterity in this manner, it is certain that they were rarely read. We must endeavour to realise the difference between ancient Greece and our own times. During the most flourishing period of Athenian literature manuscripts were indifferently written, without division into parts, and without marks of punctuation. They were scarce and costly, could be obtained only by the wealthy, and read only by those who had had considerable literary training. Under these circumstances the Greeks could never become a reading people; and thus the great mass even of the Athenians became acquainted with the productions of the leading poets of Greece only by hearing them recited at their solemn festivals and on other public occasions. This was more strikingly the case at an earlier period. The Iliad and the Odyssey were not read by individuals in private, but were sung or recited at festivals or to assembled companies. The bard originally sung his own lays to the accompaniment of his lyre. He was succeeded by a body of professional reciters, called Rhapsodists, who rehearsed the poems of others, and who appear at early times to have had exclusive possession of the Homeric poems. But in the seventh century before the Christian era literary culture began to prevail among the Greeks; and men of education and wealth were naturally desirous of obtaining copies of the great poet of the nation. From this cause copies came to be circulated among the Greeks; but most of them contained only separate portions of the poems, or single rhapsodes, as they were called. Pisistratus, the tyrant or despot of Athens, is said to have been the first person who collected and arranged the poems in their present form, in order that they might be recited at the great Panathenaic festival at Athens.

Three works have come down to us bearing the name of Hesiod--the 'Works and Days,' the 'Theogony,' and a description of the 'Shield of Hercules.' Many ancient critics believed the 'Works and Days' to be the only genuine work of Hesiod, and their opinion has been adopted by most modern scholars. We learn from this work that Hesiod was a native of Ascra, a village at the foot of Mount Helicon, to which his father had migrated from the AEolian Cyme in Asia Minor. He further tells us that he gained the prize at Chalcis in a poetical contest; and that he was robbed of a fair share of his heritage by the unrighteous decision of judges who had been bribed by his brother Perses. The latter became afterwards reduced in circumstances, and applied to his brother for relief; and it is to him that Hesiod addresses his didactic poem of the 'Works and Days,' in which he lays down various moral and social maxims for the regulation of his conduct and his life. It contains an interesting representation of the feelings, habits, and superstitions of the rural population of Greece in the earlier ages. Respecting the date of Hesiod nothing certain can be affirmed. Modern writers usually suppose him to have flourished two or three generations later than Homer.

The commencement of Greek lyric poetry as a cultivated species of composition dates from the middle of the seventh century before the Christian era. No important event either in the public or private life of a Greek could dispense with this accompaniment; and the lyric song was equally needed to solemnize the worship of the gods, to cheer the march to battle, or to enliven the festive board. The lyric poetry, with the exception of that of Pindar, has almost entirely perished, and all that we possess of it; consists of a few songs and isolated fragments.

The great satirist ARCHILOCHUS was one of the earliest and most celebrated of all the lyric poets. He was a native of the island of Paros, and flourished about the year 700 B.C. His fame rests chiefly on his terrible satires, composed in the Iambic metre, in which he gave vent to the bitterness of a disappointed man.

TYRTAEUS and ALCMAN were the two great lyric poets of Sparta, though neither of them was a native of Lacedaemon. The personal history of Tyrtaeus, and his warlike songs which roused the fainting courage of the Spartans during the second Messenian war, have already been mentioned. Alcman was originally a Lydian slave in a Spartan family, and was emancipated by his master. He lived shortly after the second Messenian war. His poems partake of the character of this period, which was one of repose and enjoyment after the fatigues and perils of war. Many of his songs celebrate the pleasures of good eating and drinking; but the more important were intended to be sung by a chorus at the public festivals of Sparta.

ARION was a native of Methymna in Lesbos, and lived some time at the court of Periander, tyrant of Corinth, who began to reign B.C. 625. Nothing is known of his life beyond the beautiful story of his escape from the sailors with whom he sailed from Sicily to Corinth. On one occasion, thus runs the story, Arion went to Sicily to take part in a musical contest. He won the prize, and, laden with presents, he embarked in a Corinthian ship to return to his friend Periander. The rude sailors coveted his treasures, and meditated his murder. After imploring them in vain to spare his life, he obtained permission to play for the last time on his beloved lyre. In festal attire he placed himself on the prow of the vessel, invoked the gods in inspired strains, and then threw himself into the sea. But many song-loving dolphins had assembled round the vessel, and one of them now took the bard on its back, and carried him to Taenarum, from whence he returned to Corinth in safety, and related his adventure to Periander. Upon the arrival of the Corinthian vessel, Periander inquired of the sailors after Arion, who replied that he had remained behind at Tarentum; but when Arion, at the bidding of Periander, came forward, the sailors owned their guilt, and were punished according to their desert. The great improvement in lyric poetry ascribed to Arion is the invention of the Dithyramb. This was a choral song and dance in honour of the god Dionysus, and is of great interest in the history of poetry, since it was the germ from which sprung at a later time the magnificent productions of the tragic Muse at Athens.

ALCAEUS and SAPPHO were both natives of Mytilene in the island of Lesbos, and flourished about B.C. 610-580. Their songs were composed for a single voice, and not for the chorus, and they were each the inventor of a new metre, which bears their name, and is familiar to us by the well-known odes of Horace. Their poetry was the warm outpouring of the writers' inmost feelings, and present the lyric poetry of the AEolians at its highest point.

Alcaeus took an active part in the civil dissensions of his native state, and warmly espoused the cause of the aristocratical party, to which he belonged by birth. When the nobles were driven into exile, he endeavoured to cheer their spirits by a number of most animated odes, full of invectives against the popular party and its leaders.

Of the events of Sappho's life we have scarcely any information; and the common story that, being in love with Phaon and finding her love unrequited, she leaped down from the Leucadian rock, seems to have been an invention of later times.

ANACREON was a native of the Ionian city of Teos. He spent part of his life at Samos, under the patronage of Polycrates; and after the death of this despot he went to Athens at the invitation of Hipparchus. The universal tradition of antiquity represents Anacreon as a consummate voluptuary; and his poems prove the truth of the tradition. His death was worthy of his life, if we may believe the account that he was choked by a grape-stone.

SIMONIDES, of the island of Ceos, was born B.C. 556, and reached a great age. He lived many years at Athens, both at the court of Hipparchus, together with Anacreon, and subsequently under the democracy during the Persian wars. The struggles of Greece for her independence furnished him with a noble subject for his muse. He carried away the prize from AEschylus with an elegy upon the warriors who had fallen at the battle of Marathon. Subsequently we find him celebrating the heroes of Thermopylae, Artemisium, Salamis, and Plataea. He was upwards of 80 when his long poetical career at Athens was closed with the victory which he gained with the dithyrambic chorus in B.C. 477, making the 56th prize that he had carried off. Shortly after this event he repaired to Syracuse at the invitation of Hiero. Here he spent the remaining ten years of his life, not only entertaining Hiero with his poetry, but instructing him by his wisdom; for Simonides was a philosopher as well as a poet, and is reckoned amongst the sophists.

PINDAR, though the contemporary of Simonides, was considerably his junior: He was born either at, or in the neighbourhood of, Thebes in Boeotia, about the year 522 B.C. Later writers tell us that his future glory as a poet was miraculously foreshadowed by a swarm of bees which rested upon his lips while he was asleep, and that this miracle first led him to compose poetry. He commenced his professional career at an early age, and soon acquired so great a reputation, that he was employed by various states and princes of the Hellenic race to compose choral songs. He was courted especially by Alexander, king of Macedonia, and by Hiero, despot of Syracuse. The praises which he bestowed upon Alexander are said to have been the chief reason which led his descendant, Alexander the Great, to spare the house of the poet when he destroyed the rest of Thebes. The estimation in which Pindar was held is also shown by the honours conferred upon him by the free states of Greece. Although a Theban, he was always a great favourite with the Athenians, whom he frequently praised in his poems, and who testified their gratitude by making him their public guest, and by giving him 10,000 drachmas. The only poems of Pindar which have come down to us entire are his Epinicia or triumphal odes, composed in commemoration of victories gained in the great public games. But these were only a small portion of his works. He also wrote hymns, paeans, dithyrambs, odes for processions, songs of maidens, mimic dancing songs, drinking songs, dirges and encomia, or panegyrics on princes.

The Greeks had arrived at a high pitch of civilization before they can be said to have possessed a HISTORY. The first essays in literary prose cannot be placed earlier than the sixth century before the Christian aera; but the first writer who deserves the name of an historian is HERODOTUS, hence called the Father of History. Herodotus was born in the Dorian colony of Halicarnassus in Caria, in the year 484 B.C., and accordingly about the time of the Persian expeditions into Greece. He resided some years in Samos, and also undertook extensive travels, of which he speaks in his work. There was scarcely a town in Greece or on the coasts of Asia Minor with which he was not acquainted; he had explored Thrace and the coasts of the Black Sea; in Egypt he had penetrated as far south as Elephantine; and in Asia he had visited the cities of Babylon, Ecbatana, and Susa. The latter part of his life was spent at Thurii, a colony founded by the Athenians in Italy in B.C. 443. According to a well-known story in Lucian, Herodotus, when he had completed his work, recited it publicly at the great Olympic festival, as the best means of procuring for it that celebrity to which he felt that it was entitled. The effect is described as immediate and complete. The delighted audience at once assigned the names of the nine Muses to the nine books into which it is divided. A still later author (Suidas) adds, that Thucydides, then a boy, was present at the festival with his father Olorus, and was so affected by the recital as to shed tears; upon which Herodotus congratulated Olorus on having a son who possessed so early such a zeal for knowledge. But there are many objections to the probability of these tales.

Herodotus interwove into his history all the varied and extensive knowledge acquired in his travels, and by big own personal researches. But the real subject of the work is the conflict between the Greek race, in the widest sense of the term, and including the Greeks of Asia Minor, with the Asiatics. Thus the historian had a vast epic subject presented to him, which was brought to a natural and glorious termination by the defeat of the Persians in their attempts upon Greece. The work concludes with the reduction of Sestos by the Athenians, B.C. 478. Herodotus wrote in the Ionic dialect, and his style is marked by an ease and simplicity which lend it an indescribable charm.

THUCYDIDES, the greatest of the Greek historians, was an Athenian, and was born in the year 471 B.C. His family was connected with that of Miltiades and Cimon. He possessed gold-mines in Thrace, and enjoyed great influence in that country. He commanded an Athenian squadron of seven ships at Thasos, in 424 B.C., at the time when Brasidas was besieging Amphipolis; and having failed to relieve that city in time, he went into a voluntary exile, in order probably to avoid the punishment of death. He appears to have spent 20 years in banishment, principally in the Peloponnesus, or in places under the dominion or influence of Sparta. He perhaps returned to Athens in B.C. 403, the date of its liberation by Thrasybulus. According to the unanimous testimony of antiquity he met with a violent end, and it seems probable that he was assassinated at Athens, since it cannot be doubted that his tomb existed there. From the beginning of the Peloponnesian war he had designed to write its history, and he employed himself in collecting materials for that purpose during its continuance; but it is most likely that the work was not actually composed till after the conclusion of the war, and that he was engaged upon it at the time of his death. The first book of his History is introductory, and contains a rapid sketch of Grecian history from the remotest times to the breaking out of the war. The remaining seven books are filled with the details of the war, related according to the division into summers and winters, into which all campaigns naturally fall; and the work breaks off abruptly in the middle of the 21st year of the war (B.C. 411). The materials of Thucydides were collected with the most scrupulous care; the events are related with the strictest impartiality; and the work probably offers a more exact account of a long and eventful period than any other contemporary history, whether ancient or modern, of an equally long and important aera. The style of Thucydides is brief and sententious, and whether in moral or political reasoning, or in description, gains wonderful force from its condensation. But this characteristic is sometimes carried to a faulty extent, so as to render his style harsh, and his meaning obscure.

XENOPHON, the son of Gryllus, was also an Athenian, and was probably born about B.C. 444. He was a pupil of Socrates, who saved his life at the battle of Delium (B.C. 424). His accompanying Cyrus the younger in his expedition against his brother Artaxerxes, king of Persia, formed a striking episode in his life, and has been recorded by himself in his ANABASIS. He seems to have been still in Asia at the time of the death of Socrates in 399 B.C., and was probably banished from Athens soon after that period, in consequence of his close connexion with the Lacedaemonians. He accompanied Agesilaus, the Spartan king, on the return of the latter from Asia to Greece; and he fought along with the Lacedaemonians against his own countrymen at the battle of Coronea in 394 B.C. After this battle he went with Agesilaus to Sparta, and soon afterwards settled at Scillus in Elis, near Olympia. He is said to have lived to more than 90 years of age, and he mentions an event which occurred as late as 357 B.C.

Probably all the works of Xenophon are still extant. The ANABASIS is the work on which his fame as an historian chiefly rests. It is written in a simple and agreeable style, and conveys much curious and striking information. The HELLENICA is a continuation of the history of Thucydides, and comprehends in seven books a space of about 48 years; namely, from the time when Thucydides breaks off, B.C. 411, to the battle of Mantinea in 362. The subject is treated in a very dry and uninteresting style; and his evident partiality to Sparta, and dislike of Athens, have frequently warped his judgment, and must cause his statements to be received with some suspicion. The CYROPAEDIA, one of the most pleasing and popular of his works, professes to be a history of Cyrus, the founder of the Persian monarchy, but is in reality a kind of political romance, and possesses no authority whatever as an historical work. The design of the author seems to have been to draw a picture of a perfect state; and though the scene is laid in Persia, the materials of the work are derived from his own philosophical notions and the usages of Sparta engrafted on the popularly current stories respecting Cyrus. Xenophon displays in this work his dislike of democratic institutions like those of Athens, and his preference for an aristocracy, or even a monarchy. Xenophon was also the author of several minor works; but the only other treatise which we need mention is the MEMORABILIA of Socrates, in four books, intended as a defence of his master against the charges which occasioned his death, and which undoubtedly contains a genuine picture of Socrates and his philosophy. The genius of Xenophon was not of the highest order; it was practical rather than speculative; but he is distinguished for his good sense, his moderate views, his humane temper, and his earnest piety.

The DRAMA pre-eminently distinguished Athenian literature. The democracy demanded a literature of a popular kind, the vivacity of the people a literature that made a lively impression; and both these conditions were fulfilled by the drama. But though brought to perfection among the Athenians, tragedy and comedy, in their rude and early origin, were Dorian inventions. Both arose out of the worship of Dionysus. There was at first but little distinction between these two species of the drama, except that comedy belonged more to the rural celebration of the Dionysiac festivals, and tragedy to that in cities. The name of TRAGEDY was far from signifying any thing mournful, being derived from the goat-like appearance of those who, disguised as Satyrs, performed the old Dionysiac songs and dances. In like manner, COMEDY was called after the song of the band of revellers who celebrated the vintage festivals of Dionysus, and vented the rude merriment inspired by the occasion in jibes and extempore witticisms levelled at the spectators. Tragedy, in its more perfect form, was the offspring of the dithyrambic odes with which that worship was celebrated. These were not always of a joyous cast. Some of them expressed the sufferings of Dionysus; and it was from this more mournful species of dithyramb that tragedy, properly so called, arose. The dithyrambic odes formed a kind of lyrical tragedy, and were sung by a chorus of fifty men, dancing round the altar of Dionysus. The improvements in the dithyramb were introduced by Arion at Corinth; and it was chiefly among the Dorian states of the Peloponnesus that these choral dithyrambic songs prevailed. Hence, even in attic tragedy, the chorus, which was the foundation of the drama, was written in the Doric dialect, thus clearly betraying the source from which the Athenians derived it.

In Attica an important alteration was made in the old tragedy in the time of Pisistratus, in consequence of which it obtained a new and dramatic character. This innovation is ascribed to THESPIS, a native of the Attic village of Icaria, B.C. 535. It consisted in the introduction of an actor for the purpose of giving rest to the chorus.

Thespis was succeeded by Choerilus and Phrynichus, the latter of whom gained his first prize in the dramatic contests in 511 B.C. The Dorian Pratinas, a native of Philius, but who exhibited his tragedies at Athens, introduced an improvement in tragedy by separating the Satyric from the tragic drama. As neither the popular taste nor the ancient religious associations connected with the festivals of Dionysus would have permitted the chorus of Satyrs to be entirely banished from the tragic representations, Pratinas avoided this by the invention of what is called the Satyric drama; that is, a species of play in which the ordinary subjects of tragedy were treated in a lively and farcical manner, and in which the chorus consisted of a band of Satyrs in appropriate dresses and masks. After this period it became customary to exhibit dramas in TETRALOGIES, or sets of four; namely, a tragic trilogy, or series of three tragedies, followed by a Satyric play. These were often on connected subjects; and the Satyric drama at the end served like a merry after-piece to relieve the minds of the spectators.

The subjects of Greek tragedy were taken, with few exceptions, from the national mythology. Hence the plot and story were of necessity known to the spectators, a circumstance which strongly distinguished the ancient tragedy from the modern. It must also be recollected that the representation of tragedies did not take place every day, but only, after certain fixed intervals, at the festivals of Dionysus, of which they formed one of the greatest attractions. During the whole day the Athenian public sat in the theatre witnessing tragedy after tragedy; and a prize was awarded by judges appointed for the purpose to the poet who produced the best set of dramas.

Such was Attic tragedy when it came into the hands of AESCHYLUS, who, from the great improvements which he introduced, was regarded by the Athenians as its father or founder, just as Homer was of Epic poetry, and Herodotus of History. AEschylus was born at Eleusis in Attica in B.C. 525, and was thus contemporary with Simonides and Pindar. He fought with his brother Cynaegirus at the battle of Marathon, and also at those of Artemisium, Salamis, and Plataea. In B.C. 484 he gained his first tragic prize. In 468 he was defeated in a tragic contest by his younger rival Sophocles; shortly afterwards he retired to the court of king Hiero, at Syracuse, He died at Gela, in Sicily, in 456, in the 69th year of his age. It is unanimously related that an eagle, mistaking the poet's bald head for a stone, let a tortoise fall upon it in order to break the shell, thus fulfilling an oracle predicting that he was to die by a blow from heaven. The improvements introduced into tragedy by AEschylus concerned both its form and composition, and its manner of representation. In the former his principal innovation was the introduction of a second actor; whence arose the dialogue, properly so called, and the limitation of the choral parts, which now became subsidiary. His improvements in the manner of representing tragedy consisted in the introduction of painted scenes, drawn according to the rules of perspective. He furnished the actors with more appropriate and more magnificent dresses, invented for them more various and expressive masks, and raised their stature to the heroic size by providing them with thick-soled cothurni or buskins. AEschylus excels in representing the superhuman, in depicting demigods and heroes, and in tracing the irresistible march of fate. His style resembles the ideas which it clothes: it is bold, sublime, and full of gorgeous imagery, but sometimes borders on the turgid.

SOPHOCLES, the younger rival and immediate successor of Aeschylus in the tragic art, was born at Colonus, a village about a mile from Athens, in B.C. 495. We have already adverted to his wresting the tragic prize from AEschylus in 468, from which time he seems to have retained the almost undisputed possession of the Athenian stage, until a young but formidable rival arose in the person of Euripides. The close of his life was troubled with family dissensions. Iophon, his son by an Athenian wife, and therefore his legitimate heir, was jealous of the affection manifested by his father for his grandson Sophocles, the offspring of another son, Ariston, whom he had had by a Sicyonian woman. Fearing lest his father should bestow a great part of his property upon his favourite, Iophon summoned him before the Phratores, or tribesmen, on the ground that his mind was affected. The old man's only reply was--"If I am Sophocles I am not beside myself; and if I am beside myself I am not Sophocles." Then taking up his OEDIPUS AT COLONUS, which he had lately written, but had not yet brought out, he read from it a beautiful passage, with which the judges were so struck that they at once dismissed the case. He died shortly afterwards, in B.C. 406, in his 90th year. As a poet Sophocles is universally allowed to have brought the drama to the greatest perfection of which it is susceptible. His plays stand in the just medium between the sublime but unregulated flights of AEschylus, and the too familiar scenes and rhetorical declamations of

Euripides. His plots are worked up with more skill and care than the plots of either of his great rivals. Sophocles added the last improvement to the form of the drama by the introduction of a third actor; a change which greatly enlarged the scope of the action. The improvement was so obvious that it was adopted by AEschylus in his later plays; but the number of three actors seems to have been seldom or never exceeded.

EURIPIDES was born in the island of Salamis, in B.C. 480 his parents having been among those who fled thither at the time of the invasion of Attics by Xerxes. He studied rhetoric under Prodicus, and physics under Anaxagoras and he also lived on intimate terms with Socrates. In 441 he gained his first prize, and he continued to exhibit plays until 408, the date of his Orestes. Soon after this he repaired to the court of Macedonia, at the invitation of king Archelaus, where he died two years afterwards at the age of 74 (B.C. 406). Common report relates that he was torn to pieces by the king's dogs, which, according to some accounts, were set upon him by two rival poets out of envy. In treating his characters and subjects Euripides often arbitrarily departed from the received legends, and diminished the dignity of tragedy by depriving it of its ideal character, and by bringing it down to the level of every-day life. His dialogue was garrulous and colloquial, wanting in heroic dignity, and frequently frigid through misplaced philosophical disquisitions. Yet in spite of all these faults Euripides has many beauties, and is particularly remarkable for pathos, so that Aristotle calls him "the most tragic of poets."

Comedy received its full development at Athens from Cratinus, who lived in the age of Pericles. Cratinus, and his younger contemporaries Eupolis and Aristophanes, were the three great poets of what is called the Old Attic Comedy. The comedies of Cratinus and Eupolis are lost; but of Aristophanes, who was the greatest of the three, we have eleven dramas extant. ARISTOPHANES was born about 444 B.C. Of his private life we know positively nothing. He exhibited his first comedy in 427, and from that time till near his death, which probably happened about 380, he was a frequent contributor to the Attic stage. The OLD ATTIC COMEDY was a powerful vehicle for the expression of opinion; and most of the comedies of Aristophanes turned either upon political occurrences, or upon some subject which excited the interest of the Athenian public. Their chief object was to excite laughter by the boldest and most ludicrous caricature; and provided that end was attained the poet seems to have cared but little about the justice of the picture. Towards the end of the career of Aristophanes the unrestricted licence and libellous personality of comedy began gradually to disappear. The chorus was first curtailed and then entirely suppressed, and thus made way for what is called the Middle Comedy, which had no chorus at all. The latter still continued to be in some degree political; but persons were no longer introduced upon the stage under their real names, and the office of the chorus was very much curtailed. It was, in fact, the connecting link between the Old Comedy and the New, or the Comedy of Manners. The NEW COMEDY arose after Athens had become subject to the Macedonians. Politics were now excluded from the stage, and the materials of the dramatic poet were derived entirely from the fictitious adventures of persons in private life. The two most distinguished writers of this school were PHILEMON and MENANDER. Philemon was probably born about the year 360 B.C., and was either a Cilician or Syracusan, but came at an early age to Athens. He is considered as the founder of the New Comedy, which was soon afterwards brought to perfection by his younger contemporary Menander. The latter was an Athenian, and was born in B.C. 312. He was drowned at the age of 52, whilst swimming in the harbour of Piraeus. He wrote upwards of 100 comedies, of which only fragments remain; and the unanimous praise of posterity awakens our regret for the loss of one of the most elegant writers of antiquity. The comedies, indeed, of Plautus and Terence may give us a general notion of the New Comedy of the Greeks, from which they were confessedly drawn; but there is good reason to suppose that the works even of the latter Roman writer fell far short of the wit and elegance of Menander.

The latter days of literary Athens were chiefly distinguished by the genius of her ORATORS and PHILOSOPHERS. There were ten Attic orators, whose works were collected by the Greek grammarians, and many of whose orations have come down to us. Their names are Antiphon, Andocides, Lysias, Isocrates, Isaeus, AEschines, Lycurgus, Demosthenes, Hyperides and Dinarchus. ANTIPHON, the earliest of the ten was born B.C. 480. He opened a school of rhetoric, and numbered among his pupils the historian Thucydides. Antiphon was put to death in 411 B.C. for the part which he took in establishing the oligarchy of the Four Hundred.

ANDOCIDES, who was concerned with Alcibiades in the affair of the Hermae, was born at Athens in B.C. 467, tend died probably about 391.

LYSIAS, also born at Athens in 458, was much superior to Andocides as an orator, but being a METIC or resident alien, he was not allowed to speak in the assemblies or courts of justice, and therefore wrote orations for others to deliver.

ISOCRATES was born in 436. After receiving the instructions of some of the most celebrated sophists of the day, he became himself a speech-writer and professor of rhetoric; his weakly constitution and natural timidity preventing him from taking a part in public life. He made away with himself in 338, after the fatal battle of Chaeronea, in despair, it is said, of his country's fate. He took great pains with his compositions, and is reported to have spent ten, or, according to others, fifteen years over his Panegyric oration.

ISAEUS flourished between the end of the Peloponnesian war and the accession of Philip of Macedon. He opened a school of rhetoric at Athens, and is said to have numbered Demosthenes among his pupils. The orations of Isaeus were exclusively judicial, and the whole of the eleven which have come down to us turn on the subject of inheritances.

AESCHINES was born in the year 389, and he was at first a violent anti-Macedonian; but after his embassy along with Demosthenes and others to Philip's court, he was the constant advocate of peace, Demosthenes and AEschines now became the leading speakers on their respective sides, and the heat of political animosity soon degenerated into personal hatred. In 343 Demosthenes charged AEschines with having received bribes from Philip during a second embassy; and the speech in which he brought forward this accusation was answered in another by AEschines. The result of this charge is unknown, but it seems to have detracted from the popularity of AEschines. We have already adverted to his impeachment of Ctesiphon, and the celebrated reply of Demosthenes in his speech DE CORONA. After the banishment of AEschines on this occasion (B.C. 330), he employed himself in teaching rhetoric at Rhodes. He died in Samos in 314. As an orator he was second only to Demosthenes.

Of the life of his great rival, DEMOSTHENES, we have already given some account. The verdict of his contemporaries, ratified by posterity, has pronounced Demosthenes the greatest; orator that ever lived. The principal element of his success must be traced in his purity of purpose, which gave to his arguments all the force of conscientious conviction. The effect of his speeches was still further heightened by a wonderful and almost magic force of diction. The grace and vivacity of his delivery are attested by the well-known anecdote of AEschines, when he read at Rhodes his speech against Ctesiphon. His audience having expressed their surprise that he should have been defeated after such an oration "You would cease to wonder," he remarked, "if you had heard Demosthenes."

The remaining three Attic orators, viz. LYCURGUS, HYPERIDES, and DINARCHUS, were contemporaries of Demosthenes. Lycurgus and Hyperides both belonged to the anti-Macedonian party, and were warm supporters of the policy of Demosthenes. Dinarchus, who is the least important of the Attic orators, survived Demosthenes, and was a friend of Demetrius Phalereus.

The history of Greek PHILOSOPHY, like that of Greek poetry and history, began in Asia Minor. The earliest philosopher of distinction was THALES of Miletus, who was born about B.C. 640, and died in 554 at the age of 90. He was the founder of the IONIC school of philosophy, and to him were traced the first beginnings of geometry and astronomy. The main doctrine of his philosophical system was, that water, or fluid substance was the single original element from which everything came and into which everything returned. ANAXIMANDER, the successor of Thales in the Ionic school, lived from B.C. 610 to 547. He was distinguished for his knowledge of astronomy and geography, and is said to have been the first to introduce the use of the sun-dial into Greece. ANAXIMENES, the third in the series of the Ionian philosophers, lived a little later than Anaximander. He endeavoured, like Thales, to derive the origin of all material things from a single element; and, according to his theory, air was the source of life.

A new path was struck out by ANAXAGORAS Of Clazomenae, the most illustrious of the Ionic philosophers. He came to Athens in 480 B.C., where he continued to teach for thirty years, numbering among his hearers Pericles, Socrates, and Euripides. He abandoned the system of his predecessors, and, instead of regarding some elementary form of matter as the origin of all things, he conceived a supreme mind or intelligence, distinct from the visible world, to have imparted form and order to the chaos of nature. These innovations afforded the Athenians a pretext for indicting Anaxagoras of impiety, though it is probable that his connexion with Pericles was the real cause of that proceeding (see Ch. IX). It was only through the influence and eloquence of Pericles that he was not put to death; but he was sentenced to pay a fine of five talents and quit Athens. The philosopher retired to Lampsacus, where he died at the age of 72.

The second school of Greek philosophy was the ELEATIC which derived its name from Elea or Velia, a Greek colony on the western coast of Southern Italy. It was founded by XENOPHANES of Colophon, who fled to Elea on the conquest of his native land by the Persians. He conceived the whole of nature to be God.

The third school of philosophy was the PYTHAGOREAN, founded by PYTHAGORAS. He was a native of Samos and was born about B.C. 580. His father was an opulent merchant, and Pythagoras himself travelled extensively in the East. He believed in the transmigration of souls; and later writers relate that Pythagoras asserted that his own soul had formerly dwelt in the body of the Trojan Euphorbus, the son of Panthous, who was slain by Menelaus, and that in proof of his assertion he took down, at first sight, the shield of Euphorbus from the temple of Hera (Juno) at Argos, where it had been dedicated by Menelaus. Pythagoras was distinguished by his knowledge of geometry and arithmetic; and it was probably from his teaching that the Pythagoreans were led to regard numbers in some mysterious manner as the basis and essence of all things. He was however more of the religious teacher than of the philosopher; and he looked upon himself as a being destined by the gods to reveal to his disciples a new and a purer mode of life. He founded at Croton in Italy a kind of religious brotherhood, the members of which were bound together by peculiar rites and observances. Everything done and taught in the fraternity was kept a profound secret from all without its pale. It appears that the members had some private signs, like Freemasons, by which they could recognise each other, even if they had never met before. His doctrines spread rapidly over Magna Graecia, and clubs of a similar character were established at Sybaris, Metapontum, Tarentum, and other cities.

At Athens a new direction was given to the study of philosophy by Socrates, of whom an account has been already given. To his teaching either directly of indirectly may be traced the origin of the four principal Grecian schools: the ACADEMICIANS, established by Plato; the PERIPATETICS, founded by his pupil Aristotle; the EPICUREANS, so named from their master Epicurus; and the STOICS, founded by Zeno.

PLATO was born at Athens in 429 B.C., the year in which Pericles died. His first literary attempts were in poetry; but his attention was soon turned to philosophy by the teaching of Socrates, whose lectures he began to frequent at about the age of twenty. From that time till the death of Socrates he appears to have lived in the closest intimacy with that philosopher. After that event Plato withdrew to Megara, and subsequently undertook some extensive travels, in the course of which he visited Cyrene, Egypt, Sicily, and Magna Graecia. His intercourse with the elder and the younger Dionysius at Syracuse has been already related His absence from Athens lasted about twelve years; on his return, being then upwards of forty, he began to teach in the gymnasium of the Academy. His doctrines were too recondite for the popular ear, and his lectures were not very numerously attended. But he had a narrower circle of devoted admirers and disciples, consisting of about twenty-eight persons, who met in his private house; over the vestibule of which was inscribed--"Let no one enter who is ignorant of geometry." The most distinguished of this little band of auditors were Speusippus, his nephew and successor, and Aristotle. He died in 347, at the age of 81 or 82, and bequeathed his garden to his school.

ARISTOTLE was born in 381 B.C., at Stagira, a seaport town of Chalcidice, whence he is frequently called THE STAGIRITE. At the age of 17, Aristotle, who had then lost both father and mother, repaired to Athens. Plato considered him his best scholar, and called him "the intellect of his school." Aristotle spent twenty years at Athens, during the last ten of which he established a school of his own. In 342 he accepted the invitation of Philip of Macedon to undertake the instruction of his son Alexander. In 335, after Alexander had ascended the throne, Aristotle quitted Macedonia, to which he never returned. He again took up his abode at Athens, where the Athenians assigned him the gymnasium called the Lyceum; and from his habit of delivering his lectures whilst walking up and down in the shady walks of this place, his school was called the PERIPATETIC. In the morning he lectured only to a select class of pupils, called ESOTERIC. His afternoon lectures were delivered to a wider circle, and were therefore called EXOTERIC. It was during the thirteen years in which he presided over the Lyceum that he composed the greater part of his works, and prosecuted his researches in natural history, in which he was most liberally assisted by the munificence of Alexander. The latter portion of Aristotle's life was unfortunate. He appears to have lost from some unknown cause the friendship of Alexander; and, after the death of that monarch, the disturbances which ensued in Greece proved unfavourable to his peace and security. Being threatened with a prosecution for impiety, he escaped from Athens and retired to Chalcis; but he was condemned to death in his absence, and deprived of all the rights and honours which he had previously enjoyed. He died at Chalcis in 322, in the 63rd year of his age.

Of all the philosophical systems of antiquity, that of Aristotle was best adapted to the practical wants of mankind. It was founded on a close and accurate observation of human nature and of the external world; but whilst it sought the practical and useful, it did not neglect the beautiful and noble. His works consisted of treatises on natural, moral and political philosophy, history, rhetoric, criticism, &c.; indeed there is scarcely a branch of knowledge which his vast and comprehensive genius did not embrace.

EPICURUS was born at Samos in 342, and settled at Athens at about the age of 35. Here he purchased a garden, where he established his philosophical school. He taught that pleasure is the highest good; a tenet, however, which he explained and dignified by showing that it was mental pleasure that he intended. The ideas of atheism and sensual degradation with which the name of Epicurus has been so frequently coupled are founded on ignorance of his real teaching. But as he denied the immortality of the soul, and the interference of the gods in human affairs,--though he held their existence,--his tenets were very liable to be abused by those who had not sufficient elevation of mind to love virtue for its own sake.

ZENO was a native of Citium in the island of Cyprus, and settled at Athens about B.C. 299. Here he opened a school in the Poecile Stoa, or painted porch, whence the name of his sect. He inculcated temperance and self-denial, and his practice was in accordance with his precept.

www.bookjungle.com email: sales@bookjungle.com fax: 630-214-0564 mail: Book Jungle PO Box 2226 Champaign, IL 61825

The Codes Of Hammurabi And Moses
W. W. Davies

QTY

The discovery of the Hammurabi Code is one of the greatest achievements of archaeology, and is of paramount interest, not only to the student of the Bible, but also to all those interested in ancient history...

Religion   **ISBN: *1-59462-338-4***   Pages:132
MSRP $12.95

The Theory of Moral Sentiments
Adam Smith

QTY

This work from 1749. contains original theories of conscience amd moral judgment and it is the foundation for systemof morals.

Philosophy   **ISBN: *1-59462-777-0***   Pages:536
MSRP $19.95

Jessica's First Prayer
Hesba Stretton

QTY

In a screened and secluded corner of one of the many railway-bridges which span the streets of London there could be seen a few years ago, from five o'clock every morning until half past eight, a tidily set-out coffee-stall, consisting of a trestle and board, upon which stood two large tin cans, with a small fire of charcoal burning under each so as to keep the coffee boiling during the early hours of the morning when the work-people were thronging into the city on their way to their daily toil...

Childrens   **ISBN: *1-59462-373-2***   Pages:84
MSRP $9.95

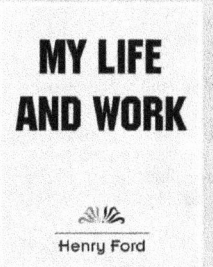

My Life and Work
Henry Ford

QTY

Henry Ford revolutionized the world with his implementation of mass production for the Model T automobile. Gain valuable business insight into his life and work with his own auto-biography... "We have only started on our development of our country we have not as yet, with all our talk of wonderful progress, done more than scratch the surface. The progress has been wonderful enough but..."

Biographies/   **ISBN: *1-59462-198-5***   **Pages:300**
MSRP $21.95

www.bookjungle.com *email: sales@bookjungle.com fax: 630-214-0564 mail: Book Jungle PO Box 2226 Champaign, IL 61825*

The Art of Cross-Examination
Francis Wellman

QTY

I presume it is the experience of every author, after his first book is published upon an important subject, to be almost overwhelmed with a wealth of ideas and illustrations which could readily have been included in his book, and which to his own mind, at least, seem to make a second edition inevitable. Such certainly was the case with me; and when the first edition had reached its sixth impression in five months, I rejoiced to learn that it seemed to my publishers that the book had met with a sufficiently favorable reception to justify a second and considerably enlarged edition. ...

Reference   ISBN: *1-59462-647-2*   Pages:412   MSRP *$19.95*

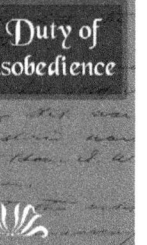

On the Duty of Civil Disobedience
Henry David Thoreau

QTY

Thoreau wrote his famous essay, On the Duty of Civil Disobedience, as a protest against an unjust but popular war and the immoral but popular institution of slave-owning. He did more than write—he declined to pay his taxes, and was hauled off to gaol in consequence. Who can say how much this refusal of his hastened the end of the war and of slavery?

Law   ISBN: *1-59462-747-9*   Pages:48   MSRP *$7.45*

Dream Psychology Psychoanalysis for Beginners
Sigmund Freud

QTY

Sigmund Freud, born Sigismund Schlomo Freud (May 6, 1856 - September 23, 1939), was a Jewish-Austrian neurologist and psychiatrist who co-founded the psychoanalytic school of psychology. Freud is best known for his theories of the unconscious mind, especially involving the mechanism of repression; his redefinition of sexual desire as mobile and directed towards a wide variety of objects; and his therapeutic techniques, especially his understanding of transference in the therapeutic relationship and the presumed value of dreams as sources of insight into unconscious desires.

Psychology   ISBN: *1-59462-905-6*   Pages:196   MSRP *$15.45*

The Miracle of Right Thought
Orison Swett Marden

QTY

Believe with all of your heart that you will do what you were made to do. When the mind has once formed the habit of holding cheerful, happy, prosperous pictures, it will not be easy to form the opposite habit. It does not matter how improbable or how far away this realization may see, or how dark the prospects may be, if we visualize them as best we can, as vividly as possible, hold tenaciously to them and vigorously struggle to attain them, they will gradually become actualized, realized in the life. But a desire, a longing without endeavor, a yearning abandoned or held indifferently will vanish without realization.

Self Help   ISBN: *1-59462-644-8*   Pages:360   MSRP *$25.45*

www.bookjungle.com email: sales@bookjungle.com fax: 630-214-0564 mail: Book Jungle PO Box 2226 Champaign, IL 61825

QTY

	Title	ISBN	Price
☐	**The Rosicrucian Cosmo-Conception Mystic Christianity** by *Max Heindel*	ISBN: 1-59462-188-8	$38.95

The Rosicrucian Cosmo-conception is not dogmatic, neither does it appeal to any other authority than the reason of the student. It is; not controversial, but is: sent forth in the, hope that it may help to clear... New Age/Religion Pages 646

☐ **Abandonment To Divine Providence** by *Jean-Pierre de Caussade* ISBN: 1-59462-228-0 $25.95
"The Rev. Jean Pierre de Caussade was one of the most remarkable spiritual writers of the Society of Jesus in France in the 18th Century. His death took place at Toulouse in 1751. His works have gone through many editions and have been republished..." Inspirational/Religion Pages 400

☐ **Mental Chemistry** by *Charles Haanel* ISBN: 1-59462-192-6 $23.95
Mental Chemistry allows the change of material conditions by combining and appropriately utilizing the power of the mind. Much like applied chemistry creates something new and unique out of careful combinations of chemicals the mastery of mental chemistry... New Age Pages 354

☐ **The Letters of Robert Browning and Elizabeth Barret Barrett 1845-1846 vol II** ISBN: 1-59462-193-4 $35.95
by *Robert Browning* and *Elizabeth Barrett* Biographies Pages 596

☐ **Gleanings In Genesis (volume I)** by *Arthur W. Pink* ISBN: 1-59462-130-6 $27.45
Appropriately has Genesis been termed "the seed plot of the Bible" for in it we have, in germ form, almost all of the great doctrines which are afterwards fully developed in the books of Scripture which follow... Religion/Inspirational Pages 420

☐ **The Master Key** by *L. W. de Laurence* ISBN: 1-59462-001-6 $30.95
In no branch of human knowledge has there been a more lively increase of the spirit of research during the past few years than in the study of Psychology, Concentration and Mental Discipline. The requests for authentic lessons in Thought Control, Mental Discipline and... New Age/Business Pages 422

☐ **The Lesser Key Of Solomon Goetia** by *L. W. de Laurence* ISBN: 1-59462-092-X $9.95
This translation of the first book of the "Lernegton" which is for the first time made accessible to students of Talismanic Magic was done, after careful collation and edition, from numerous Ancient Manuscripts in Hebrew, Latin, and French... New Age/Occult Pages 92

☐ **Rubaiyat Of Omar Khayyam** by *Edward Fitzgerald* ISBN:1-59462-332-5 $13.95
Edward Fitzgerald, whom the world has already learned, in spite of his own efforts to remain within the shadow of anonymity, to look upon as one of the rarest poets of the century, was born at Bredfield, in Suffolk, on the 31st of March, 1809. He was the third son of John Purcell... Music Pages 172

☐ **Ancient Law** by *Henry Maine* ISBN: 1-59462-128-4 $29.95
The chief object of the following pages is to indicate some of the earliest ideas of mankind, as they are reflected in Ancient Law, and to point out the relation of those ideas to modern thought. Religion/History Pages 452

☐ **Far-Away Stories** by *William J. Locke* ISBN: 1-59462-129-2 $19.45
"Good wine needs no bush, but a collection of mixed vintages does. And this book is just such a collection. Some of the stories I do not want to remain buried for ever in the museum files of dead magazine-numbers an author's not unpardonable vanity..." Fiction Pages 272

☐ **Life of David Crockett** by *David Crockett* ISBN: 1-59462-250-7 $27.45
"Colonel David Crockett was one of the most remarkable men of the times in which he lived. Born in humble life, but gifted with a strong will, an indomitable courage, and unremitting perseverance... Biographies/New Age Pages 424

☐ **Lip-Reading** by *Edward Nitchie* ISBN: 1-59462-206-X $25.95
Edward B. Nitchie, founder of the New York School for the Hard of Hearing, now the Nitchie School of Lip-Reading, Inc. wrote "LIP-READING Principles and Practice". The development and perfecting of this meritorious work on lip-reading was an undertaking... How-to Pages 400

☐ **A Handbook of Suggestive Therapeutics, Applied Hypnotism, Psychic Science** ISBN: 1-59462-214-0 $24.95
by *Henry Munro* Health/New Age/Health/Self-help Pages 376

☐ **A Doll's House: and Two Other Plays** by *Henrik Ibsen* ISBN: 1-59462-112-8 $19.95
Henrik Ibsen created this classic when in revolutionary 1848 Rome. Introducing some striking concepts in playwriting for the realist genre, this play has been studied the world over. Fiction/Classics/Plays 308

☐ **The Light of Asia** by *sir Edwin Arnold* ISBN: 1-59462-204-3 $13.95
In this poetic masterpiece, Edwin Arnold describes the life and teachings of Buddha. The man who was to become known as Buddha to the world was born as Prince Gautama of India but he rejected the worldly riches and abandoned the reigns of power when... Religion/History/Biographies Pages 170

☐ **The Complete Works of Guy de Maupassant** by *Guy de Maupassant* ISBN: 1-59462-157-8 $16.95
"For days and days, nights and nights, I had dreamed of that first kiss which was to consecrate our engagement, and I knew not on what spot I should put my lips..." Fiction/Classics Pages 240

☐ **The Art of Cross-Examination** by *Francis L. Wellman* ISBN: 1-59462-309-0 $26.95
Written by a renowned trial lawyer, Wellman imparts his experience and uses case studies to explain how to use psychology to extract desired information through questioning. How-to/Science/Reference Pages 408

☐ **Answered or Unanswered?** by *Louisa Vaughan* ISBN: 1-59462-248-5 $10.95
Miracles of Faith in China Religion Pages 112

☐ **The Edinburgh Lectures on Mental Science (1909)** by *Thomas* ISBN: 1-59462-008-3 $11.95
This book contains the substance of a course of lectures recently given by the writer in the Queen Street Hall, Edinburgh. Its purpose is to indicate the Natural Principles governing the relation between Mental Action and Material Conditions... New Age/Psychology Pages 148

☐ **Ayesha** by *H. Rider Haggard* ISBN: 1-59462-301-5 $24.95
Verily and indeed it is the unexpected that happens! Probably if there was one person upon the earth from whom the Editor of this, and of a certain previous history, did not expect to hear again... Classics Pages 380

☐ **Ayala's Angel** by *Anthony Trollope* ISBN: 1-59462-352-X $29.95
The two girls were both pretty, but Lucy who was twenty-one who supposed to be simple and comparatively unattractive, whereas Ayala was credited, as her Bombwhat romantic name might show, with poetic charm and a taste for romance. Ayala when her father died was nineteen... Fiction Pages 484

☐ **The American Commonwealth** by *James Bryce* ISBN: 1-59462-286-8 $34.45
An interpretation of American democratic political theory. It examines political mechanics and society from the perspective of Scotsman James Bryce Politics Pages 572

☐ **Stories of the Pilgrims** by *Margaret P. Pumphrey* ISBN: 1-59462-116-0 $17.95
This book explores pilgrims religious oppression in England as well as their escape to Holland and eventual crossing to America on the Mayflower, and their early days in New England... History Pages 268

www.bookjungle.com email: sales@bookjungle.com fax: 630-214-0564 mail: Book Jungle PO Box 2226 Champaign, IL 61825

			QTY
The Fasting Cure by *Sinclair Upton*	ISBN: *1-59462-222-1*	**$13.95**	☐
In the Cosmopolitan Magazine for May, 1910, and in the Contemporary Review (London) for April, 1910, I published an article dealing with my experiences in fasting. I have written a great many magazine articles, but never one which attracted so much attention...		New Age/Self Help/Health Pages 164	
Hebrew Astrology by *Sepharial*	ISBN: *1-59462-308-2*	**$13.45**	☐
In these days of advanced thinking it is a matter of common observation that we have left many of the old landmarks behind and that we are now pressing forward to greater heights and to a wider horizon than that which represented the mind-content of our progenitors...		Astrology Pages 144	
Thought Vibration or The Law of Attraction in the Thought World	ISBN: *1-59462-127-6*	**$12.95**	☐
by *William Walker Atkinson*		Psychology/Religion Pages 144	
Optimism by *Helen Keller*	ISBN: *1-59462-108-X*	**$15.95**	☐
Helen Keller was blind, deaf, and mute since 19 months old, yet famously learned how to overcome these handicaps, communicate with the world, and spread her lectures promoting optimism. An inspiring read for everyone...		Biographies/Inspirational Pages 84	
Sara Crewe by *Frances Burnett*	ISBN: *1-59462-360-0*	**$9.45**	☐
In the first place, Miss Minchin lived in London. Her home was a large, dull, tall one, in a large, dull square, where all the houses were alike, and all the sparrows were alike, and where all the door-knockers made the same heavy sound...		Childrens/Classic Pages 88	
The Autobiography of Benjamin Franklin by *Benjamin Franklin*	ISBN: *1-59462-135-7*	**$24.95**	☐
The Autobiography of Benjamin Franklin has probably been more extensively read than any other American historical work, and no other book of its kind has had such ups and downs of fortune. Franklin lived for many years in England, where he was agent...		Biographies/History Pages 332	

Name	
Email	
Telephone	
Address	
City, State ZIP	

☐ Credit Card   ☐ Check / Money Order

Credit Card Number	
Expiration Date	
Signature	

Please Mail to: Book Jungle
　　　　　　　　　PO Box 2226
　　　　　　　　　Champaign, IL 61825
or Fax to:　　　 630-214-0564

ORDERING INFORMATION
web: *www.bookjungle.com*
email: *sales@bookjungle.com*
fax: *630-214-0564*
mail: *Book Jungle PO Box 2226 Champaign, IL 61825*
or PayPal *to sales@bookjungle.com*

Please contact us for bulk discounts

DIRECT-ORDER TERMS

20% Discount if You Order Two or More Books
Free Domestic Shipping!
Accepted: Master Card, Visa, Discover, American Express

www.ingramcontent.com/pod-product-compliance
Lightning Source LLC
Chambersburg PA
CBHW080537170426
43195CB00016B/2588